SHOULD AMERICA GO TO WAR?

SHOULD AMERICA GO TO WAR?

THE DEBATE OVER
FOREIGN POLICY IN
CHICAGO, 1939–1941

JAMES C. SCHNEIDER

The University of North Carolina Press
Chapel Hill and London

© 1989 The University of North Carolina Press
All rights reserved
Manufactured in the United States of America

The paper in this book meets the guidelines for
permanence and durability of the Committee
on Production Guidelines for Book Longevity
of the Council on Library Resources.

93 92 91 90 89   5 4 3 2 1

Library of Congress
Cataloging-in-Publication Data

Schneider, James C.
Should America go to war?: the debate over
foreign policy in Chicago, 1939–1941
/ by James C. Schneider.
p.   cm.
Bibliography: p.
Includes index.
ISBN 0-8078-1801-1 (alk. paper)
1. United States—Foreign relations—
1933–1945. 2. United States—
Neutrality. 3. World War, 1939–1945—
Diplomatic history. I. Title.
E806.S35 1988
940.53'22'73—dc19   88-10644
                                        CIP

To my father
and the memory
of my mother

CONTENTS

PREFACE

This is an exploration of how Americans struggled to define their nation's role in international affairs at a particularly crucial point in world history. When the European half of World War II began with the German invasion of Poland in 1939, United States policy reflected a degree of isolationism extreme by the standards of twentieth-century America. As embodied in the Johnson and Neutrality Acts, the policy was designed to reduce the danger of American involvement in a European war by placing restrictions on the international operations of U.S. business and financial concerns. Public support for this policy was widespread. Opinion polls revealed that an overwhelming majority of Americans wished to avoid war and believed that our involvement in World War I had been a mistake.

The two years following the outbreak of World War II would display profound modifications in the policy of noninvolvement and in the public attitudes that undergirded it. By the autumn of 1941, the United States was engaged in economic and naval warfare against Nazi Germany and was moving toward a showdown with Imperial Japan. Public majorities supported all these more belligerent actions, but in fact the nation was bitterly divided over foreign affairs. The division was multifaceted. While most Americans endorsed the Roosevelt administration's package of economic aid to the Allies and limited U.S. military involvement, a substantial minority continued to denounce these steps as likely to result in full-scale war. Interventionists disagreed among themselves over the necessity and desirability of outright war, with many supporting Roosevelt out of a belief that his program was the best remaining chance to avoid full military participation. Others hoped FDR's program would draw the United States into belligerency. Only the Japanese raid on Pearl Harbor rendered these disagreements moot. The president's true motives remain a matter of dispute, but it is interesting to remember that Roosevelt did not call for a declaration of war against Germany and Italy even after Pearl Harbor. America joined the conflict in Europe because Hitler, usually the least trustworthy of men, honored his alliance with the Japanese and declared war on the United States.

The way by which war came to America is significant in several senses, not least among them that conflict was thrust upon a people who, on the whole, had been reluctant to enter it. That Pearl Harbor taught a generation of Americans a lesson about the futility of isolationism has long been a commonplace observation. However, the questions of why such a catalytic event was necessary, of why so many questions and controversies still surrounded American policy in the autumn of 1941, and why consensus remained so elusive have been relatively neglected. To work toward an answer to these questions is the purpose of this study. It examines which groups within society became involved in the debate, what sort of information was available to them to form their judgments on foreign policy issues, the nature of their response to those issues, and what signals the participants tried to send to decision makers. Public involvement was both extensive and intensive, because many Americans believed that the future of their country and even civilization itself depended on the course America adopted.[1]

Certainly the prewar period has been the subject of a vast and continually growing historical literature, but the writing has focused on international events and on policy formation in Washington. This emphasis reflects the traditional focus of political and diplomatic history, reinforced by the special stature of Franklin D. Roosevelt. Much of the initial postwar literature centered on one aspect of the prewar debate itself, namely the intent behind Roosevelt's policies. Various writers attacked the president for allegedly scheming to involve the United States in war with the Axis alliance. These accusations were bitter in tone and provoked sharp responses. In this exchange, as in the prewar debate, the administration position gained the upper hand. At least in scholarly circles, if not in popular writing, the question of whether Roosevelt contrived to bring about the attack on Pearl Harbor has been resolved. But the issue of Roosevelt's intentions and expectations continues to engage scholars. What has emerged is a portrait of a complex man whose motivations and policies defy simple categorization. Historians continue to echo the complaint Harold Ickes once made to FDR, "You keep your cards too close up against your belly." To Robert Dallek, for example, surveying the whole of Rooseveltian foreign policy actions is like "peering into a kaleidoscope." The constantly changing patterns Dallek observes are due not only to the elusive qualities of Roosevelt himself. They result as well from the president's tendency to react to events and to design policies that allowed him the widest possible latitude for action.[2]

This fact is especially important to bear in mind when examining the period from the Munich conference to Pearl Harbor. Roosevelt's prestige and influence were at their weakest early in 1939. His second term was drawing to a close and all precedent indicated it would be his last. Both his court reorganization package and his attempt to intervene in the 1938 congressional elections had failed dismally. A bitter recession in 1937 highlighted the shortcomings of his economic policies. So low had Roosevelt's political stock fallen by the spring of 1939 that he deliberately refrained from lobbying Congress for a revised Neutrality Act out of fear that his intervention would damage the bill's chances. At least until the autumn of 1939, FDR was in no position to dominate even American foreign policy, still less events overseas. The outbreak of general war in Europe revived his influence. The invasion of Poland dramatically demonstrated the aggressive nature of Hitlerian Germany and proved Roosevelt's warnings in this regard correct. But of course the Nazi war effort was successful as well as aggressive, and in that combination lies a paradox. The same sequence of events that bolstered FDR's influence at home also weakened America's international position and restricted the president's room to maneuver. People turned to him precisely because trends overseas were so disastrous. As France staggered and collapsed under the weight of the blitzkrieg, a sense of crisis gripped the United States. This apprehension helped Roosevelt gain re-election. But the magnitude of German conquests, combined with Japan's determination to expand, the precarious state of the British and American military positions, and the division within American public opinion, put severe restrictions on his ability to shape world events. Roosevelt's third term, like his first, began amid catastrophe.[3]

The domestic context in which Roosevelt operated has received extensive, but selective, study. Most of the key presidential foreign policy advisors—Cordell Hull, Sumner Welles, Henry Stimson, Henry Morganthau, and Harold Ickes—have left inside accounts of their activities. Only Harry Hopkins left no first-hand record, but this gap was substantially filled by Robert Sherwood. Many lower-level officials have left their own records, and the State Department, the military, and the defense production effort have attracted scholarly attention. Work on departmental bureaucracies has only just begun to appear. Thus the literature on the executive branch very much reflects the traditional focus on elites and the Washington scene.[4]

Coverage of other aspects of the foreign policy debate in the prewar years is extremely uneven. Congress has been the subject of work by some of the most distinguished scholars on the prewar period. More such detailed work on Congress is needed, especially since the memoirs of such key legislators as Arthur Vandenberg, Burton Wheeler, Joseph Martin, and others shed relatively little light on events in the legislature.[5]

Antiwar efforts have attracted some attention. "Isolationism" was a subject of considerable interest during the 1950s, despite the pronouncement by Samuel Lubell, one of the first scholars to investigate the concept seriously, that it was a "myth" and should be "discarded." Pacifism has a literature of its own as well. Aside from the important memoirs of such key figures as Dorothy Detzer and Frederick J. Libby and the path-breaking work of Merle Curti, the peace movement was neglected until the Vietnam debate helped rekindle scholarly interest.[6]

The literature on other organizations involved in the foreign policy debate is generally of much older vintage. The standard works on the leading crisis committees, America First and the Committee to Defend America by Aiding the Allies, ably survey their national activities but ignore their grassroots operations. Ignoring these local chapters, which the national director of America First once called the backbone of his organization, leaves a major gap in our knowledge of the period—and one that this study aims in part to fill.[7]

Much recent work on participants in the prewar foreign policy debate has tended to focus on individuals. Efforts to investigate the impact of the foreign policy crisis on domestic groups and to recount their involvement in the debate are conspicuous by their scarcity. Despite the impact of the New Left school of diplomatic history, which places great stress on the inseparability of domestic concerns and foreign policy, historians have been slow to examine this issue in depth. Valuable works have appeared on the steel industry and on liberal publicists, as well as a fine study of public perceptions of American-Soviet relations. But much more work is needed.[8]

Mass media are vital agents that help shape the interaction between the body politic and the government. As Richard Steele has shown, the Roosevelt administration was acutely conscious of the role of media during the foreign policy crisis and took steps to influence it. If the historical literature on the role of media is far from abundant, it is at least growing both in quantity and sophistication. Curiously, in light of the traditional prestige given print media, print has received the least attention. Newspapers, and to a much lesser extent magazines, have long been taken by historians as expressions of public opinion and cited as evidence of public reaction to a particular policy or measure under discussion. But general surveys of how the press has handled foreign affairs, of editorial opinion on foreign affairs, and even of monographs on such important individual organs as the *New York Times* are absent from the historical literature. Radio coverage is also a largely unexplored subject, though this is more understandable owing to the fact that few records were made of news broadcasts. This shortcoming is serious because by 1940 radio had become the principal news source for most Americans, in no small part due to the immediacy of its coverage of the war in Europe. The work of David Culbert, who has examined the foreign affairs views of six leading radio commentators of the late 1930s in the context of their treatment by both networks and sponsors, remains unique. Writings on the subject of film are, by contrast, voluminous. There, at least, the product exists to be viewed and analyzed. However, with film and radio alike, the absence of appropriate survey data precludes us from answering a crucial question—the effect the product had on audiences. Even when evidence does suggest how popular a particular film or commentator was, it does not reveal what sort of person was attracted to a certain commentator or what an audience liked about a certain film.[9]

The entire subject of public opinion is fraught with difficult questions, starting with whether the study is worth the effort. Skepticism on this account would seem especially pertinent when considering opinion about foreign policy, where public ignorance on most matters is matched in magnitude by public indifference to them. At least since the classic work of Walter Lippmann in the 1920s, the literature on public opinion has consistently emphasized the shortcomings of popular understanding of foreign affairs—its shallowness, lack of continuity, provincialism, and lack of sophistication to name only a few. Some of the literature also contends that policymakers heed public opinion very little. But most observers agree that leaders do value public support, or at least acquiescence, as a factor necessary for the success of a policy.[10]

In the specific context of this study, there is no question that governmental officials, from the president on down, regarded public opinion as a factor of vital importance. First of all, Roosevelt said so. Time and again in private messages to foreign leaders and in conversations with officials, FDR cited public opinion as one determinant of his actions. In October 1940, for example, the president pressed the Vichy government not to deliver the French fleet to German control by emphasizing the bitter consequences such an action would have on public attitudes toward France. The following April he also backed away from plans to have the Navy begin escorting Atlantic convoys, out of a belief the public would not accept such a provocative step. Here, as at other times, FDR may have employed public opinion as a rationale in lieu of disclosing other motives, or as a means of strengthening an argument on behalf of a favored policy. But there are reasons for believing that Roosevelt respected the importance of public opinion. Robert Sherwood has written that Woodrow Wilson's experience in 1918– 19 always lurked in FDR's consciousness. Roosevelt kept a portrait of Wilson over the mantle in the cabinet room and would mull over his predecessor's fate as he sat there preparing speeches. Moreover, the president had felt the power of an aroused public in his own conduct of foreign affairs. In 1935 the Senate, bowing to pressure inspired by Father Charles Coughlin and the Hearst press, had refused to approve membership in the World Court. Michael Leigh argues in *Mobilizing Consent* that the fairly crude indices Roosevelt of necessity employed to measure opinion led him to magnify its strength. I think that it is more pertinent to emphasize that the memory of Wilson led FDR to desire a very high level of public consensus before making any move that would increase significantly American involvement in war overseas. In any case, preparedness very much included public relations. Both governmental and private groups sought to build popular awareness of the foreign crisis and generate support for administration efforts to meet it. The various agencies involved in the defense effort each had its own public relations staff and the White House encouraged the activities of such private groups as the Committee to Defend America by Aiding the Allies. While the administration sought to avoid the excesses of the Committee on Public Information, which had helped create domestic hysteria during World War I, the government was attempting once again to shape opinion. And as will become clear, it was not always successful at keeping emotionalism out of public discourse.[11]

Public opinion was therefore a factor of significance in the foreign policy crisis of the late 1930s and early 1940s. But who, or what, was "the public"? The term itself is misleading, since society is no monolith. Anything approaching a genuine consensus on an important public issue is extraordinarily rare. Pearl Harbor produced one on the war; the German conquest of France achieved one on defense increases. Yet even in these cases there were disagreements of some consequence and latent ambiguities on points of importance. The tremendous upsurge of support for drastically increased preparedness efforts in the summer of 1940 did not prevent a sizable segment of Congress from opposing conscription. A majority of the legislators insisted on imposing limitations on where the draftees could be sent. But the divisions over the nature, extent, and desirability of American involvement overseas during the 1939–41 period differed greatly from the preparedness debate. The controversy surrounding intervention was open, deep, and bitter, far in excess of the disputes over levels of preparedness or any other contemporaneous foreign policy issue. Complicating the situation still further was the degree to which the foreign policy divisions disrupted existing political cleavages. As the congressional votes on major foreign policy and defense bills show, partisan differences remained significant, probably paramount. But some internationalist Republicans rallied to Roosevelt. So too did Southern Democrats who had become confirmed opponents of the New Deal during FDR's second term. Moving into leading opposition roles were progressives like Gerald Nye and Hiram Johnson, who had been staunch backers of domestic reform.

The divisions outside of Congress were similarly complex and scrambled. One example is furnished by the Irish-Americans, traditional stalwarts of the Democratic party. Substantial numbers of them left the fold in 1940 for foreign policy reasons, according to Samuel Lubell. John L. Lewis also abandoned the Democrats, though he failed to take along rank-and-file labor. Such shifting reflected the seriousness with which people viewed the international situation and its consequences for the United States. The rapid growth of such mass organizations as the Committee to Defend America by Aiding the Allies and America First also attests to the intensity of public concern. At bottom the issue between these groups was how best to preserve American society, but their disagreements over which course of action would do so were profound. Because the United States occupied such a pivotal position in world affairs, all the more acutely important after the fall of France, and because public opinion was so crucial a factor in forming policy under those circumstances, had the debate paralyzed or crippled national policy, the results could have been calamitous. Huge stakes hung on the outcome of the public debate.[12]

The importance of the debate is matched by the difficulty of studying it. The literature on public opinion is vast and contentious. One of the few areas of agreement is that the study of past opinion is extraordinarily difficult. At least for the 1939–41 period, 'scientific' polling exists. These surveys are an invaluable resource, but a number of factors limit their utility. By modern standards the samples are inadequately drawn, usually in ways that induce an underrepresentation of the poor. The wording of questions also raises problems. Gallup and others were aware that wording could affect how a respondent might answer, but they sometimes failed to design questions accordingly. Most seriously for the historian, pollsters did not ask the "right" questions, specify the characteristics of the respondents as precisely as one might wish, or repeat questions over time at suitable intervals. Despite these shortcomings, flawed polls are preferable to none at all. But even at their best, polls do not begin to reveal everything we wish to know about public responses to an issue. They will be used in this study, but they are not its primary focus.[13]

The overall approach adopted here is to examine the public debate of 1939–41 from the standpoint of an informed and interested contemporary observer. Initially, this involves investigating how both domestic and international events were reported in the media. It is possible to construe a particular media organ, such as a local newspaper, as an expression of public opinion, and, to the degree that politicians and other leaders did so, this is a valid use. But that is not how they will be used here. Instead, I wish to examine coverage for itself, that is, what it reveals about how some contemporary observers portrayed and interpreted changing events. Secondly, the goal is to discover what conclusions a reader or listener might reasonably reach in light of the information and interpretations then available. So much subsequent scholarship has added to our knowledge of World War II that it is easy to forget that contemporaries operated with much more restricted information. Such a perspective is especially essential when dealing with the opponents of American involvement. Their position has fared poorly under the weight of Pearl Harbor and the Holocaust. Of course it is no part of my purpose to make a brief on behalf of any position—certainly not that one—but as Roberta Wohlstetter, for one, has shown so well, something that can be perceived clearly in retrospect can be blurred beyond recognition in the clutter of contemporary events. Hindsight can distort as well as clarify. To give each side of the debate its due, one must try to see events as participants did.[14]

A second focus of this study will be those who participated in the debate. At a time of international crisis, with war a genuine, if uncertain, possibility for the United States, public interest and in-

volvement in foreign policy issues were in all likelihood at their
peak, providing an opportunity to gauge who the "people" were.
Who did get involved and how extensively? What vehicles did people use to express opinion? We know something of the activities of
the so-called crisis committees, America First and the rest, though
very little beyond the upper leadership of those groups. What of
the lower echelons? And what of existing interest groups—labor,
business, the church, ethnics, veterans, and so forth? Did such
groups get seriously involved? If so, what forms did their participation take? Did it involve the rank and file, or lower leadership at
least, or did national officials speak for their organizations? And,
ultimately, what came of all this involvement? What "signals" did
such groups send to government leaders, and to their fellow citizens? The answers are important not only for what they reveal
about the immediate situation, but also because the 1939–41 debate was a period of unusually intense and extensive discussion of
foreign policy and of America's role in the modern world. The
debate, ending as it did with Pearl Harbor, provided a sort of
national catharsis. Precisely because the issues involved were so
fundamental and salient, and because the level of public interest
was so extraordinarily high, the attitudes formed as a result would
carry over for a generation. Ernest R. May articulated what many
observers have long known when he wrote that the "lessons" of
World War II oriented American policy for two decades. Not until
Vietnam exposed the dangers of misapplying such lessons was
their influence weakened.[15]

The final thrust of this study is to explain the dilemma that
bedeviled American opinion up to the moment Japanese planes
swept down over the United States Pacific Fleet. Stimson, Knox,
Morganthau, Ickes, and (perhaps) Roosevelt believed that full
American belligerency was necessary for the defeat of Nazi Germany. Hindsight indicates their judgment was correct. Why then
did so few Americans grasp this point? As late as November 22,
1941, two weeks prior to the raid on Pearl Harbor, Gallup found
that only 26 percent of those surveyed approved of an immediate
declaration of war. These results came near the close of a second
year of resounding Axis triumph. True, the British had sunk the
German battleship *Bismarck*, conquered the Italians in East Africa,
and averted an invasion of the Home Islands. Otherwise the

record was bleak. The Wehrmacht succeeded everywhere it struck —in the Balkans, in Greece and North Africa against the British, and in Russia against the Red Army. By November the British were locked in a furious struggle to relieve their besieged garrison at Tobruk, and the Russians were struggling to prevent the capture of Moscow. The war at sea presented a similarly grim picture. U-boats were sinking British shipping at such an alarming rate that Roosevelt felt compelled to ask Congress for a repeal of the strictures against the use of American shipping in war zones. Congress responded by approving both the arming of merchantmen and the convoying of ships to Britain. To compound matters further, it was evident that relations with Japan had reached a crisis. More than half the American public expected war in the near future. Yet with all this—the Allies losing the war and the prospect of a new conflict in the Pacific—Americans balked at full military participation.

To answer these questions and keep the project at a reasonable length, I have largely restricted the geographic scope of my study to Chicago and its immediate environs. Both the restrictions and the choice of location merit explanation. Looking at local activity was precisely the point of the study. Because the number of groups involved in the debate was potentially so large and diverse, and because their views were not drawn together in any single source, the amount of sifting to be done was mammoth. To have available as many different segments of the population and interest groups as possible, a major metropolitan center offered clear advantages. The choice of Chicago was based on several factors: the diversity of its media and the views they contained, the diversity of its population, its importance as a regional center. The presence in Chicago of the national headquarters of a crisis committee afforded superior opportunities to examine the functioning of such an organization at all levels. New York City would also have served, and it offered the tempting advantage of a larger number of newspapers, one of which was indexed! However, both New York City and the *Times* have often been consulted as guides to popular opinion, and I wanted to break fresh ground. Neither New York nor Chicago nor any single community (even Muncie) can be taken as representative of the overall population in any rigorous sense. Certainly I make no such claim. The presence of

Robert McCormick and the *Tribune* are alone enough to make Chicago unique. By the same token, this is not simply a local study. Chicago was influential in itself and its voices were heard around the country, as we shall see. Moreover, embracing as it did so many of the diverse elements of the larger society, Chicago does allow us to see the nature and extent of foreign affairs activity below the level of a national elite. I have also attempted to examine activities in other major cities, albeit to a much reduced extent, for comparative purposes. The result will, I hope, shed new light on a crucial period of national reappraisal, when Americans looked anew at their nation's role in the world and battled over which course to set. In so doing, they revealed a great deal about this country's political process—in the widest sense of that term—and about themselves. The debate of 1939–41 offers an important example of how American society performs during a crisis when it has to reach important judgments on matters of foreign policy. On the outcome of that debate rested stakes of immense value, and the results are influencing us still.

ACKNOWLEDGMENTS

My debts are numerous and my creditors dwell from coast to coast.

The staffs of many libraries aided me with courtesy as well as information. I wish particularly to thank those at the Joseph Regenstern Library at the University of Chicago; the Seely G. Mudd Library at Princeton University; the Hoover Institution on War, Revolution, and Peace at Stanford University; the New York Public Library; and the Library of Congress. Librarians at two state universities provided me with measureless help. The State Historical Society of Wisconsin, and those who labor in it, are genuine treasures. The staff of the John Peace Library at the University of Texas at San Antonio invariably fulfilled my extensive demands for interlibrary loan materials promptly and without complaint. To all, my thanks.

Those correspondents whose names appear in the bibliography took time to share their invaluable insights as participants in the story that follows. Special appreciation goes to Robert Douglas Stuart, Jr., Clark M. Eichelberger, and T. Walter Johnson. Each viewed the events in a different light; each exhibited similar kindness and patience toward a young graduate student.

Many people at the University of Wisconsin contributed advice and encouragement to this project. David Shepard, Michael McManus, and George Sweet put aside their own graduate work to serve as sounding boards for my ideas and to offer suggestions and good cheer. George Brown deserves special mention for his help on opinion polls and on the 1940 election. Professor Bernard

C. Cohen shared many insights on the relationship between public opinion and foreign policy. Professor Stanley K. Schultz helped acquaint me with Chicago and tried to civilize my prose. Above all, John Milton Cooper, Jr., who first suggested Chicago as a focus for my dissertation, furnished wise counsel throughout the project and served as a critic in the best sense of the term. I am sure that I could not have had better guidance.

My colleagues at the University of Texas at San Antonio, David R. Johnson and Woodruff D. Smith, read the manuscript with care. They provided vital encouragement and some much-needed prodding. Their suggestions regarding the preface were especially useful.

I have never met three other people to whom great thanks are due. Kathy A. Brown combed the League of Women Voters papers for me and unearthed a wealth of information. The readers who reviewed the manuscript for the University of North Carolina Press offered many wise suggestions. I have met Lewis Bateman, but I am sure that had nothing to do with his patience and consideration as an editor. To him, Ron Maner, Margaret Morse, and all the other members of the UNC Press staff who helped in the preparation of this book, my thanks.

Finally, there is Denise—who volunteered for some of the drudgery and lived with all of the anxiety. She bore everything with her own good humor, and that has been the most valuable aid of all.

SHOULD AMERICA GO TO WAR?

ONE

A WORLD LITTLE CHANGED

"War! bomb warsaw" exclaimed the *Chicago Tribune*'s headline on the morning of September 1, 1939. That evening the city's other leading newspaper, the *Daily News*, announced simply "war!" The wording was apt; it summarized a salient concern of most Americans as they regarded the foreign crisis that late summer day. War itself, more than any of the circumstances attending its outbreak, seemed to most Americans the main threat to their well-being. Armed conflict among the major European powers made this concern even more pronounced. It compelled Americans to confront issues of international politics and to ponder what courses the United States might adopt in dealing with changing world conditions. Over the next twenty-six months an extensive and often fierce public debate reflected both the divergent viewpoints Americans came to hold on foreign policy issues and the intensity with which many Americans defended their positions. Yet the debate would not really be joined until the following summer. So long as Americans remained confident of Allied victory, so long as participation in the war therefore remained the only serious threat to American society, complacency reigned. The outpouring of national opinion which surrounded revision of the Neutrality Act, while significant, is therefore misleading. During the lull in fighting that followed the conquest of Poland, foreign affairs receded from the headlines and also from the consciousness of Americans, if the decline in popular activity relating to foreign policy provides a measure of public interest in events abroad.[1]

Cities like Chicago were the centers of the national debate over foreign policy. Although historians like Thomas A. Bailey have called Chicago the "capital of isolationism," a city so large, so ethnically, socially, and economically diverse, hardly could have held to a monolithic position on so controversial a matter as American foreign policy. A host of meetings, rallies, and informal debates in the months before Pearl Harbor bore witness to the divisions among Chicagoans, reflecting the debate that raged across the United States. The leading citizens' pressure group to oppose expanding American involvement in the war, the America First Committee (AFC), was founded in the Windy City. There, until its dissolution after Pearl Harbor, the committee maintained both its national headquarters and many local chapters. But the America Firsters did not go unchallenged. Their leading organizational adversary maintained a chapter in Chicago that included such able and respected men as Adlai E. Stevenson and Paul H. Douglas among its leaders. This was the Committee to Defend America by Aiding the Allies (CDAAA), whose name sacrificed elegance for accuracy in describing its program. Later the even more militant Fight For Freedom (FFF) committee also established an outpost. The faculty, staff, and student body at the University of Chicago divided over American policy toward the war. Republican stalwarts in the city's northern suburbs eyed President Franklin D. Roosevelt's foreign policy maneuvers with suspicion and hostility, while denizens of its ethnic enclaves welcomed his actions in support of their homelands. Chicago's press was similarly at odds. The *Tribune* opposed with unflagging vigor Roosevelt's developing program of aid to the Allied cause, whereas the *Daily News*, the smaller *Chicago Journal of Commerce*, and radio news commentator Clifton Utley lent Roosevelt consistent and important backing. The *Chicago Defender*, with the largest circulation of any black-owned newspaper in the country, reflected the uncertainty within the black community over how to respond to the foreign crisis.[2]

As a setting for the debate, Chicago was large enough to contain most of the diverse elements found in the nation as a whole. It was not one community but many, sprawling across two hundred square miles south and west of Lake Michigan. The city's population of 3,396,808 made it second in size only to New York, a fact which exercised a subtle influence on the attitudes of many

Chicagoans toward the eastern metropolis. As in most other major cities, decades of rapid growth had come to an end by the 1930s. Its population had grown by less than 1 percent during the Depression decade, and the increase in the 1940s would be little larger. In fact, a significant migration to the suburbs had already begun. The surrounding region had grown by 11.5 percent in the 1930s and the pace was accelerating. This exodus consisted disproportionately of Chicagoans who were affluent, Protestant, well educated, and of older ethnic stocks.[3]

Fundamental to Chicago were its neighborhoods. By 1940 they housed residents drawn from across Europe and, increasingly, from Africa by way of the American South. The human tide of Eastern and Southern European immigrants had long since pushed its predecessors toward the city's periphery and formed itself into largely undiluted pockets around the urban core. Of the older stock, only the Germans remained on the near north side and the Irish on the near south. Italians took their place west of the Germans, with the Poles nearby along Division Street. Jews settled on the west side, and Bohemians on the southwest. All maintained their vigorous cultures, making Chicago's neighborhoods a babel of different tongues. Ties to the home countries remained strong, encouraged by dozens of local newspapers, institutions, and organizations. The ethnic groups formed the basis of the largest Catholic archdiocese in the United States, headed in 1939 by the most eminent and influential Catholic cleric in the country, George Cardinal Mundelein. Under his leadership, the church was a major influence in both local and national affairs, far more so than its Protestant or Jewish counterparts. Blacks were concentrated in Bronzeville, as locals of both races referred to the near-south-side neighborhood. Alone among the ethnic minorities in Chicago, their population continued to swell during the 1930s, growing by almost 19 percent.[4]

One of the most significant facts about the ethnic composition of Chicago was the lack of a dominant ethnic group. Whites whose parents had been born in the United States comprised little more than a quarter of the population. Poles were the largest single group of foreign born, with less than 12 percent of the city's total population. Chicago housed more Poles than any other city outside the homeland. Germans ranked just behind, at more than 11 percent, while Russians followed at 7 percent. Chicago contained almost identical numbers of Irish and Scandinavians, about 6.5 percent of the citizenry in each case. Italians, Czechs, and Slavs followed in that order. Even the smaller groups like the Czechs numbered in excess of 100,000, and therefore comprised a sizable and viable subcommunity.[5]

Ethnics were no more monolithic in their beliefs than any other large population segment. Studies of Chicago's ethnics in the Depression era are surprisingly sparse. Those accounts that do treat the 1930s suggest the ferment and multiplicity of the ethnic neighborhoods. The Poles, for example, were split along three axes by religion alone. Polish Catholics were divided into nonconformists and those whose loyalty to the church was virtually unquestioning. The Polish National Alliance was dominated by secular Poles. Only the Alliance cooperated in more than a minimal way with Polish Jews. The church was far more of a factor in the education of Chicago's Poles than among its Italians. Only 10 percent of the Italian parishes had established schools as late as 1910, but by 1920 every Polish parish had one. Perhaps 60 percent of Polish children attended a parochial school. Religion was less of a factor dividing the city's 270,000 Jews than was national origin, though the two factors overlapped. German Jews had settled first, and by 1940 were already leaving Hyde Park and Grand Boulevard for the far northern suburbs. Eastern European Jews, more heavily Orthodox in belief on average than the Germans, were just beginning to spread into the near west side. Differences among these and other groups would be muted somewhat by the impact of events abroad, which reinforced nationalism in every ethnic group.[6]

The configuration of political power in Chicago was more elaborate than the popular tales of crime and corruption might suggest. Full-blown machine politics came late to Chicago. Not until Anton Cermak forged a citywide Democratic coalition among the various ward organizations in 1931 did the components of the modern Chicago machine merge. The lack of a dominant ethnic group had inhibited the growth of machine politics. Cermak seized upon the widespread hatred of Prohibition to forge his coalition. When he was slain the following year, control passed to a group of Irish politicians led by Patrick J. Nash and Edward H. Kelly. Kelly served as mayor from 1933 until 1948, when Richard J. Daley began his ascendancy over Chicago politics. The Irish maintained a lock on the key city policymaking jobs, ruled the electoral machinery, and controlled the patronage that sustained the machine. Other positions, especially the visible ones, they apportioned carefully among Chicago citizenry. Moreover, the organization in the Kelly-Nash period was always more of an assemblage of barons— ward bosses and aldermen—than its critics understood. Every major ethnic group controlled at least one ward and so elected a national as alderman. Jacob Arvey represented the Russian Jews, Benjamin Adamowski and Edmund Jarecki the Poles, and so forth. Machine corruption was so legendary it inspired a kind of perverse pride among some Chicagoans. But graft and influence peddling told only part of the story. Chicago politicians succeeded in bringing their city more than its share of federal government largess as Kelly tied the machine to the New Deal. According to one estimate, perhaps 80 percent of the blue-collar workers in Chicago received relief at some point during the Depression.[7]

The 1930s were hard times indeed for Chicago and for Illinois. Approximately one-fifth of the state's workers were on relief at any given time, amounting to half the total work force over the course of the decade. The figures for blacks, though unreliable, were surely much greater. Prosperity was still a stranger in Bronzeville in 1939. Amid the depths of the Depression Chicago payrolls fell off by 75 percent, and 40 percent of the work force was unemployed. Conditions gradually improved thereafter. But, as was true for the nation as a whole, most city industries had barely regained pre-Depression levels of output when the war in Europe began.[8]

While the Irish dominated Chicago politics, the city's great private wealth lay in other hands: the McCormick fortune in farm machinery, the Field retail millions, Dawes in banking, and the Rosenwalds of Sears Roebuck. The city was also an important center of steel making, the electronics industry, and food processing, as well as being the hub of the nation's railroad network. The Kelly-Nash machine provided superior urban services and a favorable business climate. Kelly utilized New Deal assistance to help keep down city taxes and indebtedness. The machine also fought against a proposed state income tax and provided favorable property valuations for cooperative businesses. Moreover, until after the Memorial Day Massacre at the Republic Steel plant in 1937, Kelly set Chicago police against organized labor. City hall and the LaSalle Street financial interests accommodated each other, verbally at odds but in practice content to rule separate dominions, while the ethnic wards received rewards sufficient to keep them in line. Thus did the metropolis function.[9]

Despite the celebrated battle at Republic Steel, labor relations in Chicago were generally more peaceful than in other major cities. The unions attained a measure of power and influence with surprisingly little violence. Until World War II, Chicago was dominated by the American Federation of Labor (AFL). The Federation claimed some 330,000 members in 1940, to 60,000 for the Congress of Industrial Organizations (CIO). Together they represented about one-quarter of the labor force in the Windy City. Reflecting the national pattern, the CIO was strongest in mass production industries like steel and meat packing. The AFL enjoyed its greatest success among teachers, the building trades, teamsters, and service workers. Locals from the latter three industries had formed the Chicago Federation of Labor (CFL) in an effort to achieve greater cooperation in coordinating strikes, organizing consumer boycotts, and encouraging political action. Under the leadership of John Fitzgerald, the CFL maintained its own radio station, WCFL, and extended a lenient contract to the financially troubled *Chicago Times* as a means of making labor's voice heard in the city. Fitzgerald shied away from independent political action and welcomed overtures from Edward Kelly when the mayor moved to patch up his relations with labor after the Memorial Day Massacre. Though Fitzgerald personally favored trying to organize mass production industries, hostility between the AFL and the CIO at the national level led to bitter local rivalry by the late 1930s. In Chicago both factions concentrated on expanding their memberships during the defense boom and did not take a leading part in the foreign policy debate.[10]

News, and in particular foreign news, reached Chicago via many channels. There were still several foreign-language newspapers published in the city, though these tended to concentrate on local affairs. The national print media—a plethora of magazines, journals, and news magazines—were of course available to Chicagoans.

A World Little Changed

Above all there was radio, just coming into its own as a purveyor of news in the late 1930s. Until then, radio news departments had been minor adjuncts of the networks. In most cases they provided, literally, a headline service only. Both NBC and CBS kept small staffs in Europe, but prior to the war their main function was to provide exotic entertainment for American audiences. The networks provided extensive coverage of the Munich crisis, but both CBS and NBC retreated to their previous patterns of inattention during the months following its resolution. As the European situation again grew ominous in the summer of 1939, the networks improved their foreign staffs and again expanded their coverage. Whether or not radio created a mass interest in foreign affairs, as one historian has claimed, it certainly brought events in Europe into American homes with an urgency and immediacy that print media could not match. This was true for European news only, however, since technological shortcomings precluded broadcasting across the Pacific. Thus radio helped to focus American attention on Europe and relegate Asia to a secondary status. By 1941 Americans indicated that radio had surpassed newspapers as their primary source of news. Nevertheless, newspapers retained huge followings and provided a depth of coverage that radio could seldom equal. Moreover, the papers provided insight into local thinking and activities in a way that no national medium could match.[11]

In the *Chicago Tribune* the city had a newspaper as colorful and brash as its own popular image. The *Tribune* boasted the largest circulation of any standard-sized newspaper in America. Over a million copies sold on Sundays and just under a million each weekday. Only the *New York Daily News* reached more American homes. To serve its readership, the *Tribune* offered a lively package of hard news and features. During the 1939–41 period it contained extensive coverage of foreign affairs and maintained one of the largest foreign staffs on any paper in America. Like the staffs of the wire services, the radio networks, and the other independent newspapers, the *Tribune*'s people were concentrated in Europe. Just one reporter, a native Japanese, was based in Asia. *Tribune* editorials castigated the New Deal, and its pronounced views often surfaced in its news stories as well. A 1937 poll of Washington correspondents voted the paper second only to the Hearst press as a distorter of news. Other critics claimed its features were the real source of the paper's popularity. Whatever its biases, the *Tribune* was seldom dull and few rivals could match in extent its coverage of world and national affairs.[12]

Colonel Robert Rutherford McCormick was the undisputed master of the *Chicago Tribune*. Grandson of the Joseph Medill who built the *Tribune*, grandnephew of Cyrus McCormick, son of an ambassador to three European capitals, McCormick was born in 1880 into the heart of Chicago's business and social elite. Educated in England and at Groton and Yale, he received everything from his parents except their attention. "Bertie" McCormick grew into a tall, ramrod straight, lonely, and reserved young man. Earmarked for the law, Robert instead drifted into local politics, where he helped supervise construction of the Wilmette-Joliet Canal. On the project he befriended a young Irish engineer named Edward J. Kelly. Their personal regard survived even Kelly's rise to the top of the Cook County Democratic machine and McCormick's acerbic Republicanism.[13]

When Robert's older brother Medill decided in the 1910s that politics interested him more than the *Tribune*, "Bertie" and his cousin Joseph Patterson gradually assumed operating control of the paper. Although poles apart politically, the cousins soon rebuilt the languishing *Tribune* and trounced the Hearst press in a vicious circulation war. Following service in World War I, their journalistic partnership ended when Patterson left Chicago to found the *New York Daily News*. Robert McCormick then forged the *Tribune* into an extension of his own formidable personality.

He conducted himself as the aristocrat he probably conceived himself to be. In manners, lifestyle, and speech—though seldom in his political views—McCormick was an open anglophile. He dressed in tweeds, groomed his mustache impeccably, was fond of polo and riding to the hounds, and wore knickers for decades after they had become unfashionable. McCormick so enjoyed serving in France during World War I that he named his Wheaton farm "Cantigny" after an American battle there. All his life he liked to be addressed as "colonel." He seems to have participated in little actual combat, but became a serious and capable student of military history. McCormick made few real friends and despised the idlers and dilettantes whom he believed filled high society. Aloof by nature, the colonel went out of his way to cultivate the independence he so prized in a newspaper man. Following his first wife's death in the summer of 1939, he lived as a virtual recluse for five years.[14]

With the *Tribune*, McCormick shed his stiffness and restraint and became a flamboyant maverick. Himself childless, he ruled paternally over the *Tribune* staff. Employees were abruptly fired, but received top wages and fringe benefits for so long as they retained the colonel's good will. Soon after assuming control, he and Patterson had christened the *Tribune* "The World's Greatest Newspaper." McCormick wrote little himself but conveyed his ideas through editorial writers like Leon Stolz and Clifford Raymond. The *Tribune* embarked on dozens of crusades. It opposed Prohibition, political corruption, and British imperialism; it boosted opera, safety on the Fourth of July, and balanced budgets. The colonel hated Communists and labor unions and, after 1933, Franklin D. Roosevelt. One *Tribune* story on prostitution carried the headline "Roosevelt Area in Wisconsin a Hotbed of Vice." As eccentric and excessive as McCormick was, it has been easy to dismiss him as a relic. "The best mind of the 14th century," said one bit of Chicago lore. But there was substance as well as silliness to McCormick's career. He conducted a lifelong defense of freedom of the press that has had enduring importance. In fact, First Amendment considerations account in part for his break with Roosevelt, whom he initially had supported. The colonel regarded the National Recovery Administration code for the newspaper industry as an infringement on the independence of the press and broke with Roosevelt accordingly. Throughout his career McCormick was an intense nationalist whose views on American foreign policy were rooted in his understanding of the principles of the founding fathers. He cherished the Monroe Doctrine, with its emphasis on noninvolvement with Europe, as the enduring foundation of American foreign policy.[15]

Over at the city's leading evening paper, the *Daily News*, its publisher William Franklin Knox based his ideas not on the founding fathers, but on his mentor Theodore Roosevelt. Born in 1874, Knox was the son of a Canadian immigrant. His family migrated several times between New England and the midwest in an unsuccessful effort to better their modest circumstances. By 1898 young Frank Knox had worked his way through Alma College in Michi-

gan. When the Spanish-American War began, Knox rushed to enlist as a private in Theodore Roosevelt's Rough Riders and saw
action at San Juan Hill. The war was brief, but a lasting friendship developed between Knox and Roosevelt. Knox cheered TR
throughout his presidency and served him as a trusted lieutenant
in the 1912 Progressive campaign for the White House. Later he
echoed Roosevelt in calling for an early American entry into
World War I. Again enlisting as a private when war came, Knox
fought in France and rose to become a lieutenant colonel of
artillery.[16]

Knox had begun his newspaper career upon returning from
Cuba in 1898. He advanced swiftly, mastering all facets of the
newspaper business. In 1927 he joined the Hearst organization
and within a year was general manager for the entire press chain.
Three years later he broke with Hearst, resigned, and bought control of the *Chicago Daily News*.

The new owner-publisher remained under the spell of Theodore Roosevelt. Knox's rugged individualism, pride in physical
vigor, bluff speech, and engaging grin were all patterned after his
old leader. He also shared TR's intense nationalism and his fasci-
nation with things naval, though, much to his own disgust, Knox
suffered from sea sickness and kept off ships whenever possible.
He lacked Roosevelt's intellectual depth, but similarly cloaked his
moralism in no-nonsense talk of power politics. Wrote *Daily News*
columnist Howard Vincent O'Brien, "There is no swank about
him. He is essentially and permanently democratic and is as de-
void of guile as any man I have ever known." But, continued
O'Brien, he had "tabasco in his blood."[17]

In the depths of the Depression, Knox rebuilt the moribund
Daily News through exposés on gambling and the rackets. By 1939
daily circulation exceeded one-third of a million. Knox's Republican loyalty and his fiscal orthodoxy overcame his attraction to the
Roosevelt family. He broke with the New Deal in August 1933, on
the grounds that the administration had intervened too far in the
economy. During a European vacation the following year he became alarmed over fascism. Nominated for vice-president on the
1936 GOP ticket, Knox was a vigorous and often strident critic of
the New Deal and remained so in 1939. But the rising specter of
fascism prompted Knox to begin to support administration for-

eign policy early in 1938. Coverage of foreign affairs was a special strength of the *Daily News*. An independent foreign staff, led by Edgar Ansell Mowrer, who had won a Pulitzer Prize, and Leland Stowe, who was soon to win one, provided insightful and determinedly anti-Fascist reports from Europe.[18]

By the fall of 1940, their differences over foreign policy would involve McCormick and Knox in what Chicagoans would call the "battle of the two colonels," a clash symptomatic of the larger national debate. In 1939, relatively little of that impending contention was visible at any level. Opinion polls showed that an overwhelming majority of Americans desired that their country remain at peace. So strong and widespread was this revulsion against war that it muted temporarily the ongoing domestic controversies over foreign policy, including those between the two Chicago publishers. Readers of either of the two papers, surely the bulk of the attentive public in Chicago, thus received fundamentally similar views of the international situation.[19]

The similarities were pronounced in the way each paper portrayed the return of war to Europe and its meaning for America. Each emphasized the horror and carnage of war. The *Tribune*'s first wartime editorial on the European situation stressed the vast misery and destruction armed conflict would produce as well as the huge resulting debts for all participants. The *Daily News* more graphically sketched a similar picture of carnage: "A second great war has come to curse a war-sick Europe. Millions of men, armed men, have taken the field. Helpless women and children are being slaughtered in Poland by bombs from the air. Equally defenseless men, women and children are going down in torpedoed ships at sea. Great cities are blacked out, and people scurry like rats for their holes at the sounds of shrieking sirens." Each pictured, in cartoons and photographs, the devastation wrought by the last war and the sorry promise of the new.[20]

The two newspapers also agreed unequivocally about the proper course for American policy. "This is not our war," stated the *Tribune*. The *Daily News* was again more emphatic than its morning rival. The headline over a front-page editorial blared, "WE MUST KEEP OUT." Neither paper articulated the basis for such a view. In light of overwhelming evidence from public opinion polls and almost every other source, each paper evidently believed that the desire for continued peace was so widespread there was no need to justify or explain editorial support for such a policy. Few commentators elsewhere felt compelled to build a case for neutrality either, and fewer still expressed doubts about the policy itself.[21]

Both papers did fear that emotional attachments might cloud the judgment of Americans and lead the nation into war. This theme would later become a fixture in antiadministration circles, but in 1939 sentiment against involvement so pervaded the country that warnings against emotionalism were not confined to Roosevelt's enemies. Admonishments against "war hysteria" were a staple of commentary nationwide during the early days of the war. A *Tribune* editorial cautioned against the insidious power of radio to arouse excitement, and another reminded ethnic Americans that their loyalty belonged to this country. A few days later its cartoon pictured the sparks of hate and hysteria drifting across the Atlantic toward the United States. On September 9 the *Daily News* stressed the dangers of alarming the public over the scant possibility of the United States entering the war. An editorial criticized Roosevelt for using the alarming label "limited national emergency" to describe the steps he had taken in response to the outbreak of the war. With obvious relief, the *Daily News* noted in mid-September that people were turning their attention back to their own immediate concerns.[22]

Nowhere in those opening months of the war did either newspaper attempt to draw a clear moral or political distinction between the Allies and the Germans, much less suggest that such a distinction serve as the basis of United States policy. Only the *Tribune* took time to denounce persecutions by the Nazis. "It would be a strange American indeed," it wrote, "who could stomach their creed and their attitudes." The *Daily News* had been so unmistakably anti-Nazi for so long that by the outbreak of the war it no longer felt a need to declare its position. Neither did the two Chicago papers consider friendliness to the Allied nations as an appropriate basis for American policy. Such relative silence with regard to the contending sides in Europe was by no means always shared by newspapers elsewhere. Editorials from Atlantic to Pacific flayed Hitler's regime. Both Chicago dailies saved their anger for the Soviet Union's November invasion of Finland. "The invasion of Finland . . . may contain the beginnings of the greatest catastrophe with which Europe has been threatened since the Hunnish invasion," said a *Tribune* editorial. The *Daily News* and the *Tribune* agreed that the Soviet Union was likely to be the real winner in any prolonged conflict among the other European powers, an opinion shared by Charles Lindbergh and many others. But anticommunism did not dictate the foreign policy views of the two principal Chicago papers. Had the Soviet Union never been formed, their position would have been the same. For McCormick and Knox it was not that the 1939 conflict was the wrong war; it was that war itself was ruinously wrong.[23]

A final conviction that the *Tribune* and the *Daily News* shared was that the United States could control the level of its involvement in the European crisis. This was not so obvious a point as perhaps it might seem. Within a year the fantastic German successes in Western Europe would convince many Americans both in and out of government that the fate of most of the civilized world depended largely on the intentions of Adolf Hitler. Nations like the United States were never reduced to mere pawns, but by then Hitler seemed to set the tempo and control the pace of events. Other countries were forced to react to the German lead. Until the fall of France all this remained ahead. Though loathed and to some degree feared, Hitler seemed to possess no extraordinary power. America still seemed safely beyond the reach of any foreign aggression. Most Americans believed that the Allies would eventually win and of course hoped for such an outcome. Few expected a German victory; war itself was the threat to American well-being. This was one reason why the *Tribune* and others placed so much emphasis on the need to prevent emotional attachments from dictating United States policy. Since Americans controlled their own destiny, they need only keep their heads to assure the continuation of peace.

If the two papers concurred in their views on many aspects of the international situation, significant elements of disagreement lay at or near the surface. The most important of these was their differing views of the Roosevelt administration. Fear of growing federal government power, and particularly that of the presidency, remained the basis of both papers' opposition to Roosevelt's domestic programs. But such concerns marked as well the *Tribune*'s hostility toward administration foreign policy. McCormick had begun to contend that Roosevelt yearned to maneuver the nation into war. Intervention would deflect criticism from New Deal domestic failures, please Roosevelt's British friends, and provide a means for Roosevelt to retain and strengthen his grip on the country. By 1939 Knox had separated president from policy and foreign affairs from domestic issues. Knox refused to join McCormick in believing that FDR would put personal interests ahead of the nation's welfare. But the flag around which the *Daily News* rallied did not always fly over the Roosevelt White House.[24]

Calls for national unity and bipartisanship in foreign policy were frequent in the late autumn of 1939. Walter Lippmann, for one, wrote that the gravity of the European situation required Americans to put aside petty political squabbling. McCormick and Knox used the same rhetoric as Lippmann in an effort to gain advantage for the Republican party. McCormick suggested that a change to sensible—that is, Republican—leadership would insure the nation's safety. Knox subtly advanced a similar conclusion. In response to a general rallying of public support, said the *Daily News*, Roosevelt should strive to represent all the people. To Republicans who viewed New Deal measures like the Wagner Act as "class oriented," this amounted to a call for an abandonment of efforts to expand New Deal reforms. The *Daily News* further recommended that a bipartisan congressional committee hold regular meetings with the president to advise him on foreign policy matters. An editorial in mid-September suggested Roosevelt should reorganize his cabinet to include political opponents in both parties. The president was thinking along similar lines. He held secret meetings in Washington with Knox and other prominent Republicans to sound them out on the idea. Knox urged Roosevelt not to run for a third term on the grounds that to do so would impair national unity. The Chicagoan still harbored some doubts about Roosevelt's commitment to peace and the views of certain presidential advisors, most likely Harry Hopkins. In December Knox wrote Roosevelt cautioning him that the public did not believe the current situation justified cessation of the partisan debate over foreign policy.[25]

The two papers' differing assessments of the administration helped determine their positions on one of the two major foreign policy debates before the fall of France. During the 1930s, Con-

gress had passed a series of Neutrality Acts in an effort to prevent international economic entanglements from dragging America into war. By September 1939 existing neutrality legislation
banned all sales of arms to warring nations, allowed American
shipping to sail anywhere on the high seas, forbade travel on ships
of belligerent nations, and prohibited loans to nations in default of
their World War I debts to the United States. Roosevelt proposed
to repeal the embargo on arms sales and to reinstitute a lapsed
"cash and carry" provision from a previous version of the Neutrality Act. This would restore a ban on American shipping in war
zones, but allow nations to purchase American-made arms and
munitions under certain restrictions. Buyers were required to pay
cash for the material and to transport it abroad in other than
American ships. The goal, said Roosevelt, was to restore "true
neutrality."[26]

Roosevelt's real aim, retorted the *Tribune,* was to aid the Allies.
In the paper's view, repeal of the arms embargo in time of war was
an unneutral act, representing a shift of the nation's economic
weight to the side the administration regarded as more moral. The
Tribune charged that repeal would set a dangerous precedent and
risked beginning a movement toward war. "How long can people
take warlike steps short of war?" queried an editorial. "Such steps
gain momentum. Their impulses quicken." The logic behind the
proposed revision, the paper continued, implied falsely that the
Allies were fighting America's fight. Naturally the Allies would
seek to exploit such an implication to exact further advantage
from the United States. By stating that the "cash and carry" policy
would operate in favor of the Allies at the expense of the Germans, the *Tribune,* along with other administration opponents, described the true impact of the proposed change with far more
accuracy than had Roosevelt.[27]

Knox accepted the president's logic. The *Daily News* refused to
admit that the new policy would reward one side. Instead, in common with other proponents of repeal, the paper turned the
charge of partiality around. "Taking sides? We are taking sides
now. Hitler's side," roared one editorial. "By refusing to sell arms
to belligerents we are playing Hitler's game." Stripped of their
emotional baggage such charges were true. But both Roosevelt's
and Knox's sympathy for the opponents of fascism were well

known. By failing to admit the obvious fact that "cash and carry" favored the Allies, backers of the plan cast doubt on the honesty of their motives and further alarmed their critics.[28]

Why did the administration forces reject candor in their desire to aid the Allies? At one point the *Daily News* did raise a key question of the entire embargo debate. "Is it neutral on our part," inquired an editorial, "to deprive France and Britain under the neutrality act, of the benefits of their superiority at sea, and so increase the relative strength of Hitler's superiority on land and in the air?" But the *Daily News* never offered a direct answer to its own question. The *Tribune*'s reply to a similar query was clear. Americans, an editorial suggested, "should ask themselves if going to war a little bit is possible. Can the United States adopt a cause and then stand aside?" Not only would an innate American sense of activism and responsibility come into play, but those emotions would be exploited by an administration bent on aligning the United States with Britain and France. If one discards McCormick's conviction that the administration was resolved to take America into war, there were many points at which the country could stop short of actual fighting. To those who distrusted FDR, however, the *Tribune*'s reasoning must have seemed acute. To those people mindful of the gradual way in which the country had become enmeshed in Allied affairs prior to U.S. entry into World War I, probably a larger group than the Roosevelt haters, the argument was at least plausible.[29]

The central concern for peace shared by the Chicago newspapers and virtually every other element of American society blinded many to America's altered place in the modern world. A consensus agreed on the possibility and desirability of America remaining a nonbelligerent. In that sense she could also remain a neutral, deciding for herself the precise dimensions of her neutrality. Yet by 1939 the international ramifications of American policy had become immense. The concept of neutrality no longer carried the comfortable connotation that the United States was inconsequential and hence easily ignored by foreign nations. The direct implication of this argument was that American inaction mattered as much as purposeful action, that passivity no longer represented impartiality. Even as they first exposed this truth, however, men like Knox and McCormick balked at accepting it. McCormick came closer, noting the risks of becoming tied to "the mistakes of statesmanship, the ambitions of rulers, and the fate of empires far away." Yet this theme appeared less often than his attacks on the ambitions of scheming New Dealers. Knox, the disciple of Theodore Roosevelt, refused to confront the issue. His newspaper stressed instead a return to traditional international law as its reason for supporting repeal of the arms embargo, an argument widely used by proponents of change. They did not suggest that the United States was, in effect, inescapably forced to choose sides in international conflicts, regardless of the level of active American involvement. To appreciate the vast consequences of American policy was to admit a level of American responsibility for international affairs that Knox, to say nothing of McCormick, was unprepared to recognize in the fall of 1939. So the readers of neither paper were educated to the underlying realities of America's place in the world.[30]

The *Chicago Journal of Commerce* presented the implications of America's position in the modern world better than either of the city's leading dailies. As a business newspaper, its columns touched national and international politics only tangentially. Editorials did address these subjects on occasion. The *Journal* presented its analysis of the international situation in its first weekly issue following the outbreak of hostilities. The editorial recognized that nothing the United States could do, not even maintaining the status quo, would be seen abroad as impartial. So the paper saw no sense in striving for a posture the nation could never achieve. Instead, the United States should choose the policy that minimized the risk of involvement in war. People differed over what constituted the safest course, the *Journal* admitted, but the paper itself supported the administration's recommendations.[31]

The *Chicago Defender* contained little more international news than the *Journal of Commerce*, but a far greater range of commentary. Founded in 1905 by Robert S. Abbott, the *Defender* reached more American blacks than any other black-owned newspaper in the United States. It sold 26,000 copies in Chicago and another 10,000 nationwide. Accordingly, the *Defender* covered not only the news of Chicago's Bronzeville, but racial matters throughout the country. The racial focus very much extended to the paper's coverage of foreign news as well. If blacks were directly involved in an overseas story, the *Defender* often contained a brief account. Otherwise the paper ignored both national and international affairs in its news columns. Commentary was a far different matter. Abbott was as staunch a Republican as Robert McCormick, but unlike the colonel, he filled his paper with divergent viewpoints. "The World's Greatest Weekly," as the *Defender* called itself, contained everything from Marxism to McCormick Republicanism. Racial pride and a refusal to accept discrimination were the common elements, as well as the dominant themes, of the editorial page itself. The paper's various columnists also devoted considerable attention to international events. Readers thus encountered only a narrow spectrum of the news, but a fairly extensive commentary on events they presumably learned about through radio or daily newspapers. Joe Louis received much more space on the *Defender*'s front page than the war, which did not even make the paper's list of the top twenty stories of 1939. But *Defender* readers got by far the widest range of commentary, measured ideologically, to be found in any Chicago paper.[32]

The *Defender* was anti-Fascist, but the desire for progress toward racial equality at home eclipsed every other issue in its pages. The paper acknowledged that fascism was fundamentally racist and opposed to democratic capitalism, but the shortcomings of both the United States and the Western European democracies precluded a policy of militant opposition to the Axis powers. Congressional unwillingness to pass an antilynching law symbolized the oppressive racial situation in America. Abroad, the imperialistic policies of France and Great Britain belied their pretensions as defenders of democracy. The memory of Ethiopia lingered. France and Britain had done nothing to help when a black nation was destroyed by aggression. Rather than calling for aid to the Allies, the *Defender* urged blacks everywhere to exploit the international situation to gain the rights they were unjustly denied.[33]

As this exhortation implies, the *Defender*, like the other Chicago papers, was in effect telling its readers that the outbreak of war ought not to override more immediate considerations. The paper's position fit the overall pattern of press opinion in other ways as well. War itself, rather than fascism, emerged as the principal danger to America. Lucius C. Harper, whose column "Dustin' off the News" appeared on the front page, wrote on September 9 that, "War is a rich man's game in which the poor man is called upon to pay the price and to render patriotic service with some mythical hope of reward." A Jay Jackson cartoon pictured a pro-war activist being haunted by a skeletal World War I doughboy. Furthermore, the figure was pointing to the betrayal of American blacks, British colonial peoples, and Ethiopia. "This is obviously not a war for the defense of democracy," noted an editorial, "but rather for the preservation of the imperialist status quo." The *Defender* also made clear that the administration would have to earn black support for its foreign policy. "President Roosevelt calls for the unity of our nation around his program of neutrality," the paper observed. "There can be no unity short of equality of opportunity for all." The *Defender* directed its readers to maintain their focus on injustice at home. Where events seemed to have no relevance for blacks, the paper ignored them. The most outstanding instance involved revision of the neutrality legislation, which the *Defender* never mentioned.[34]

The diverse attitudes toward foreign affairs found in Chicago papers also existed around the country. In particular, the level of insight into the issues underlying the arms embargo question varied widely. Differences existed over all phases of the matter. As the *New York Times* noted, both opponents and proponents of repeal insisted their concerns were confined to America. Few would admit either a desire to help the Allies or a dislike of them. Each side emphasized that its position offered the best chance to preserve peace, though the embargo's defenders were more emphatic on this point. Each side proffered a range of explanations, justifications, and warnings. The warnings came mostly from opponents of repeal, reflecting American perceptions of the international situation. Serious fighting between the major powers had yet to begin, the American public remained confident of Allied victory, and therefore Americans perceived the war itself, rather than Nazism, as the main danger to the national well-being. Roosevelt's proposal to alter American neutrality policy, coming after the outbreak of the war, amounted to changing the rules so as to favor one side after the game had begun, his opponents charged. By showing favoritism, the move might provoke the Nazis.

Spokesmen for "cash and carry" countered in a variety of ways. A few, like columnist Jay Franklin, acknowledged the favoritism inherent in any change in policy. Franklin sensed that the twin aims of continued peace and the defeat of Germany might not be compatible, but he too stressed the former. Most proponents of repeal ignored the favoritism issue and defended "cash and carry" as a return to the traditional American doctrine of freedom of the seas. The thrust of their argument was American rights, not the impact abroad. Observers proceeding from similar apprehensions sometimes reached opposite conclusions on the embargo question. The *Atlanta Constitution*, for example, supported repeal of the ban against weapons sales but agreed with the *Tribune* that participation in another war might consume the American democratic process. The two papers thus sought to avoid the same danger by pursuing opposite lines of action. By late 1940 the concern with war's effect on American democracy would be largely confined to the forces opposing the "aid short of war" program. But in the autumn of 1939, positions had yet to crystalize.[35]

Seldom, in Chicago or elsewhere, did genuine bitterness cloud the analyses of issues. The debate between the *Daily News* and the *Tribune* over repeal of the arms embargo and attendant issues contained only occasional elements of heat. Little real friction resulted, and, after final passage of the bill on November 2, they muted their quarrel. Each remained fearful that war might ensnare America. The *Tribune* underscored continuing public opposition to U.S. intervention in the European war and doubted any benefits other than an increase in business profits would come from such interventions. Peace plainly outweighed profit. The *Daily News* continued to fear volatility in public opinion and suspected that Roosevelt yearned to take part in the peacemaking, something the paper contended was "not our job." On this point McCormick surely concurred. Now that the embargo had been repealed, the extensive agreement between the two major Chicago dailies again became evident. Only the *Defender*, fueled by outrage over discrimination in America and toward colonial peoples overseas, sustained bitterness through the winter of 1939–40.[36]

Throughout the period of the Phony War, during the winter of 1939–40, coverage of American foreign policy and the European war lacked focus in most American media, including the *Daily News* and the *Tribune*. As military activity reached a virtual standstill and the diplomatic front became quiet, the volume of coverage shrank. Foreign affairs had dominated the front pages in the autumn; by February stories were scarcely to be found. Each Chicago paper pursued its own particular interests and seldom confronted its rival. In November both papers condemned the Russian invasion of Finland. The *Daily News* urged Washington to supply the Finns with arms and to provide loans to pay for such shipments. The *Tribune* remained silent on the matter of aid. It emphasized instead the wisdom of the Monroe Doctrine, especially the principle of noninterference in European affairs. Most pieces echoed earlier themes, such as a *Tribune* series on the administration's plotting of "dictatorship" for the country should the United States enter the war. As proof, reporters like Chesly Manley cited contingency plans to mobilize various segments of the economy for war. The *Daily News* dismissed all such allegations outright. But such direct feuding was exceptional. Basically the *Tribune* and *Daily News* agreed that foreign affairs were not of critical interest to Chicagoans. Their mutual lack of attention to it in the spring of 1940 attested to this belief. Each paper insisted moreover that New Deal domestic excesses should be the primary issue in the upcoming election. The public could ignore the siren call of foreign affairs when it entered the voting booth.[37]

During the winter lull of 1939–40, one of the few direct sources of continuing contention between the two Chicago dailies was Great Britain. Even here the clash was muted. Many historians have claimed that McCormick was anti-British. As his views appeared in print during the Phony War, McCormick emerged as less a rabid anglophobe than a nationalist. Britain received far milder treatment in the *Tribune* than in the *Defender*. The *Tribune* gave extensive and unbiased coverage to a speech by the British ambassador, Lord Lothian, before the Chicago Council on Foreign Relations (CCFR), to cite one example. Within a week, however, the *Tribune* was again chiding Britain for failing to repay her World War I debts. *Tribune* criticism centered on the issues of dictatorship and imperialism. Such wartime measures as food rationing and press censorship were equated with the imposition of a permanent dictatorship. The *Tribune* also repeatedly drew its readers' attention to Britain's record in Ireland and elsewhere. Editorials questioned whether Britain fought for anything more noble than preservation of the status quo and cited as evidence British rebuffs to Gandhi's drive for Indian independence. Other stories did little more than twist the lion's tail. Conversely, the *Tribune*'s St. Patrick's Day cartoon was a tribute to British sea power.[38]

Although willing to print material unflattering to Great Britain, the general tenor of the *Daily News* remained favorable. It agreed with the *Tribune* that Britain's policy of searching American ships and inspecting overseas mails was an affront. Knox was sufficiently upset to suggest that the United States consider embargoing arms sales to Great Britain should her policy persist, a more extreme reaction than anything in the *Tribune*. The *Daily News* agreed that Britain's imperial policies embarrassed her position as a champion of democracy. But no careful reader of the *Daily News* would have gained the impression that a basis existed for serious American grievances toward Britain. In general the paper's coverage of the European situation was done in tones supportive of the Allies, but it was also restrained, often insightful, and usually balanced.[39]

The East Asian situation received far less coverage than Europe in the Chicago press. The same held true for American media across the nation, though newspapers on the Pacific coast gave somewhat greater attention to Asia than those in other regions. Even during the lull of the Phony War, articles on Asia were a rarity anywhere. Of the two major Chicago papers, the supposedly isolationist *Tribune* contained the more extensive reporting on Asia than did its evening rival. The *Tribune*'s Asian policy was an extension of its general foreign and domestic views. The real danger to the United States came not from the Japanese, with whom the United States had no quarrel, but from the Roosevelt administration and its susceptibility to British influence. While deploring Tokyo's use of force, the paper doubted Japanese actions were significantly worse than Western imperialism in the region. The *Tribune* warned Americans against allowing themselves to front for "occidental imperialism." As for American economic interests, said an editorial, "our China trade is not worth the life of a single American marine." McCormick believed that the United States should retire from the Philippines as soon as possible and make Hawaii an impregnable and impassable base.[40]

At first the *Daily News* prescribed no definite course of action in Asia, nor did it specify the interests or holdings America should insist upon in her dealings with Japan. Knox at one point allowed that the United States might decide to withdraw from Asia. His real hope was for an attitude of determination in American foreign policy and a consistency of goals. Roosevelt's seemingly aimless tacking was intolerable. By late spring, however, the *Daily News* had decided upon a concrete policy of firmness. An editorial in mid-April recommended an embargo on all war supplies to Japan. As an inferior power she would be forced to accede to American demands. Fear of trouble should not inhibit our policy. Weakness or vacillation by the United States would only encourage Japanese leaders to undertake new aggression and thus would lead to further deterioration in relations between the two nations. Citing the pattern of Hitler's expansion in Europe, a later editorial intimated that a small war now might prevent a major conflict in the future.[41]

This sharp and explicit disagreement over Far Eastern policy was a portent of coming feuds. But the split was as yet confined to Asia, an area of secondary concern in early 1940. The difference looms far larger in hindsight than it must have to readers at the time. Asia scarcely received mention in either the *Journal of Commerce* or the *Defender*. Polls showed that Americans felt somewhat more threatened by Germany than by Japan, and even Hitler did not yet create great concern in Chicago.[42]

The pattern of public reaction to the opening phase of the war in Europe was one of deepening interest but sporadic and restrained activity. Coming at a time when the New Deal had spent its force and before the 1940 political campaigns had begun in earnest, the war dominated political discussions. As the months passed, the war touched an ever-growing number of Chicagoans. Ethnic groups with direct ties to the peoples of Europe were interested in the conflict from the first. So too was the League of Women Voters. Blacks looked with skepticism upon the notion that the war was somehow a struggle for civilization against the forces of barbarism. Veterans' groups addressed the problems of American security which the new situation created. American foreign policy was a subject of heated debate on the University of Chicago campus. Business leaders pondered the war's probable effects on the economy, as did their counterparts in organized labor. Everyone talked of their desire for peace. As one Chicagoan said, "the only war we are looking forward to is that between the New York Yankees and the Cincinnati Reds in October."[43]

Demand for war information soared. Bit by bit consciousness of the war spread off the editorial and news pages of American newspapers and into the society sections, the gossip columns, the entertainment pages, and the comics. The hostilities caught *Tribune* society reporter "Cousin Eve" on vacation in France. From her, Chicagoans read reports of daily life in Paris, of frantic contingency planning by tourists whose returning voyages were cancelled, and of the nervous fear that the Germans might soon attack. The *Defender* featured similar stories of American blacks, and added an account of how the closing of Paris nightclubs was throwing black performers out of work. On September 5 Ed Sullivan's popular Hollywood column contained an imaginary interview with celebrated World War I hero, Father Francis P. Duffy. War, Duffy had found, was nothing more than aimless carnage. At all costs it should be avoided. In November, the *Tribune* discovered that the war already was influencing women's fashions. It approved of the new, simpler, more masculine look, but worried that the impact had come so much sooner than in 1914. "Ole Nosey," gossip columnist in the *Defender*, insisted the war was having an even more drastic effect on the social lives of blacks. "Now that it looks like we may be going to war," she reported, "the guys and gals are getting down to the marriage license bureau as fast as they can." A *Daily News* reader often could find more outspoken opposition to fascism in Sterling North's book review column than appeared on the editorial page. North contended that Western civilization was at stake in the present war, and his hatred of Nazism infused many of his reviews. Nor was he a solitary prophet. The cartoon strip *Don Winslow*, whose lantern-jawed hero served as a troubleshooter for the United States Navy, repeatedly featured foreign powers greedy to capture this nation's wealth. An October strip decried foreign rulers who deluded their people with "chosen people propaganda." That fall, the war seemed to show up everywhere in Chicago's newspapers.[44]

Diverse signs indicated community reaction. On the evening of September 1, Hitler was burned in effigy at six different points within the city. Throughout the autumn requests for books on

international affairs skyrocketed at various Chicago libraries, reflecting a national trend. Hermann Rauschning's *The Revolution of
Nihilism*, a strong denunciation of Hitler by a former Nazi official, enjoyed special popularity. The *Defender* occasionally recommended recent books on the European situation to its readers.
Chairman George A. Ranney justified increased Community Fund
goals on the grounds that the war was already driving up prices. A
small group in Evanston formed the "American Gas Mask Society"
to oppose war propaganda. The society soon disappeared, but the
concerns that it exemplified endured.[45]

The Veterans of Foreign Wars (VFW) was probably the first major organization to take a public stand in response to the war. At its
national convention in Boston on September 2, the VFW endorsed
a policy of strict neutrality for the United States, called for a special session of Congress to safeguard American interests during
the current crisis, and endorsed the principle of "cash and carry."
The American Legion held its national convention in Chicago
during the last week of September and took up issues arising from
the war. Outgoing national commander Stephen F. Chadwick
urged the country to preserve its existing posture of neutrality.
America's exclusive concern should be to bolster her own defenses. Chadwick told the Chicago Bar Association that he opposed repeal of the arms embargo because he believed that the
country ought to be either all the way in the war or all the way out
of it. Following Chadwick's address, William Collins, newly in-
ducted president of the Cook County American Legion, vowed
that his organization would spearhead efforts to keep the United
States at peace. Frank Knox led the applause for Collins's declaration. Some local chapters debated neutrality issues, at times heat-
edly. In general, the legionnaires avoided taking stances on the
embargo, rejected any need for American military involvement,
and endorsed strong national defense. At the national convention,
the Legion's foreign relations committee bowed to pressure from
the Roosevelt administration and dodged the specific issue of embargo repeal. The convention in turn adopted the committee's
recommendations.[46]

No organization was better prepared to adopt a stance in response to the war than the League of Women Voters (LWV). Since
its inception in 1921, the League had supported the principle of

U.S. cooperation with collective efforts to prevent war. Of course such a principle was sufficiently elastic to embrace a variety of specific interpretations. For many of the LWV rank and file, foreign affairs were doubtless of secondary interest at best, and they may not have paid much attention to that part of the policy program. So, as events were to reveal, the League was no more unanimous in its foreign policy views than any other mass organization, especially one that encouraged its members to voice their opinions. But the nature of the League and the caliber of its membership insured that the internal debate, as well as the formal positions adopted by the group, would be unusually well thought out and articulated. Chicagoans occupied three of sixteen chairs on the national board of directors, and one board member, Louise Leonard Wright, also held a key executive post as head of the Department of Government and Foreign Policy. Mrs. Wright was scarcely less of a foreign affairs expert than her husband, Quincy Wright, who was acknowledged to be one of the nation's premier scholars of international law. Skilled in both verbal and written argument, Mrs. Wright was a powerful voice for collective security within the uppermost councils of the League.[47]

When the war began the League was operating under policy principles adopted at its biennial convention in 1938. Such principles provided broad guidelines to the national board, which could then organize the membership to lobby on behalf of specific proposals. The 1938 gathering had endorsed the concept of an arms embargo in a form essentially identical to Roosevelt's preferred alternative to the existing law. The League favored granting the president discretionary authority to impose an embargo, which it wished to see used in cooperation with friendly nations against aggressive powers. In short, the embargo was to be part of the arsenal of collective security, not a means of withdrawal from international affairs. The League had joined the abortive effort to repeal the embargo in the spring of 1939, so it wasted little time the following autumn in supporting Roosevelt's renewed drive for revisions. Problems arose with the "cash and carry" provision, however. Many League members, including Mrs. Wright, did not believe existing guidelines authorized the board to take a stand on such a measure. League president Marguerite M. Wells convinced the board to support the administration nevertheless. She contended that only Roosevelt's proposal had a realistic chance of passage and that "cash and carry" fell within the convention's mandate to support collective security. The League thus endorsed revision on September 19, in a statement emphasizing that "cash and carry" seemed likely to prevent incidents that might involve the United States in war.[48]

The Illinois League undertook its part of the national effort to support neutrality revision. Through its forty-seven local chapters, the state LWV sought to educate its members and to influence the Illinois congressional delegation. State president Lolita E. Bogert sent all chapter heads copies of a letter from President Wells explaining the national board's position. Neutrality was the most widely discussed topic at chapter meetings in October and November. League women distributed thousands of flyers outlining the organization's analysis of the current options available to the country and sought time over local radio stations for brief talks on neutrality. Chapter chairwomen and individual members with political contacts wrote local congressmen and party officials on behalf of the Roosevelt bill. At the direction of Wells's office, the Illinoisans focused their lobbying efforts on the Republican delegation. Bogert targeted chapters represented by Republicans for special prompting. She also contacted individual members with ties to GOP leaders, and got Frank Knox to lobby two Republican National Committeemen. League efforts were particularly vigorous because its leaders expected a close vote in Congress.[49]

All this activity led to criticism. Bogert anticipated trouble from the *Tribune* and dismissed it, though she was dismayed that the "World's Greatest Newspaper" seldom saw fit to publish letters from League members regarding embargo repeal. Internal turmoil came as a surprise. Dissention in Chicago seems to have centered in the Evanston and Highland Park chapters, adjoining Northwestern University and the University of Chicago respectively. Frayn Utley, head of the Government and Foreign Policy Department of the Illinois League, reported that the Evanston chapter was split wide open over the embargo issue. Many members of her own Highland Park group, she noted, had resigned in protest, as had members in other chapters. The precise extent of dissent is impossible to gauge, but it seems not to have outlasted the embargo controversy or to have caused any serious damage to the League in Illinois.[50]

The Illinois American Federation of Labor (IAFL) also found itself embroiled in controversy over foreign policy issues. Two representatives of Chicago's Milk Wagon Drivers Union placed a resolution approving Roosevelt's neutrality policy before the September IAFL convention. Rather than endorsing revision of the Neutrality Act, the proposed resolution stressed the country's desire to stay out of the war and noted that this was Roosevelt's goal as well. Even so, the measure provoked sharp debate. Fears of a renewed depression, following the dislocations of a wartime economy, were uppermost in the minds of many federationists. The state executive board managed to kill the resolution, saying the IAFL would await the guidance of national headquarters.[51]

Chicago-area business groups also took no formal stands, but as elsewhere foreign affairs were the subject of intense interest and a common topic for luncheon meetings. The *Chicago Journal of Commerce* surveyed local business leaders at the outbreak of hostilities. Caution marked their replies. Businessmen emphasized the uncertainty of the future, but most saw little likelihood of immediate economic disruption. The country had gained experience from 1914, now knew how to handle the economic situation, and had anticipated the present war more that it had the earlier one. Prolonged conflict would certainly stimulate the American economy across the board, a majority believed, regardless of what course the country chose to adopt. Chicago businessmen, according to the *Journal*, judged that the real opportunity for the United States was to supplant the trade of belligerent nations in nonwarring areas. The *New York Times* at first gave a somewhat different view of Chicago business opinion, claiming that businessmen anticipated security benefits and increased profits should the embargo be repealed. Later the *Times* reported that most of the city's business leaders wished to retain the embargo. Whatever the local consensus, if any, businessmen received varying advice on the proper course for America. The *Daily News* business editor, Royal F. Munger, cautioned that companies would have to gauge carefully the altered climate. "In the first place," he wrote, "let us realize that any hope of remaining aloof from the conflict and its economic repercussions is an idle dream." A. Homer Hartz, president of the Illinois Manufacturers Association, told its members that he feared war would cause the imposition of "state socialism." In October the elite and impeccably conservative Union League Club heard Minnesota meat-packing magnate Jay Hormel predict a severe postwar depression if the American economy became geared to war-based production. Hormel voiced concerns similar to those of AFL chief William Green and leaders of the nation's steel industry. National Association of Manufacturers president Howard Coonly told the Chicago Association of Commerce that his organization desired peace in order to focus on the country's unsolved economic ills. So vigorously did he champion his association's opposition to war, Coonly reported, that people had commented "it sounds as though you were building an alibi." Coonly was encountering the lingering impact of the Nye Committee investigations, which had helped convince many Americans that big business welcomed war as an opportunity for enlarged profits. Such sentiments formed an undercurrent of public opinion in the opening stages of the war.[52]

The least equivocal message on foreign policy issues came from Chicago's Protestant churches. Overwhelmingly they spoke out against either joining the fighting or tampering with existing neutrality legislation. "How to keep America at peace" was the main topic among delegates at the Chicago Church Federation youth conference. Several hundred Chicago ministers, representing nineteen denominations, gathered in late September to discuss church affairs. A floor resolution which backed retention of the arms embargo passed by a huge majority. The editor of the Chicago-based *Christian Century* magazine, Paul Hutchinson, announced formation of a People's Program for Peace. Established for the duration of the embargo debate, the organization favored retention of the arms embargo and wished to add a rigid "cash and carry" system for all American exports to warring nations. Black church leaders were also active. Leaders of the national Baptist Ministers' Conference wrote President Roosevelt urging him to preserve peace by all possible means and to promote "genuine democracy" in the United States. Dr. L. K. Williams, president of the National Baptist Convention, conducted a mass prayer for peace at the New York World's Fair. Williams was only one of many black ministers who led prayer drives for peace.[53]

Efforts to revise the Neutrality Act did receive support from one enormously influential religious leader in Chicago, George Cardinal Mundelein; but the cardinal died in the opening stages of the debate, before making public his support for "cash and carry." His barely veiled denunciation of Father Coughlin's opposition to repeal of the embargo was read to a nationwide audience over NBC by Bernard Sheil, the auxiliary bishop of Chicago. The loss of Mundelein was a blow to the Roosevelt administration. For years the cardinal had been a staunch backer of the president and an outspoken opponent of fascism. He was the first cardinal to attack Adolf Hitler openly, and his May 1937 blast created a serious diplomatic incident between Berlin and the Vatican. Mundelein's successor, Samuel Cardinal Strich, would lack both the late cardinal's outspokenness in support of the administration and his enormous prestige. By February 1940 the official publication of the archdiocese, *The New World*, was criticizing New York clergy for their "anglophile prejudice." American neutrality, said the article, should be maintained regardless of the ethical case for aiding the Allies. Death had robbed the administration of an invaluable ally in Chicago.[54]

Most of Chicago's huge ethnic enclaves supported the late cardinal's concerns rather than the neutralism of *The New World*. The largest concentration of Poles outside Poland, almost 700,000 in 1940, made Chicago their home. Smaller Czech and Jewish populations were well organized and articulate. Nazi sympathy among Chicago's German-Americans created occasional headlines, but the numbers involved were small. Local Italian-Americans maintained a low profile throughout the period between the invasion of Poland and Pearl Harbor, as did the Irish community. But the peoples from Eastern Europe were active and vocal.

Chicago's Czechs swung into action first. On September 5, a member of the Czechoslovak Chicago Council promised aid to the Poles in their struggle against the Nazis. The next day, Jan Papanuk, consul for Eduard Beneš's Czechoslovak government in exile, announced his government's pledge to form an army to aid the Poles. Local Czech leaders applauded this action. Three weeks later, exiled Czech leader Jan Masaryk addressed a Chicago gathering on the subject of "Civilization in Peril." The national convention of the Slovak National Alliance of America took place in Chicago during late October. Its delegates endorsed repeal of the arms embargo and demanded restoration of a free Czechoslovakia.[55]

Most ethnic groups eschewed formal pronouncements on American policy and concentrated instead on aiding their ancestral homelands. Efforts by local communists to convince Chicago Poles to hail the "liberation of their homeland" by the Red Army fell flat. A Polish War Relief Fund was founded the opening day of the war, one of many charitable organizations that subsequently appeared. Under the direction of the Polish National Alliance, Chicago's largest Polish group, the Relief Fund staged a mass rally in February 1940. Twenty thousand people attended and heard speeches by former president Herbert Hoover, Robert R. McCormick, and several others. This was the first of many mass meetings held in Chicago as a result of the war, but one of the few organized before the fall of France. Other relief organizations, such as the Finnish War Relief, were controlled by the business community. Chicagoans filled their quota in the Finnish Relief drive earlier than citizens of any other American city. The more populous ethnic groups retained control over their respective campaigns. Zionist leader Chaim Weizmann visited Chicago in January to launch a drive which netted $2.5 million for Jewish War Relief. Whatever their personal feelings, Chicago's Jewish leaders were restrained in their public views on foreign policy issues. Although given repeated warnings of Jewish sufferings under Hitler, local leaders like Rabbi Jacob Weinstein urged the United States to stay out of the war.[56]

Chicago's black neighborhoods tended not to view antifascism as a cause to be embraced, despite universal repugnance over Nazi racism and the Italian conquest of Ethiopia. Black churches were overwhelmingly pacifist. So too were the various left-wing groups active in Bronzeville. But the Nazi-Soviet Pact was an especially difficult pill for many black communists to swallow and their ranks were in disarray by year's end. One local leader urged blacks to make common cause with American Jews in a campaign for equality in the United States. David Ward Howe, whose column

"The Observation Post" appeared frequently in the *Defender*, reported that the war was a widespread topic of conversation among young blacks. Many looked forward to increased economic opportunity, especially in an enlarged military. Yet other young blacks participated in the student antiwar demonstrations that were a fixture on campuses around the country. A letter to the *Defender* also indicated that the war was a frequent subject of discussion out on the streets. Black opinion was mixed, wrote Jessie Johnson. He encountered many sympathizers for the Allies and many others who saw no real democracy on either side of the Atlantic. Judging from the volume of letters urging the *Defender* to increase its foreign affairs coverage, interest in the European crisis ran high in Bronzeville. Correspondence also suggested that the memory of Ethiopia remained strong, though its impact was mixed. Some readers pointed to Ethiopia as a lesson in the dangers of failing to halt aggression; others believed that it showed the racism and self-serving nature of the Allies. Cartoonist Jay Jackson had his own interpretation. He pictured the natives of Africa gazing across the Mediterranean to "civilization's unending wars" and concluding it was better to remain "savage."[57]

Black leaders around the nation seemed generally to have shared the *Defender*'s view that American blacks should focus on racism at home. L. Hollingsworth Wood, chairman of the National Urban League, told the 1939 convention that the action of Britain and France on behalf of a beleaguered Poland might shame the United States into reviewing the plight of its own minority groups. Kappa Alpha Psi, one of the largest black fraternal organizations in America, heard its national leader declare that the race issue showed that Britain and the United States had no claim to being defenders of civilization. Fascism and communism were worse, James E. Scott told the Kappans, but American weaknesses only helped Hitler's cause and correcting them should therefore get top priority. The *Norfolk Journal and Guide* concurred, adding that World War I had taught American blacks the futility of crusades for democracy. Among blacks then, no less than among whites, a virtual consensus existed that America had no reason to embroil itself in the European conflict.[58]

Near Bronzeville lay the University of Chicago, where the crisis in Europe immediately became a major subject of contention.

While its president, the controversial Robert M. Hutchins, maintained his policy of keeping silent on political issues, faculty and students engaged in earnest and sometimes penetrating debate.

Campus forces supporting Roosevelt administration foreign policies were led by Professor Quincy Wright. In letters to Illinois congressional representatives, a speech to the Chicago Legal Club, and in many articles appearing in the campus newspaper, the *Daily Maroon*, Wright endorsed neutrality revision. Regardless of the forum, Wright presented his views with honesty and developed his arguments with care. He stressed that the "cash and carry" policy removed a weapon from Hitler, accorded with traditional American policy, and would probably shorten the war. He doubted that arms sales or propaganda could get the United States into the fighting and emphasized that "cash and carry" would avoid the potential dangers of "incidents" at sea. Wright's position was strikingly close to that of Frank Knox in the *Daily News*, whom he may have influenced.[59]

The *Daily Maroon* provided a forum for a wide range of campus viewpoints on the embargo issue. Student spokesmen presented what they described as "liberal," "conservative," and "Trotskyite" outlooks on the question. Various professors also contributed opinions. *Maroon* editorials were cautious during the early stages of the debate. On October 12 the paper suggested that potential danger lurked along whatever path the United States chose to follow. Above all the country needed to exercise great care in making its choice, a call similar to the position then being advanced in the *Daily News*. The following day the *Maroon* declared its support of "cash and carry." Without American support, the Allies faced a serious prospect of defeat. Imperfect as the Allied nations were, Nazi Germany was far worse. An October 17 editorial stressed that the war's outcome was bound to have economic and political effects on the United States, so the nation needed to take such precautions as it could to make certain that those effects were not harmful. Having stated its position, the paper thereafter refrained from further editorializing.[60]

The political left led campus opposition to an altered position on neutrality. Its most prominent spokesman was a young economics professor, Maynard C. Krueger. A witty lecturer who had taken up politics as a hobby, Krueger was a leader in the Socialist party and would be their vice-presidential candidate in 1940. Like many businessmen and some labor leaders, Krueger based his opposition to repeal of the embargo on its potential danger to the American economy. He predicted that the economic boom which attended the war trade would create massive inflation while it lasted and a serious depression when it broke. Hardship and misery would result. Campus communists organized a Keep America Out of War conference early in November. The *Maroon* dismissed the gathering as a front for leftist propaganda, attracting few not already won over. Antiwar activities continued throughout the winter, but the numerous factions were unable to unify. At one point, four different groups could not even agree on an acceptable slogan. A common desire for peace sometimes produced joint demonstrations, but they often ended with disgruntled factions denouncing communist attempts to dominate the proceedings.[61]

Late in April 1940, a self-described "liberal faction" began to form as an alternative to the communists. The American Student Union (ASU) was the main political organization on campus and, as elsewhere, communist activity within the Union had alienated many members. When communists within ASU blocked passage of a resolution to condemn the Soviet invasion of Finland, twenty-five members walked out. Led by two graduate students, Robert Merriam and Adele Rose, they issued a statement denouncing ASU's refusal to combine a peace program with a firm opposition to totalitarianism. Whether the dissidents could create an alternative organization was not then clear.[62]

The campus turmoil stood in stark contrast to the general climate of opinion in Chicago and across the nation. As winter gave way to spring the long lull in Europe dulled American interest in the clash overseas. Few signs suggested that the public felt more than a vague unease over what the year would bring, and the desire for peace remained strong. One poll found that three-quarters of those surveyed thought the Allies should try to make peace with Hitler. The major Chicago newspapers reflected the general belief that the war was still a safe distance away, and very little in their columns would have led a reader to conclude otherwise. The *Tribune* and the *Daily News* had quarreled several times over the wisdom and virtue of the Roosevelt administration, but never over the fundamental course of American foreign policy. Other disputes had been short-lived and, allowing for the usual tenor of the *Tribune*, moderate in tone. In retrospect, they loom as portents of the bitter battles soon to come. But through the spring, divisions were yet largely latent and of limited importance. They would likely have remained so had not events forced them to surface. For weeks the *Tribune* ran excerpts from George Washington's farewell address, admonishing the United States to avoid foreign entanglements. A February editorial then commented, "The world as he saw it then has changed very little from the world as we see it now." Though not so firmly wedded to the past, the other Chicago newspapers agreed that traditional neutrality was the soundest posture for America. Nor did any major spokesperson challenge this assumption. To Chicagoans during the opening period of the war, the foreign crisis seemed ominous, but remote. America still controlled its future.[63]

Elsewhere the sense of concern regarding the situation overseas was generally no more urgent. While a few observers claimed that the United States had a vital stake in the war's outcome, isolationism still existed among some informed circles. The *Denver Post*, for example, claimed that "the smallest domestic problem is more important to the American people than the most momentous European crisis." No doubt this overstated matters greatly, but it contained some truth. Judging by the vast attention given to the premiere of *Gone With the Wind*, Atlantans that winter seemed more interested in the Civil War than the current European strife. The national radio networks and their local affiliates received countless complaints from listeners who objected to having war bulletins interrupt scheduled programming. Looking ahead to the congressional session of 1940, the *Chicago Journal of Commerce* did not foresee a single defense or foreign policy issue on the agenda. Even among those who held that isolationism was impossible or immoral, few called for American involvement. Confidence persisted that the country could avoid fighting. As late as April 1940, in the final hours of the Phony War, a *Fortune* survey uncovered the prevalence of peace sentiment in America. More than 85 percent of the respondents agreed that the next administration should go to war only in the case of a direct attack, regardless of events abroad. *Fortune* also asked for a ranking of national priorities, and peace received more than three times as many votes as

the next most cited choice. Looking back on the winter of 1939–
40 from a year's vantage point, the *New York Times* would write that
"the impact of war in Europe had been, so far as the United States
was concerned, only a tap." In 1940, the *Times* noted, the tap
would become a punch.[64]

TWO

THE BATTLE OF
THE TWO COLONELS

The German army took just eleven weeks to smash six European nations and American complacency. Beginning on April 9, 1940, Denmark, Norway, the Netherlands, Belgium, and Luxembourg fell in rapid succession to the Nazi onslaught. Hitler's crowning achievement came when his legions knifed through France, slashing her from the war and forcing the dazed formations of Britain's expeditionary forces to flee continental Europe shorn of their equipment.

The French collapse reordered the balance of military power in Europe and the world. The impact of this shift was magnified because the events unfolded as high drama. Quiescent months of Phony War provided a stark backdrop to the sudden flurry of activity. Hitler's methods underscored his reputation for moral bankruptcy. Without warning or provocation he attacked a succession of neutral nations. The new German method of warfare, the blitzkrieg, was unprecedented in its ruthlessness toward civilian populations and its effectiveness against opposing armies. Like a well-crafted stage play, the fall of France lasted long enough to enthrall and impress the audience without numbing it. The drama even provided a surprise ending, for few had anticipated that the French would collapse. This unexpected turn shattered the implicit analogy to World War I that many Americans had used in appraising the new conflict and justifying the limitations to American involvement.

The massive German success created a palpable sense of danger among the public, but it left the overwhelming American resolve to remain at peace largely intact. By early 1941 more people cited international affairs as their greatest worry than mentioned personal finances or any other factor. The war was also by far the biggest single topic of conversation, though men discussed it with significantly more frequency than women did. National opinion polls showed that only a small minority favored an immediate declaration of war, while a slight majority favored war if it could be proven that Germany would eventually attack the United States. Preparedness was another matter. A *Fortune* survey revealed that almost 94 percent of the public was willing to spend whatever was necessary to build up American defenses. The fall of France also produced two important shifts in American policy. Each reflected the perception that the Axis powers in some way menaced the security and well-being of the United States; each respected the continuing desire for peace. As the scale of German success became clear, the Roosevelt administration proposed enormous increases in the level of American military preparedness. Almost without opposition, Congress approved a series of appropriations for the expansion and modernization of the armed forces. Only a bill to institute the first peacetime conscription in the nation's history provoked serious controversy, due in large part to congressional fears that the men might be sent abroad. So powerful was sentiment favoring preparedness that Congress passed the conscription bill in an election year.[1]

The second departure from the existing American position came on the issue of economic aid to Great Britain. The British suffered from a critical shortage of many types of war materials and weaponry. From August onward, England endured a heavy aerial bombardment while German submarines continued to menace her ocean lifelines. British industrial capacity, moreover, could not match that of a German-dominated Europe. London bought massive quantities of supplies from the United States under the "cash and carry" formula, supplemented by purchases of weapons that Roosevelt made available from America's own scanty supply. The most important of these transactions came in September, when the president authorized transfer of fifty destroyers to Britain in exchange for rights to bases in the Western Hemisphere.

The destroyer deal and similar efforts lent important material and symbolic support to the British, but in a legal sense they represented discrete responses to specific needs. Agreement by Washington to furnish one batch of weapons guaranteed nothing about the fate of future requests. By December 1940 the British had almost exhausted their ability to pay for American supplies. In response to an urgent appeal from Prime Minister Winston Churchill, Roosevelt submitted to Congress his lend-lease plan. The president proposed that the United States now pay for continuing aid to Britain. Lend-lease constituted an enduring commitment of America's full economic power to the struggle against Nazi aggression. Passage of the bill ended the political question of whether or not to furnish material aid to Britain. Such a momentous measure provoked an intense national debate—far more bitter, more sustained, and more inclusive of the population than anything the country had seen previously.

The press made clear that issues of profound importance were at stake. How those issues were defined, however, varied considerably according to the source. Readers of Chicago's two leading dailies, for example, received quite different pictures of the foreign policy situation. The *Daily News* and the *Tribune* disagreed over the seriousness of the German menace, the wisdom of the administration's foreign policy, and the fundamental goal of that policy. The *Daily News* argued that Hitlerian Germany menaced American security and needed to be stopped. The *Tribune* held that Roosevelt was advocating unneutral and unnecessary action in a disguised but deliberate attempt to provoke full American participation in the fighting. Their differences in viewpoint soon spread off the editorial page and came to infuse the entire content of each newspaper. By early 1941 readers often received nearly opposite treatments of news in the *Tribune* and the *Daily News*. Bias and emotionalism on both sides cheapened the debate, obscuring issues of fundamental importance to the determination of foreign policy and contributing to the growth of bitter divisions within the American public.

As the German storm rolled westward, few could doubt the seriousness of events in Europe. The clash in Europe dominated the headlines and filled the airwaves from mid-April onward. Nothing but war news appeared on the front page of either Chicago daily in late May and early June. One *Tribune* editorial read: "Every-thing at Stake in Europe." The campaign developing in the Low Countries, it said, would determine who would dominate the Con-tinent. The editorial noted that the spectacle overseas was having effects on American sentiment and extended sympathy for the plight of the Dutch and Belgians. The *Daily News* already had voiced similar opinions. Coverage in the *Defender* and the *Journal of Commerce* was much less extensive, but no attentive reader of either paper could fail to grasp the importance of the Nazi on-slaught. "America today is facing the greatest crisis in its history," the *Defender* told its readers.[2]

Nazi success brought hitherto dormant divisions over foreign policy into stark relief. The controversy raged nationwide, but no-where was it more sharply drawn than between the two leading dailies in Chicago.

Initially the *Tribune* worried about the temptation to involve America more deeply in the European struggle, while the *Daily News* began to contend that the outcome would affect the nation's vital interests. Their respective editorials on the plight of the Low Countries suggested the emerging differences. In saddened tones, the *Tribune* pleaded with Americans to restrain their sympathies for the unfortunates of the Old World. McCormick continued to insist on the imperative need to preserve civilization in this hemi-sphere by remaining at peace. The *Daily News* waffled in its initial editorial policy. On May 6 the paper emphasized that German domination of Europe would pose a grave threat to American se-curity. Hitler eventually would covet the Western Hemisphere and war would result. Thus, said the *Daily News*, the United States should prevent Nazi expansion—while major allies existed. The editorial did not specify a form of appropriate action. Although vague, this position placed the paper in the forefront of those advocating a stern policy against Germany. Reiterated throughout the summer, the theme anticipated the paper's later stance. How-ever, the *Daily News* often adopted an inward-looking posture and implied that America ought really to concentrate on its own af-fairs.[3]

Both dailies stressed the urgent need to boost American military preparedness. The *Daily News* placed more emphasis on prepared-ness than on aid to the Allies. The United States was doing all it could to help in the struggle against Hitler, the *News* contended, but arms production for its own use remained by all measures inadequate. As late as August 28, with France surrendered and Britain reeling under the Luftwaffe's bombs, the paper would urge the United States to look to its own defenses. "Is it not . . . our most urgent duty to put ourselves in a position to meet the worst, if it comes, rather than take the desperate chance that it may not come?" The *Daily News* supported each of Roosevelt's emergency requests for increases in military appropriations.[4]

The *Tribune* was equally vocal in backing preparedness, but used its support to attack the administration and to deter efforts to escalate aid to the Allies. McCormick charged that Roosevelt had squandered billions on defense and had produced only an anemic military force. The *Tribune* hoped citizens would remember this and vote Republican in November. Meanwhile the defense effort should be turned over to private industry and experts like Charles Lindbergh and Edward Rickenbacker. In the *Tribune's* view, American weakness made it foolhardy to risk war with Germany or to deplete slender U.S. stockpiles by sending arms abroad. These positions were staples among Roosevelt's Republican critics everywhere in 1940. The *Chicago Journal of Commerce*, for example, flayed the New Deal almost every week for mishandling defense funds.[5]

More than mere Republican loyalty and a dislike of the president underlay McCormick's attack on the Roosevelt defense record. Military matters fascinated him, and he read widely on the subject. In his view, simple expansion of the armed forces was not the proper remedy for defense shortcomings. The colonel advocated tailoring the American military establishment to the tasks it was designated to fulfill. He called on the administration to declare what specific threats to the nation it foresaw and to gear the expansion program toward dealing with them. McCormick himself favored a modestly sized, highly trained, and heavily mechanized force designed to operate in North America. Given American naval strength and the enormous difficulties any opponent would face in attempting a cross-ocean invasion, he thought such an army could adequately defend the continent. McCormick further believed that a force of more than half a million trainees would swamp existing facilities and delay the creation of a viable defensive force. Mass conscription was therefore counterproductive. Roosevelt wanted so many men in order to build a new expeditionary force for use in Europe, not for purposes of defense. Such measured criticism of the preparedness drive was quite rare in the summer of 1940. Columnist Boake Carter adopted a stance similar to McCormick's, but most Americans seemed willing to leave defense planning to the government.[6]

The nation's black press also supported the need for preparedness, though at times with misgivings. The *Cleveland Guide* endorsed proposed defense increases without reservation. The *Defender* agreed that Hitler menaced the Western Hemisphere, but continued to give highest priority to the grievances of American blacks. In fact the paper sought to turn the crisis atmosphere to its own ends. Arms alone were insufficient to prepare America, declared one editorial. Fascism fed on public discontent. Therefore the United States needed to build popular loyalty by perfecting genuine democracy for citizens of all races. The Chicago weekly was the only black newspaper in the country to oppose the conscription bill. Until the military abandoned Jim Crow, it said, blacks must consider their government unworthy of sacrifice. The *Pittsburgh Courier* supported the draft but pondered the less obvious costs of the preparedness effort. The *Courier* anticipated the diversion of resources from pressing social needs and the increased militarization of American life. As always, it said, blacks would bear a disproportionate share of the burden.[7]

Stances on preparedness necessarily involved evaluations of the larger international situation. Here both the *Defender* and the *Tribune* retained their views of the previous autumn almost intact, while the *Daily News* gave evidence of considerable evolution in its thinking.

In the wake of the fall of France, the *Daily News* put forth a case for the existence of what it called the "Atlantic Civilization." This was a "tightly woven net of mutual exchanges, values and interests" that had grown up during the nineteenth century and embraced every American. Hitler threatened both the values and the interests. Britain was the nexus of international commerce. Her fall, maintained the *Daily News*, "would call for a radical readjustment of the business life of every American citizen and community." Foreign staff editor Carroll Binder called the collapse of

France "nothing short of a disaster for the values we cherish and an immense boon to those who aim at the destruction of our political and economic order." For the *Daily News,* as for many others, the war had ceased to be yet another exercise in the recurring feuds between rival European powers and had emerged as a defense of all that was good in Western life. Said one July editorial, "the people know the choice. It is religion, justice, moral decency, courage 'to speak out and act' versus godlessness, brute force, the firing squad, and the false lullaby of appeasement." This conviction of a "civilization imperiled" underpinned the paper's position on foreign policy for the duration of World War II.[8]

Variations on this theme appeared in scores of articles, editorials, and broadcasts following the Nazi conquest of France. Most agreed that a community of values existed and that fascism threatened to destroy it. The two ideas in fact formed the basis of Walter Lippmann's foreign policy prescriptions, though in public Lippmann tended to emphasize factors of power, especially sea power, as the key determinants in the present war. Others were less reticent about openly proclaiming the moral dimension of the struggle. Archibald MacLeish chided American young people for their alleged failure to appreciate the cynicism and brutality of the aggressor nations. It was vital, MacLeish wrote to the *New York Times,* for Americans to regain the conviction that "there are final things for which democracy will fight." Two days later in the *Times,* Allan Nevins advanced similar themes in a review of Raymond L. Buell's *Isolated America* and Charles A. Beard's *A Foreign Policy for Americans.* Nevins praised Buell for demonstrating the links that bound America to foreign nations. Beard received criticism for an excessive materialism that blinded him to the moral nature of the present conflict. The *Times* itself denounced "the complete recklessness and irresponsibility, the moral insanity of Nazi leaders." The *Chicago Journal of Commerce* argued that the danger to democracy posed by fascism was what differentiated the new world war from its predecessor. The message to readers from this line of argument was clear. The United States ought not to remain aloof from a conflict that would affect the future of civilization itself.[9]

The *Defender* evidenced little sympathy for the concept of an "Atlantic civilization." The paper spoke with many voices, but they united on this point. One editorial on the fall of France dealt as harshly with the victims of aggression as with the victors. The current conflict was in no sense a people's war. "Hitler is reaching for loot, as France and Britain reached for loot in 1918." Moreover, France's fall and Britain's danger were due largely to the misguided and self-serving policies of their respective ruling elites. "The political bankruptcy of the leadership of France and Britain has never been equalled," declared the *Defender*. Similar sentiments appeared in Lucius Harper's column. Harper viewed the war as just another clash among rival groups of white exploiters, whose outcome would make little difference to the world's blacks. Incoming editor John H. Sengstacke echoed Harper's views. "The prize of this war," he wrote, "is the colonial world, the enslavement of small nations, and the control of waterways." The paper's foreign editor, Metz T. P. Lochard, came closest to accepting the "civilization imperiled" argument. But Lochard used the concept to make a different point than the *Daily News* was trying to establish. Lochard focused blame for the debacle in Western Europe on the Allies for failing to enforce the Versailles treaty. Moreover, his account made war itself seem the greatest danger to civilization. *Defender* articles continued to spotlight racial injustice in Britain and the evils of imperialism. The paper suggested that because Britain and France had practiced appeasement during the Ethiopian war the man in the street had little sympathy for their present plight. Certainly they received very little in the *Defender*, whose coverage of the Soviet Union was far more favorable.[10]

The *Tribune* dismissed the "world civilization" argument as mere "emotionalism" and "hysteria." Roosevelt at once preyed on such emotionalism and suffered from it himself. "He couldn't keep his shirt on if it was buttoned to his pants and weighted down with lead," grumbled one *Tribune* editorial. Rejecting any concept of a world civilization, the *Tribune* desired that calculations of the world balance of power serve as the basis for United States policy. Such views were rare in the heated atmosphere created by the success of the German blitz. The *Boston Globe* was one of the few papers to decry alarmism and belittle the military danger to the United States in words similar to those of McCormick. Never one to fear taking an unpopular stance, the colonel continued his attack on the "civilization imperiled" argument by recalling America's last great international adventure. The *Tribune* denied that the present conflict was unique and traced its origins to resentments left over from World War I. This was but another entry into an endless ledger of quarrels. The *Tribune* reminded its readers that American intervention in the last war had resolved few European tensions. The United States could not control the course of affairs on the continent, nor should it try to do so. The paper attacked the logic of the "common foe" theory with what proved to be one of the most widely used challenges to the "aid short of war" formula. "If the welfare of the United States is wholly dependent upon an allied victory . . . then it is both cowardly and absurd to withhold an ounce of our power from the battlefields of Europe." The logic and public appeal of this argument were of such strength that few of the paper's opponents in Chicago were ever willing to debate the point directly.[11]

Other aspects of the *Tribune* position provided critics with more inviting targets. McCormick stated that, regardless of who won the war, the dominant power to emerge in Europe would be unfriendly to the United States. He may have meant that Britain's days of supremacy were over and that either Germany or the Soviet Union was bound to replace her. If such was his meaning, however, his wording was ambiguous and misleading. The editorial instead implied that Nazi Germany was no more hostile or dangerous than Great Britain, a view that the *Tribune*'s own calls for preparedness belied. Arguably McCormick's concentration on a balance-of-power interpretation of world politics was just as sound as the advocacy of world civilization appearing in the *Daily News*, which also included some hard-headed calculation of economic interest. But McCormick's balance-of-power approach could also be turned to favor some form of intervention, as Lippmann and others had in fact done. If a successful German invasion of the Western Hemisphere was possible, America might very well choose to fight in Europe. Indeed, on June 10 the *Tribune* admitted that Britain's Royal Navy had kept the United States insulated from foreign troubles since 1820. Should that fleet be taken or destroyed, the paper declared, America would face a drastic reformulation of her own role in world affairs. This startling and atypical admission appeared as France's doom was becoming clear. It showed how deeply the course of events had shaken Americans. But the June 10 piece stood in sharp contrast to other *Tribune* editorials of the same period.[12]

The nub of the difference between the two newspapers lay in their assessments of Germany's potential to do harm to the United States. During May and June, a portrait of an unrelenting and immensely powerful foe took form in the *Daily News* and elsewhere. Eyewitness reports from France emphasized the size of the German army and the revolutionary superiority of its striking power. Cartoon imagery changed. Huge hobnailed boots and gigantic tanks replaced the earlier symbol of the funny little dictator with the Charlie Chaplin mustache. As its visual imagery shifted from clown to juggernaut, in print the *Daily News* personalized the enemy and magnified Hitler's individual influence. References such as "those who were fighting Hitler, and all that he stood for" became increasingly common. Hitler was "the only man in the world" who conceivably could induce Congress to declare war. Americans who opposed preparedness became *his* "dupes and stooges." This picture of an awesome military machine, absolutely subject to the will of an evil mastermind, remained a fixture in the *Daily News* and other forums until the final defeat of Germany.[13]

As with so many other issues, the black perspective was filtered through the lens of racial discrimination in America. *Defender* cartoonist Jay Jackson also utilized the image of the huge hobnailed boots, but his drawing put them on the British and American armies to symbolize the oppressive treatment blacks were receiving. A most elaborate and unusual expression of this special perspective came in a lengthy *Defender* feature story about a hypothetical Nazi invasion of Georgia. Written by Violet Moten Foster, St. Clair Drake, and Enoc P. Waters, Jr., the piece illustrated many favorite *Defender* themes in fictional form. Stormtroopers landed in Savannah "because white landlords, businessmen, and politicians sold out the South and opened the gate to Hitler." The Nazis overwhelmed local resistance, despite a suicidal assault by a Jim Crow construction battalion armed only with shovels. When the German commander asked why such troops attacked unarmed, their colonel confessed, "No Negro troops have guns, especially in the South." Segregation also harmed the civilian population when blacks were slaughtered in inferior Jim Crow air raid shelters.

Southern congressmen obstructed effective countermeasures in their determination to preserve segregation. The story ended with the blitzkrieg advancing in triumph. The message here, and throughout the *Defender*, was that blacks faced even more pressing menaces than the Nazis. The fight against segregation had to come first.[14]

Those forces that did assign the German menace an overriding priority had an additional case to prove. However hostile and powerful, did Berlin intend to menace the United States, and did it have the means to do so? The *Daily News* found clues in Fascist ideology which revealed that Germany and Italy would threaten America in due course. A series of reports by several members of the *Daily News* foreign staff developed this theme. Early in June, M. W. Fodor wrote that the dictatorships' own ideology compelled them to strike at democracy because freedom was an intolerable affront to the Fascist system of slave labor. The most detailed analysis came from John T. Whitaker in Rome. A series of his articles pictured fascism as a bid for world revolution. "To the fascists such a conflict is rudimentary, not merely because of ideological differences, but because as realists they have always said that economically and socially it must be 'we or they.'" Whitaker contended that the forces that impelled Fascist expansion were too dynamic to rest content with even the conquest of Europe. While the American republics squandered their time with "oratorical breast beatings," he wrote, Nazi agents were plotting a campaign to undermine hemispheric solidarity. Other correspondents echoed Fodor and Whitaker. During the height of the lend-lease debate in January 1941, Wallace R. Deuel wrote a series of articles entitled "Where Hitler Stands." Reprising many of Whitaker's earlier themes, Deuel began his series by saying, "If Adolf Hitler wins the war, sooner or later he will force the issue with the United States." The litany of Nazi conquests proved it. The views of all these foreign correspondents ran in the regular news columns and often received front-page exposure. Well-written and vigorously argued by eyewitnesses in Europe, they formed a persuasive and frightening picture. Most American correspondents were anti-Fascist, but seldom were they granted so much space in which to present their analysis. Few forums could match the depth of foreign coverage found in the *Daily News*.[15]

Despite the tremendous unease that swept Chicago and the country as the blitzkrieg routed the Allies, the *Tribune* maintained a measured skepticism regarding the German threat. McCormick avoided the issue of Hitler's intentions, concentrating instead on the capabilities of the German war machine. He stressed the very short operating ranges of many of its key elements, especially the air corps. In June the paper cited the opinions of several un-named American military experts who discounted the likelihood of a successful invasion of North America. These men contended that existing U.S. naval strength and the anticipated increase in her air power would enable a modestly sized, mechanized army of the type envisioned by McCormick to defeat any invader. The colonel broadcast his own case over the Mutual radio network on June 9, assuring listeners that a prepared America would be thoroughly safe. He was anything but sanguine about the state of American defenses, as the *Tribune*'s support for increased defense spending proved, yet McCormick's analysis of the shortcomings of the German armed forces holds up rather well in light of modern knowledge. On the national scene, Colonel Charles Lindbergh was saying much the same thing. But June of 1940 was not a time to voice restraint. The thunder of Nazi successes drowned out both colonels. Hitler had designed his war machine to overawe as well as to conquer, and it did both.[16]

Evidence indicating McCormick's views about Hitler's long-term intentions is sparse. An August editorial contended that the Führer desired those parts of Europe that had at any time been German, but it made no mention of whether he might reach beyond Europe. Opponents like Adlai Stevenson, Chicago leader of the Committee to Defend America by Aiding the Allies, challenged the *Tribune* in public on this issue. The paper responded by claiming ignorance concerning Berlin's ultimate designs, but insisted that America could defeat the Nazis if the necessity arose. The especially stinging abuse leveled at the CDAAA in this editorial perhaps indicated how defensive the *Tribune* felt on this subject.[17]

Latin America appeared to be a likely arena for Nazi aggression. The frequency and diversity of warnings about danger there reflected an anxiety widespread across the nation. Even the *Tribune*'s panel of nameless military experts worried about the safety of Brazil and her neighbors. In order to deter efforts to send American military equipment to Britain, McCormick at first attempted to arouse fears that Mexico might invade the southwest. This argument proved unavailing, and by August the *Tribune* was issuing earnest warnings of Nazi "fifth column" activity in Mexico and other nations. The *Daily News* carried similar reports. These fears were endemic in 1940. Citizens of the region bordering on Mexico seemed especially concerned. San Antonio mayor Maury Maverick declared that the danger of subversive activity in Mexico was so serious that the southwest lay under the threat of invasion. In an effort to protect the Alamo City, Maverick issued submachine guns to city policemen. Residents of nearby Del Rio came close to rioting when they mistook three Jehovah's Witnesses for Nazis. The trio had been passing out pamphlets on which swastika symbols appeared, and only vigorous efforts by the town sheriff and members of the American Legion prevented violence.[18]

A second fear common to both Chicago dailies, as well as the Roosevelt administration and other Americans, was of German economic penetration of Latin America. In mid-August a *Daily News* editorial contended that Hitler desired a major air base in Dakar, West Africa, for use as a commercial springboard to South America. *Tribune* correspondent Wayne Thomas described vigorous German activity aimed at undercutting U.S.–Latin American trade and cornering the market on several strategic commodities. These dual themes of trade war coupled with covert influence recurred throughout 1940 and 1941.[19]

Toward Germany's remaining foe, Great Britain, the Chicago papers remained ambivalent, though there were clear differences in the nature of their positions. As we have seen, the *Defender* held the British to account for their imperialism, segregationist policies, and their record of appeasement. The paper applauded signs of racial progress, such as the decision to drop the color bar in the Royal Air Force. Later in the year it cheered British forces as they helped restore Emperor Haile Selassie to his throne in Ethiopia. But overall the *Defender* remained wary of Britain's war aims. Knox was far friendlier, but he took care to insist that aid to Britain served American vital interests and deserved support primarily on that basis. In fact, the *Daily News* tended to phrase its appeals in terms of help for Hitler's foes rather than as aid for America's friends. Even during the depths of the blitz, the British received little outright praise. The *News* seemed determined to insure itself against charges of anglophilia. Other papers were less circumspect. Even the *Tribune* was far more outspoken in its praise for Britain's courage and perseverance, though also in its scorn for her alleged pretensions to democracy. Commenting on Winston Churchill's formation of a war government, the *Tribune* said, "The country's constitutional transition into 100 percent dictatorship was accomplished by a regimented parliament this afternoon in two hours and fifty minutes." While the *Defender* echoed this charge, it met with ridicule in the *Journal of Commerce*. Britain's emergency measures were purely temporary, the *Journal* emphasized, and unlike Nazi totalitarianism they would never outlast the war. Neither did the British glorify their government or its leader in the German fashion. The *New York Times* applauded the measure as evidence that the British were getting serious about mobilizing their power for war. Virtually all the papers, including the *Tribune*, united in paying Churchill and his nation glowing tribute for their defense of the homeland. On many occasions McCormick also praised with evident sincerity Britain's determined defense of her own interests and set this as a goal for the American government to emulate.[20]

The colonel's support for the British was confined to a verbal level, for he balked at every administration initiative to supply material to the beleaguered island. The most important of these initial efforts came in early September, when the United States transferred fifty obsolescent destroyers to Britain in return for the use of British bases in the Western Hemisphere. The reaction of both the *Tribune* and the *Daily News* to this destroyer deal epitomized their attitudes in the broader issue of aid to the Allies.

Knox had left Chicago by this time to join the administration as secretary of the navy. He remained in almost daily contact with the *Daily News* staff, however, and the paper continued its support for aid to Britain. An editorial on August 22 summarized its stance. Britain badly needed the ships. They were unnecessary for our own defense. Washington and London favored the transfer and Gallup polls indicated majority support among the American public. What then was delaying the deal? It was ludicrous to become entangled in "the fine points of international law" in light of the present world crisis. When official announcement of the transfer came two weeks later, the paper reported without question Roosevelt's assertion that the exchange boosted hemispheric defense and did not constitute a provocation for war. Thus the *Daily News* sometimes prodded the government to act with greater swiftness and decision.[21]

At the first hint that such a deal was in the offing, the *Tribune* began to attack. McCormick had long wished to obtain use of the bases, but he wished to acquire them as payment of Britain's war debts to America. The current arrangement was altogether different. "The sale of the navy's ships to a nation at war would be an act of war," an editorial bristled, even though an article in the same issue reported that legal experts in Chicago disagreed on the matter. The editorial also cast doubt on Britain's need for the destroyers. Several times during August the paper returned to its charge that the proposed deal represented a serious risk of war. Yet when the exchange went through on September 4, the *Tribune* congratulated itself for first raising the idea of acquiring the British bases and only mildly demurred at the method employed to obtain them. This rather surprising stance was surely dictated by the circumstances of party politics. Had McCormick simply denounced the agreement he would have broken openly with his party's nominee for president.[22]

The campaigns of 1940 had not gone well for McCormick. Almost within eyesight of the *Tribune* Tower, the Democratic national convention nominated the despised Franklin Roosevelt for a precedent-shattering third term. Then his own Republican party had been captured by Wendell Willkie, a man almost as suspect in his foreign policy views as FDR.

Gone were the days when the *Tribune* and the *Daily News*, Republican organs both, had yearned to suppress foreign policy issues in order to turn the 1940 election into a massive popular rebuke to the New Deal. Like so much else, these hopes became casualties of Hitler's success. By midsummer both papers, along with many others, saw foreign policy as the decisive issue of the 1940 campaign. Each scrutinized the unfolding political drama, although their reviews predictably conflicted.[23]

The *Tribune* endorsed—in fact demanded—partisan differences over foreign policy. Convinced that the public's desire for peace would overwhelm all other considerations, the paper hoped Re-

publicans could tap this sentiment to unseat Roosevelt. Conse-
quently, the *Tribune* highlighted the issues of peace and preparedness. Under the title "Our Mr. Chamberlain Should Retire," a May
16 editorial deplored the meager allotments given defense. The
New Deal instead had "lavished millions on boondoggling." This
criticism also surfaced frequently in the *Journal of Commerce* and
other antiadministration media. Having failed to prepare the nation for the current emergency, said the critics, Roosevelt was
nonetheless bent on war. From Washington, Arthur Sears Henning reported in the *Tribune* that Democratic leaders lived in fear
that the administration's secret commitments to enter the war
would surface before the election. A cartoon portrayed the president slogging down the "Wilsonian Road to War" under the banner of "aid to the Allies." In the background the mass of citizens
followed the GOP standard in the opposite direction. An editorial
the same day charged that Roosevelt "is hell bent for war, as everybody with a shred of sense all over the world now recognizes."
When Knox and Henry Stimson entered the cabinet, Henning
maintained that this move completed the Democrats' conversion
into the party of war.[24]

The other prong of the *Tribune*'s campaign was to establish the
Republicans as the party of peace. In this endeavor the presidential candidate would be of prime importance. Both Arthur Vandenberg and Robert Taft were outspoken noninterventionists, but
neither took hold with the party faithful. By the eve of the Republican national convention, McCormick had turned to Thomas E.
Dewey. The *Tribune* portrayed Dewey as a champion of its favorite
themes. To a *Tribune* reader, Dewey appeared to be running because Roosevelt had squandered American weaponry and was now
trying to provoke war in order to disguise his domestic failures. In
reality, Dewey's candidacy suffered from his relative youth and his
inexperience with foreign affairs. He too failed to gain the nomination. McCormick could at least take pleasure in the party platform. His protégé, C. Wayland Brooks, led the Illinois caucus in a
vigorous and successful push for a strong peace plank. On June
25 an editorial placed even more importance on the platform than
on the candidate. By now the *Tribune* had read the signs, for the
convention had turned to Wendell Willkie, the only outspoken advocate of aid to the Allies among the leading Republican contend-

ers. Steadfast to the end, delegate McCormick refused to vote for Willkie and denied him a unanimous nomination.[25]

Willkie's success saved the *Daily News* from a dilemma of great potential difficulty. As the Republican convention approached, the paper interpreted the bind in which the GOP found itself. While events demanded that all Americans support the administration's foreign policy, party identity required Republicans to differ. A temporary solution was to take refuge in advocacy of a strong national defense, but eventually the issue of partisanship versus national interest would have to be faced. Knox himself was pulled in both directions. In June, the colonel resolved his own personal dilemma in favor of national unity and joined the administration. Then the nomination of Willkie robbed the campaign of any clear distinctions between the candidates on the aid issue. The *Daily News* even accepted the GOP's foreign policy plank, forged by Brooks and the Illinoisans, as "harmless."[26]

For the remainder of the campaign the *Daily News* endorsed both Roosevelt's aid program and Willkie's support of that program, all the while pleading for political unity on foreign policy. The paper did fret about the ambiguity of the caveat, "except in case of attack," attached to the Democratic party's antiwar plank. Those Willkie supporters who proclaimed their overriding desire to stay out of the war also worried the *News*. More bothersome still was a late campaign effort by Willkie and Roosevelt to outdo each other in making sweeping pledges of peace. The paper labeled these claims "bunk." National policy was already set. The nation was arming feverishly and increasing its aid to Great Britain and China. Fixation on the concept of peace was misguided and naive, the *News* insisted, a single-minded attachment to political catchwords. True to the heritage of TR, Knox held that national self-interest was the only proper basis for policy. The issue of war or peace depended on events rather than wishful thinking. Vague as the paper's prescriptions often were, they did at least attempt to offset the increasingly strident rhetoric coming from the two candidates. A few other advocates of aid echoed the *Daily News* in denouncing the trend in campaign rhetoric as unrealistic and misleading. Such comments were the exception. Most of the media were content to leave unchallenged the candidates' unqualified promises of peace.[27]

McCormick blended program and partisanship into a different mixture. Such tepid support as Willkie got was based squarely on the candidate's professed devotion to the cause of peace. The title of one early editorial, "Willkie and Peace or Roosevelt and War" summed up much of the *Tribune*'s outlook. Coverage of Willkie emphasized his antiwar pledge and downplayed his stance in favor of aid to Britain. Local Republicans, especially senatorial contender Brooks, did receive enthusiastic endorsement, but Willkie's chief attraction often seemed to be that he was not Roosevelt. The *Tribune* put its energy into flogging the incumbent president. Attacks of varying tone, insight, and honesty appeared throughout the paper. Arthur Henning opened one lead news story by saying, "The most arresting aspect of the situation in Washington is the widespread opinion in official circles that, if President Roosevelt is re-elected, it will not be long before the United States will be in the war." The officials in question remained anonymous, just as the "ample evidence on hand of a conspiracy, headed by Mr. Roosevelt, to get this country into war" never surfaced. Alongside these charges came pieces probing the extent to which the government had already abandoned neutrality and questioning how long the country could balance between peace and war. Amid the innuendo and vitriol, these sober articles may have seemed like more campaign chaff.[28]

Not all observers of the 1940 campaign ascribed paramount importance to foreign policy issues. This was particularly true of anti-Roosevelt newspapers, regardless of their views about aid for Britain. The *Cleveland Plain Dealer* and the *Denver Post* agreed that the third term issue should be decisive among voters. Only unemployment outweighed the third term as an issue in the opinion of the *San Francisco Chronicle*. In Chicago, the *Journal of Commerce* denounced Roosevelt for almost everything except foreign policy, about which it made no mention during the latter days of the campaign. The *Plain Dealer* and the *Chronicle* supported the administration's foreign policy with enthusiasm, the *Journal of Commerce* did so grudgingly, and the *Post*, while somewhat erratic in its views, most often opposed the president on foreign affairs matters.[29]

The *Defender* underwent a dramatic shift in its political posture as the election neared. Founding editor Robert Abbott was a staunch Republican. Under his direction the paper had remained a GOP organ. Early coverage of the 1940 campaign continued this tradition. Roscoe Simmons, columnist and principal political reporter, was a McCormick loyalist. Simmons gave extensive space to the colonel's activities at the Philadelphia convention and spotlighted the drive to write a strong peace plank into the party platform. An article on the GOP slate in Illinois emphasized the importance of fighting the Cook County machine and the need to keep America out of war. Substantively, if not rhetorically, the *Defender*'s coverage could have come straight from the *Tribune*—until the twelfth of October. Readers must have been stunned to read the strong endorsement of Roosevelt written by new editor John Sengstacke. Hardly less surprising was his reason for backing FDR, the international emergency. "The evidence is incontrovertible," ran the endorsement, "that a crisis of titanic proportions is rapidly coming to our shores." The *Defender* called Roosevelt "a seasoned statesman" whose reelection would promote the unity necessary to meet the threat from the Axis. Later editorials would stress New Deal accomplishments, but the initial endorsement dealt only with foreign policy. The *Defender*'s shift was part of a realignment of the black vote brought about by the Depression and the New Deal. That it came with such suddenness no doubt reflects the accession of Sengstacke, but the underlying causes were profound and lasting.[30]

The *Tribune* soon had even more to worry it than the defection of black voters to the Democrats. The "World's Greatest Newspaper" invested heavily in the contention that the election was a referendum between Willkie's resolve for peace and Roosevelt's yearning for war. When voters chose FDR, the paper scrambled to cut its losses. McCormick still maintained that foreign policy had decided the election. State and local GOP candidates won where they had run hard on a strict noninterventionist platform. The success in Illinois of Brooks and gubernatorial contender Dwight Green, despite Willkie's loss there, satisfied the *Tribune* that noninterventionism had indeed been the key. The national ticket had watered down its commitment to peace and had fallen short in consequence, Willkie's strident peace pledges in late October notwithstanding.[31]

In contrast, readers of the *Daily News* learned that the Republican loss represented a laudable public rejection of a party increasingly given over to "appeasement and defeatism." Unconvinced and unafraid, Americans had "emphasized by their votes that they are not giving way, backing up, or even falling silent before the dictators." Responsibility for the misguided emphasis belonged less to Willkie, whom the paper continued to praise, than to unnamed elements within the party. Discerning readers surely guessed that one of those "elements" published a morning newspaper in Chicago. By repudiating such foolish counsels, the *News* rejoiced, voters had insured that the policy of preparedness and aid to the Allies would continue unabated. In a very different way than the *Tribune,* the *Daily News* also turned the election into a mandate on foreign policy. While its evidence seemed much stronger, events would soon show how great the divisions over aid still were.[32]

The vast outpouring of words during the 1940 campaign in fact did little to clarify the foreign policy of the United States. Almost everyone supported peace; no major political figure had yet called for war. Polls showed that Roosevelt commanded wide support for his aid policy. But the president had kept his prescriptions characteristically vague. Probably no one else was in a position to define policy. In any case, the boundaries of America's commitments to peace and to aid remained obscure. Many elements within American society, the *Daily News* among them, had already abandoned an unqualified devotion to peace. Yet few commentators had attempted to define with precision what would justify going to war. Only the absence of direct provocation by the Axis powers prevented a potentially explosive debate on this issue. Events did not extend similar protection to the clouded question of aid. Strictly speaking, FDR had established a pattern and not a policy. The destroyer deal had been only the most spectacular of several administration initiatives that had furnished war material to the British. The president had chosen not to consult Congress during the summer arms transfers in order to expedite the shipment of aid. The price of speed was to evade the process of formal decision making between the branches of government, which by tradition had served to sanction any new national policy. Now time was running out on an old policy, "cash and carry." London announced in December that funds to pay for American supplies would soon be drained. His hand forced, Roosevelt presented Congress with a plan, shortly to be labeled lend-lease, under which America would pay for further material sent abroad. Passage would make the United States a full-fledged economic partner in the struggle against Hitler, the "arsenal of democracy" in Roosevelt's phrase.[33]

Thus by the end of 1940 the elements were in place for the sort of cathartic debate on the direction of American involvement in the war that the presidential election had not provided. Lend-lease served as the focal point. Unlike the adoption of "cash and carry," this was not a return to an earlier program. Unlike the repeal of the arms embargo, lend-lease favored the Allies by open design rather than circumstance. Passage of Roosevelt's bill would signal a conscious rejection of the traditional strictures guiding neutrality, a move disturbing to many Americans even in the war-ravaged world of 1940. Backers and opponents of the measure each grasped the importance of the decision at hand. Both sides were now well organized, their arguments well rehearsed. The resulting clash was the fiercest and most pivotal of the 1939–41 period.

Immediately after the election, items in the *Daily News* began to hint that the basis of the American aid program would have to be changed. Correspondent William Stoneman wrote from London that the British could not afford to pay for supplies indefinitely. Reporter Edgar Ansell Mowrer advised readers in mid-November to "cease worrying about outmoded legal concepts which we have already violated by the transfer of destroyers." When news of the British financial pinch began to break, the *Daily News* described Washington's response in carefully measured terms. Administration leaders were not about to let their concern blind them to the national interests of the United States or the public's desire to remain at peace.[34]

The economic situation of the British filled the *Tribune* with apprehension of a different sort. The paper noted that the protracted war envisioned by Churchill was bound to place strains on the American economy. Conversion to an all-out war footing would send taxes soaring, swell the national debt, and ultimately prove ruinous. To support its position, and also to argue against extending financial credits to London, the *Tribune* repeatedly invoked the experience of World War I. The munitions makers, it predicted, would soon be leading large eastern financial interests in a joint effort to ensnare the country in foreign entanglements once again. As rumors of Britain's financial straits proliferated, the paper at first denied that any stringency existed. Bowing finally to contrary evidence, the *Tribune* then sought to settle an old grudge. Before even considering credits, the United States ought to acquire various British islands in the Western Hemisphere, such as Jamaica, in lieu of debts unpaid from World War I. An editorial in mid-December cautiously reiterated American friendship toward the British, but by this time McCormick was convinced that alone they could never defeat the Nazis. With Russia still a nominal ally of Germany, the colonel's analysis suggested that victory would require American participation in the fighting. Instead, he favored a negotiated peace based on the status quo. This notion had been outmoded in the previous winter and was a political dinosaur by December 1940, though McCormick was far from being its only advocate.[35]

Administration forces introduced the Lend-Lease Bill in Congress on January 10, 1941. The *Tribune*'s reaction was immediate and typified that of many opponents of the measure. Chesly Manly began his lead story on the proposal by writing: "Congress was stunned today by the unexampled enormity of powers requested by President Roosevelt in his bill." *Tribune* coverage emphasized the views of administration critics who charged that lend-lease "combined a declaration of war against Germany, Italy and Japan with the creation of a totalitarian dictatorship in the United States." On January 12, the paper ran one of its rare front-page editorials under the title "A Bill to Destroy the Republic." The piece introduced all future *Tribune* arguments, which centered on the broad powers granted the president. The paper soon dropped the term "lend-lease" and substituted "war dictatorship bill" in all its editorials and news columns. This apocalyptic rhetoric was typical of the paper during the debate. Most of the initial editorials eschewed substantive argument in favor of ad hominem attacks against lend-lease proponents. Readers learned that backers of the plan fell into two broad categories. One group was willing to endure dictatorship in order to aid Britain; the other desired dictatorship for its own sake. The former were blinded by their own emotional anglophilia, while the latter yearned to put over what the New Deal had failed to accomplish. Throughout the debate, which lasted until Roosevelt signed the Lend-Lease Bill on March 11, the *Tribune* slashed at the motives of aid proponents and the issue of expanding presidential power.[36]

Here McCormick's close identification with partisan politics and his well-known hatred of Franklin Roosevelt undercut the substance of his case. The powers authorized under the original lend-lease proposal were sweeping. Congressional debate focused on this issue at the outset. Administration opponents obtained a series of amendments designed to curtail presidential prerogatives somewhat. But the times lent themselves to extreme measures. Germany appeared irresistible. To date her opponents on both sides of the Atlantic had looked ineffectual by comparison. Americans had only to gaze overseas for contemporary examples of real dictatorships, against which FDR and lend-lease seemed benign indeed. The charge that FDR aspired to dictatorship was an old one in antiadministration circles. Colonel McCormick and the others had cried wolf often, regarding New Deal efforts most citizens applauded. To veteran readers his philippics may now have sounded like efforts to refight lost elections.

Another *Tribune* salvo became almost as ritualistic as the dictatorship theme. The paper also alleged that Roosevelt intended to use lend-lease as a springboard for war. FDR knew he could gain neither popular nor congressional approval for an open declaration of hostilities, so he concocted the Lend-Lease Bill as a subterfuge. McCormick here employed a tactic in wide use among all varieties of noninterventionists. By invoking the threat of war, they sought to enlist the popular desire for continued peace against a specific "short of war" measure. The *Tribune* seldom disparaged the benefits lend-lease seemed certain to provide and instead dwelt on its possible risks. As a debating strategy this had its merits. Berlin's likely response to lend-lease was a valid question to consider. Roosevelt's policy did entail risks, as the president admitted, and deserved careful scrutiny. But McCormick diluted the point by compounding it with his conspiracy theory.[37]

The antiwar appeal was further weakened because, like the concept of a negotiated peace, it implied a trust in Adolf Hitler. The logic of this argument suggested that the Führer would be unlikely to attack America unless provoked. Nothing in Hitler's record seemed to justify such an assumption. *Tribune* opponents, the *Daily*

News in particular, seized upon this point. Why worry about furnishing a pretext to a man who needed none? Advocates like the *Daily News* and the Committee to Defend America by Aiding the Allies emphasized that Hitler's appetite for conquest was insatiable. What had Norway or Czechoslovakia done to warrant Nazi aggression? Lend-lease entailed risks, they acknowledged, but at least the plan took the initiative against the Nazis.

The *Tribune* was advocating a static and defensive strategy at a time when such a position had fallen into disrepute. Contemporaries like Adlai Stevenson scorned it as a "Maginot Line mentality," a reference to the imposing string of French fortifications that the blitzkrieg had circumvented with frightening ease. Mc-Cormick did champion a policy that amounted to preparedness and passivity, in effect a strategy of deterrence. For him the hazards of an activist foreign policy remained uppermost: "If we are to dictate from time to time what shall be the course of events abroad, we shall see no end to such an enterprise. It would require continuous intervention in the affairs of the European continent and the far east. If American military forces could again overthrow European governments and scatter the present rulers in flight, what then? Must our armies remain in strength to repeat this whenever a symptom of the old trouble is rediscovered?" Hitler's imposing string of victories had not overcome McCormick's conviction that the present struggle was but a continuation of an age-old contest for domination of Europe. He expected the pendulum to swing back against the Nazis eventually without benefit of an American push. The merit attached to the colonel's view of the historical ebb and flow of European power politics, and to his sense of the pitfalls inherent in worldwide military intervention, was that his insights addressed potential dangers and long-term trends. But the evidence for their existence was necessarily vague and conjectural. His opponents possessed the considerable advantage of basing their position on immediate and concrete problems.[38]

The sense of urgency common among backers of lend-lease was conveyed by the title of a *Daily News* front-page editorial. "Hitler Won't Wait" attempted to rebut the *Tribune*'s position almost point by point. On the issue of the broad grant of presidential power, the *Daily News* began by citing its own record of opposition to such aggrandizement. The paper had denounced FDR's plan to pack the Supreme Court and his 1938 attempt to purge his party of dissident conservatives. The difference now was that rapidly moving events made the grant of power necessary in order to carry out an established national policy. At what time either the public or its congressional representatives had ever formally "established" that policy the *Daily News* did not say. Yet the paper was not alone in implying that American intervention in the war was settled policy, and its contention that the present emergency justified granting Roosevelt wide discretionary powers was echoed elsewhere. In denying the *Tribune*'s other major point, that lend-lease would lead to war, the *News* was also less than fully forthcoming to its readers. The paper chose to concentrate on narrowly legalistic grounds. Lend-lease did not represent a declaration of war because no American personnel would be sent overseas. While strictly accurate, this rejoinder ignored the blatantly unneutral aspects of the Roosevelt program and the consequent risks that attended its adoption. Rhetoric in the *News* was seldom so overblown as in the *Tribune*, but neither paper contained a full and balanced account of the possible consequences that might result from adopting lend-lease.[39]

Other lend-lease proponents were more forthright or more sophisticated in their analysis. The *Louisville Courier-Journal*, led by militant editor Herbert Agar, openly championed the bill as one example of American resolve to see Hitler defeated at any cost. Columnist Dorothy Thompson observed that lend-lease showed that the United States was "attempting to win a war without fighting it." She praised this stance as one that allowed the country to play a decisive role without tying it to the aims or obligations of foreign nations. However, the most widespread response to the war charge was to contend that all courses facing the United States involved risk, and that lend-lease offered the best chance for America to avoid war.[40]

Early in February, the *Daily News* returned to the issue of presidential power in a piece that captured both the crux of the newspaper debate in Chicago and the bitterness it produced. The paper charged correctly that lend-lease detractors never demonstrated how the bill would upset the system of checks and balances among the branches of government. Congress retained control of the purse strings and maintained its constitutional prerogative to declare war. The *News* insisted that the sole purpose of the bill was to expedite aid. Opponents resorted to the conspiracy charge against Roosevelt because they had no effective case against the aid policy itself. Then the *Daily News* went on the attack:

> Surely a crazier coalition was never assembled! Come lately German Nazis and Italian Fascists, Communists, pacifists, professional Anglophobes, Socialists, anti-Semites, rabid partisans who hate Roosevelt more than they hate Hitler, ostrich isolationists and a scattering of timid citizens afraid of they don't know what—all rally around a few vociferous anti-Roosevelt Democrats and a band of squaw Republicans to attack and calumniate the United States government in a moment of national crisis.
>
> These people, whether they know it or not—and some of them do—are performing Hitler's work in America. Hitler's one aim here is to so confuse and befuddle public opinion that aid to Britain will be hampered and delayed.

The paper closed by repeating the assertion that national policy was already resolved on the issue of aid. Lend-lease merely implemented that policy. Unity among all citizens to deal with the Axis menace was the nation's vital need.[41]

The *Defender* continued throughout the lend-lease debate to contain more diversity than either of the leading Chicago dailies. Columnist Roscoe Conkling Simmons remained faithful to the gospel according to the *Tribune*. Reporting on congressional testimony against the bill, Simmons wrote, "In came Robert R. McCormick, bravest American editor, likewise ablest Republican." His columns supplied the only continuing account of the controversy to be found in the *Defender*, and he mirrored the *Tribune* on every count. Simmons's use of the term "dictator bill" was only part of the emphasis he placed on the issue of presidential powers, and he insisted Roosevelt was bent on war. Otherwise the *Defender* largely ignored the lend-lease debate, though it did endorse the bill. Germany had to be stopped, declared one of the paper's two editorials on the measure, and the administration's proposal was the only chance to do so short of war. The same piece also reflected the growing bitterness of the debate. "The opponents of aid to Britain are either ignorant of the Gargantuan appetite of the Fascist powers or are serving some clandestine interest which they camouflage in the guise of neutrality." The only time the paper returned to the subject of lend-lease, it was largely to flay opponents for their pointless struggle to delay the bill. In a twist, the *Defender* accused the bill's critics of risking war by stalling a measure necessary to sustain America's foreign shield, Great Britain.[42]

The enactment of lend-lease gratified proponents like the *Daily News*, but success masked a larger disappointment. As knowledgeable observers had always expected, the bill received huge majorities in both houses of Congress. A vital step in the defeat of Nazi Germany, the full harnessing of the world's mightiest industrial power to the struggle against Hitler, was now mandated. A working majority in Congress and across the land had abandoned economic neutrality and rejected moderation in the level of American aid to Britain. Yet a broader purpose had not been achieved. In calling for national unity, the *Daily News* meant to solicit recognition that defeat of the Axis powers had become the overriding American goal. It was a plea for opponents to set aside their doubts about the government and its record and to eliminate all priorities conflicting with prosecution of the war—to do in short what Frank Knox had done. The loyal opposition should cease opposing and become simply loyal. This bid failed. Perhaps a third of the population remained unreconciled.

Economic involvement with Great Britain began with repeal of the arms embargo. Initiatives such as the destroyer deal eventually followed. The logical capstone of this pattern was lend-lease. Aid to Britain became established national policy. But adoption did not necessarily signify the acceptance of anything more extreme. In particular, lend-lease by no means guaranteed American intervention in the war beyond the sphere of economics. As shrewd observers noted at the time, the bill's congressional advocates refused to engage their opponents in debates on wider questions of foreign policy. Proponents confined their testimony to the merits of the lend-lease plan and the mechanics of its operation. This tactic may have eased the bill's passage, but it precluded development of the kind of open-ended endorsement that the *Daily News* envisioned. A popular majority was not ready to make victory a higher priority than peace. A sizable, vocal, and determined minority remained

opposed to the administration's program. By the later stages of
the debate they were already being attacked for obstructionism by
Walter Lippmann and others. Bitterness on both sides became intense. Attention to issues gave way to charges that were often ad
hominem in nature. The major Chicago dailies reflected this
trend, which the *Tribune* had probably helped to start.[43]

By early 1941, as exemplified by the Chicago press, fundamentally differing views of the challenges facing American foreign
policy had taken shape. Each newspaper tended to interpret developments in light of its established position. Each paper's ideas
were reflected in its news columns as well as its editorial pages. In
the *Tribune* such coloration was overt, even ostentatious. But it
could be found in the *Daily News*, the *Defender*, and in papers
around the nation as well. Those long reports from Europe in the
Daily News, to cite one example, filled as they were with grave
accounts of an implacable Fascist menace, represented messages as
surely as the *Tribune*'s use of the term "war dictatorship bill." By
1941 the differences in outlook between the *Daily News* and the
Tribune extended to virtually every facet of the foreign policy situation. Perhaps the only point of agreement was that the consequences of a mistaken policy would be ruinous. To the extent that
readers derived their own views from the way news was presented,
the press divisions contributed to deep schisms within the attentive
public. The resulting bitterness testified that polarization rather
than unity was the real product of the lend-lease debate.

THREE

THE QUICK MARCH
OF INTERVENTION

The success of Hitler's blitzkrieg in Western Europe took the foreign policy debate beyond the news sheet, out of the dining room, and onto the streets of America. Concern over Fascist expansion and the war in Europe had been growing throughout the winter of 1939–40. Coffee table discussions became common and often developed into heated arguments. Attendance reached unprecedented levels at special forums, like the League of Women Voters or the Council on Foreign Relations. A core of leadership developed that sought to mobilize opinion behind a program of heightened preparedness and expanded help for Hitler's foes. The fall of France galvanized these interventionists into action. As noted in a newsletter of the League of Women Voters, "with breathtaking rapidity national defense has become the all absorbing activity of the government and the people of the United States." Backers of increased American aid used the sense of emergency to steal a march on their opponents. The proaid forces organized with a sophistication surpassing anything the noninterventionists could muster in 1940. Interventionists were able to present political leaders with impressive evidence of public support for American aid to Great Britain. When polls asked in early summer whether it was more important to remain at peace or to help Britain at the risk of war, Americans chose peace by a two-to-one margin. Within six months opinion had reversed itself. Proponents of aid failed in their bid to achieve national unity, however. As the United States began to depart from traditional neutrality, public controversy over the benefits and risks attendant upon the policy became intense.[1]

The Chicago chapter of the Committee to Defend America by Aiding the Allies led local efforts to promote increased aid. Nationally, members of the League of Nations Association, led by its director, Clark M. Eichelberger, began the work of forming the new committee. William Allen White assumed chairmanship at the time of the committee's formation in May 1940, and served until the following January. Like Frank Knox, White was a newspaperman stamped from the old Theodore Roosevelt progressive Republican mold. His position as editor of the *Emporia* (Kansas) *Gazette* contributed to White's enormous national prestige as a venerated social and political commentator. To many people, the Kansan epitomized the decency and homespun wisdom that they associated with small-town America. Since precision and political caution had outweighed elegance as criteria for choosing the organization's formal name, the Committee to Defend America by Aiding the Allies, most people called it the "White Committee." Leadership for the Chicago chapter came from a group associated with the Council on Foreign Relations and the University of Chicago. The local CDAAA organized mass meetings, distributed literature, supplied speakers to neighborhood gatherings, and encouraged citizens to demand that the Roosevelt administration increase its support for the Allies. Chicago committee members saw themselves as a beleaguered vanguard, facing an uphill struggle in a city essentially antagonistic to their viewpoint. But they believed that CDAAA could turn opinion around, and they worked energetically to that end. Tied as it was to a program of furnishing aid, rather than to encouraging military participation, the committee's work in Chicago culminated with the struggle to secure congressional passage of the lend-lease plan.[2]

The Chicago Council on Foreign Relations furnished much of the leadership for the proaid forces in the Windy City. The Council was an educational forum that brought in speakers from around the world to discuss international affairs. Somewhat despite its leaders' wishes, by the late 1930s the Council had become a virtual conduit for anti-Fascist advocacy. The executive committee strove to prepare a balanced program season, only to discover a dearth of speakers willing to defend Fascist policies. Those who did appear, like author Colin Ross, met a hostile audience. A few visitors presented impressive cases for a restrained foreign policy. In the 1939–40 season, Herbert Hoover and Hanson W. Baldwin, the *New York Times*'s military expert, each argued against American involvement in the burgeoning overseas crisis. Far more numerous was the chorus of voices denouncing Hitler and Mussolini. In general these denunciations came from three sources. The Council routinely invited returning foreign correspondents to address its membership, and it happened that members of the *Daily News* staff came home more often than their *Tribune* counterparts. At one point the speakers' committee considered passing over Edgar Ansell Mowrer, a Pulitzer Prize winner recently back from Europe, in order to avoid the appearance of catering to the evening daily. Official representatives of the Allied nations comprised a second major element from which the Council drew its speakers. The British ambassador, Lord Lothian, headed the list appearing in the 1939–40 season. Finally, official or quasi-official representatives from Eastern European nations often spoke before the Council. Eduard Beneš, the former president of Czechoslovakia, and Jan Masaryk, son of that nation's founder, delivered addresses before large audiences in 1939. Council leaders like Clifton Utley were themselves outspoken anti-Fascists. After the fall of France at least one executive committee meeting debated whether to continue inviting defenders of fascism to appear. Ultimately the Council decided to maintain its attempts at balance, but the preponderance of anti-Fascist speakers made this a small setback at worst for supporters of the Allies.[3]

The Council's impact extended beyond its immediate membership. All regularly scheduled CCFR meetings were broadcast locally over WAAF, to an audience of nearly 200,000 Chicagoans, according to station estimates. The *Daily News* often previewed upcoming meetings and the *Tribune* covered the proceedings if the speaker was of special note.[4]

Important as CCFR's educational role was in creating an awareness of the growing menace of fascism, the Council itself never engaged in open advocacy. For its more activist members, the opportunity to do so arrived with the formation of the Committee to Defend America by Aiding the Allies.

On May 18, 1940, William Allen White dispatched hundreds of telegrams throughout the nation calling for a new committee to rouse public support for increased aid to the Allies. Three of these appeals went to Chicagoans Paul H. Douglas, Quincy Wright, and Clifton Utley. Douglas and Wright were members of Eichelberger's League of Nations Association, and Utley was the current director of the Council on Foreign Relations. Each had already spoken out against fascism. Douglas was a nationally known professor of economics at the University of Chicago, whose interest in politics had led to a successful race for alderman. Since this position engaged much of Douglas's time, Wright and Utley took the lead in organizing a local CDAAA chapter.[5]

Another of White's telegrams went to Frank Knox. The *Daily News* printed a copy on the front page, accompanied by a short article supporting the goals of the new group. Letters from interested Chicagoans soon began arriving at Eichelberger's headquarters in New York. His League of Nations Association maintained a small staff in Chicago, which became the nucleus of the future chapter's office. Eichelberger referred the Chicago-area inquiries back to the League office there for instructions about forming a CDAAA chapter. Many of these early respondents, who included Knox, Wright, Douglas, and Utley, already knew one another through mutual connections with the Council on Foreign Relations or in academic circles.[6]

Following receipt of White's telegram, Utley, Douglas, and Wright organized a luncheon meeting of about a dozen persons at the Chicago Club. There they initiated plans for a local CDAAA chapter. Most of the same group attended a second meeting on June 21 to develop ideas further. Wright and Utley reported back to White, recommending that Adlai E. Stevenson serve as chairman of the new group. White concurred and telephoned Stevenson to press him to accept the position. Stevenson agreed, after clearing the move with the partners of his law firm. The choice was a shrewd one, highly beneficial to both Stevenson and the committee.[7]

Stevenson was a forty-year-old lawyer with an impressive background and an active interest in foreign affairs. He had been born into wealth and Democratic politics in Bloomington, Illinois. His grandfather and namesake had served as Grover Cleveland's second vice-president and had established an enduring political tradition in the Stevenson family. His father, Lewis, was a lieutenant in the Hearst empire. Young Adlai received special advantages, including a tour of Europe at age eleven. He subsequently attended preparatory school at Choate, college at Princeton, and law school at Harvard. Leaving after a year, Stevenson finished his law degree at Northwestern and joined one of Chicago's most prestigious law firms, Cutting, Moore, and Sidley. From the first, Stevenson was torn between public affairs and a legal career. His commitment to public service was strong, as was his relish for acclaim and affluent living. He left Chicago during the first flush of the New Deal to enter the Agricultural Adjustment Administration, but by 1934 he had chosen to rejoin his old firm. There he stayed through 1940, although he continued to direct occasional veiled inquiries to friends in the government concerning opportunities available in Washington.

Stevenson's gifts, both of person and place, well qualified him to build the new chapter. He was a man of genuine charm and wit, with a talent for communicating these qualities in print and in person. One of the most engaging public speakers of his generation, Stevenson had sharpened his abilities during two terms as president of the Chicago Council on Foreign Relations in the mid-1930s. His tenure as the embattled head of the CDAAA in Chicago would likewise hone his writing skills. Membership in the social and professional elite enabled Stevenson to tap the wealthy for funds, a knack he had already developed through charity work. Through CCFR he made contact with Chicagoans sympathetic to the Allied cause. Stevenson also had personal links to the *Daily News* staff through Lloyd Lewis, a neighbor who wrote for the paper, and the Mowrer brothers, who were old acquaintances from Bloomington. Added to Stevenson's other attributes was a well-nurtured political sense, which aided him in guiding the fledgling group through the pitfalls of Chicago public affairs during a time of great national turbulence.[8]

A trip to Europe in the 1930s and his experience on the Council of Foreign Relations had convinced Stevenson that fascism posed a potential danger to the United States. To former vice-president Charles G. Dawes, still one of Chicago's foremost bankers and businessmen, Stevenson had forecast in January 1939 that a "clash of self-interest" was fast coming in Europe. He saw no reason "for confidence that the dictators will be reasonable." Two months later Stevenson urged Congressman John C. Martin to support an embargo on sales of all war supplies to Japan. By June 1940 he had become certain that increased material aid to the Allies was necessary in order to check Nazi expansion. Stevenson based his support for stepped-up aid on American self-interest. Such a program might enable the United States to avoid the "frightful expense and taxation" required if the country were to arm in sufficient strength to deter Hitler. Once Britain regained a position of advantage, he hoped that a lasting peace might be negotiated in Europe. As of July 1940 Stevenson saw no need for an American "army in Europe . . . yet."[9]

Under his leadership the Chicago chapter of the White Committee slowly took shape in July and August. It received some valuable early publicity when Utley broadcast an account of the committee's formation over his radio program. Over four hundred letters came in as a result. The real building process proceeded along other lines, however, as the original committee members mined their networks of friends and acquaintances for membership and financial contributions. The goal was to assemble 100 sponsors for the committee. Stevenson personally wrote dozens of letters during this period, appealing for support, explaining CDAAA's policy, and seeking out possible new contacts. Wright, Douglas, and Professor Bernadotte E. Schmidt scoured the University of Chicago. Walter Dill Scott, president emeritus of Northwestern University, and Professor Kenneth Colegrove performed the same function on the Evanston campus. Rabbi Solomon Goldman put the chapter in touch with one of its first and most important financial sources, Chicago's Jewish community. Stevenson cultivated another important Jewish leader, the businessman and philanthropist Max Epstein. Other committee members recruited among their own circles, and the group began to attract support from organized labor. All the while Eichelberger in New York routed pertinent letters to the Chicago office and furnished advice and manpower to help with organizing.[10]

The Chicago CDAAA engaged in limited public activity during the early weeks of summer. Stevenson and Utley prepared a press release which declared that "with or without military invasion, our security, our economy, our way of life is [*sic*] in deadly peril from an unappeasable, dynamic, ruthless and victorious foe." Their suggested answer to this danger was increased aid to Britain. A similar message appeared in petitions circulated in the Loop. The chapter also helped stage a mass meeting on June 28 at the University of Chicago, where both Utley and Quincy Wright spoke. Burdened by the demands of his law practice, Stevenson concentrated on seeking new sponsors and on drafting a statement for testimony before the platform committee of the Democratic national convention. Speaking as one of two representatives for the White Committee, Stevenson chose to emphasize preparedness and opposition to American overseas military involvement. His appeal for aid was confined to a brief and cautious paragraph. To increase the committee's visibility at the convention, the Chicago chapter established an office at the Stevens Hotel, which made CDAAA literature available to visiting Democratic delegates.[11]

Organizational work continued through the August dog days. Stevenson devoted an increasing proportion of his time to CDAAA work. He helped to stimulate activity in downstate Illinois and northward in Milwaukee, as well as in Cook County. Stevenson's endeavors began a pattern whereby Chicago sought to establish itself as an informal midwestern headquarters of the White Committee. Serious problems existed in the Chicago office itself, however. A visiting representative from Eichelberger's national office judged the Chicago group only moderately effective. The biggest obstacle was the limited time Stevenson could give to CDAAA work. Most of his efforts went toward raising money. Early in August, Stevenson asked the New York office for help. He wanted either a staff member who could raise funds full time or money to hire a local professional. After discussion with the national office, the chapter hired John A. Morrison as its director. Organization in the chapter was always haphazard, but Morrison's formal duties were to supervise office operations and in general to serve as Stevenson's deputy. In his mid-thirties, Morrison was a geographer, specializing in the Soviet Union, who had recently taught at the University of Chicago. He was energetic and an able public speaker, especially in small-group settings. With Morrison aboard, the tempo of CDAAA activity in Chicago accelerated.[12]

Gradually the committee brought its case before the public. For weeks Stevenson had written to local businessmen requesting display space for CDAAA literature. The committee finally secured a downtown storefront on Adams Street in early August. Under the direction of William McCormick Blair, Jr., a young cousin of the *Tribune* publisher, this outpost proved sufficiently effective to stop local traffic and attract a bomb threat. Satellite chapters in Evanston, Winnetka, and Highland Park followed Chicago's lead and established similar displays. The Winnetka group obtained a vacant shop rent free at a choice location. Members contributed lunches everyday and sold them at deliberately inflated prices. The profits financed the Winnetka chapter and the surplus went to British War Relief. Stevenson later estimated that these storefront centers circulated petitions and conducted letter-writing campaigns that together generated thousands of signatures in support of the destroyer deal.[13]

The Chicago committee also undertook to spread its viewpoint through mass meetings. On August 14 the committee scored a major success—and Stevenson achieved a personal triumph—before an overflow crowd in Mandell Hall on the University of Chicago campus. The rally was organized by dissident members of the American Student Union, who had broken from the parent group in protest over ASU's refusal to condemn the Russian invasion of Finland. Led by Adele Rose, Robert Merriam, and Hart Perry, they had formed a campus "Aid to the Allies Club." Quincy Wright helped the students obtain local celebrities as drawing cards for their rally. Paul Douglas was scheduled to address the gathering, with Edgar Mowrer of the *Daily News* as the featured speaker. When Mowrer cancelled his appearance shortly before the rally, campus organizers were concerned and somewhat resentful. Lucy McCoy, the secretary at the Chicago CDAAA office, suggested that Stevenson substitute for the absent correspondent. Students comprised the bulk of the crowd, and few had heard of Stevenson. Within minutes he won them over, in part by mimicking Mowrer's well-known and distinctive tone during the opening portion of his speech. Then Stevenson shifted into his own polished cadences and delivered an earnest appeal for the nation to end its complacency and steel itself to oppose Fascist expansion. The response was tumultuous. Before concluding, the rally adopted a resolution calling on President Roosevelt to expedite aid to Britain.[14]

One month later the Chicago committee mounted an ambitious meeting of its own. In early August a Chicago-based antiwar group, the Citizen's Keep America Out of War committee, had drawn perhaps 25,000 people to a rally at Soldier Field. To counteract this demonstration, Morrison, Utley, McCoy, and several other local leaders decided that the White Committee should stage a mass meeting of its own in mid-September. Stevenson was vacationing with his family in Ontario and did not learn for several days that he had been put in charge of planning the rally. Hurriedly, but with politic skill, Stevenson orchestrated arrangements for the assembly. The antiwar rally had attracted thousands, only to be dwarfed in mammoth Soldier Field. The White Committee elected to use the 13,000 seat Chicago Coliseum in hopes of filling it. Volunteers distributed thousands of handbills advertising the meeting. The promotional literature stressed that CDAAA based its aid policy solely on American self-interest. A series of articles in the *Daily News* further publicized the upcoming rally. "We have planned it as a demonstration of Chicago's majority opinion in favor of allied aid and as a reply to defeatists, appeasers and isolationists," Stevenson announced. The chapter also placed a large advertisement in the *Defender*, written especially for a black audience. "We don't want war," it read. "We don't want the Race problems that occur in war. We may not love the British, BUT TODAY ONLY BRITAIN STANDS BETWEEN US AND HITLER'S WILL." Stevenson also urged chairpersons of various pro-British clubs and ethnic organizations to encourage their members to attend. Chapter leaders were meticulous and emphatic in their choice of who would address the rally. Stevenson hoped to get Harold Stassen as keynote speaker. His credentials as a midwesterner and a Republican would insulate the gathering from criticism that it represented northeastern Democratic interests. When Stassen proved to be unavailable, the chapter was forced to settle for syndicated columnist Dorothy Thompson and former congressman Maury Maverick of Texas as the featured speakers. Both were effective before large crowds, but Thompson lived in New York City and Maverick was a New Deal Democrat. Other speakers were retired admiral William H. Standley, who lent an aura of military expertise to the gathering, and Hollywood's Douglas Fairbanks, Jr., who supplied drawing power. Each was introduced by a prominent Chicagoan from a different ethnic group. Stevenson urged these spokesmen to advertise their ethnicity during their introductions. The committee invited other ethnics to be present on the dais so that every major group in the city was represented. Stevenson achieved a similar concert in the religious domain, with a Catholic delivering the invocation and a Presbyterian leading the closing prayer. Gender does not seem to have been a consideration.[15]

Chapter leaders judged the rally a solid success. Stevenson gleefully told William Blair that *Tribune* photographers were unable to find the empty seats they had been sent to shoot. Many people had to be turned away. Despite a hot night and a lengthy program, few in the audience left early. John Morrison judged Standley a capable speaker and rated the other three "superb." Frequent applause interrupted both Thompson and Maverick. Local radio station WBBM recorded the entire meeting for later broadcast. By acclamation, those assembled endorsed a cautiously worded resolution supporting "all possible aid [to Britain], compatible with our defense requirements." The motive, Stevenson announced, was to gain the time to prepare American defenses. "This policy," he told the rally, "is, we think, best calculated to keep America out of war by keeping war out of America." In keeping with the national agenda of the White Committee, the gathering called for the transfer of twenty-five B-17 heavy bombers, twenty torpedo boats, and as many combat planes as possible to the British. Both resolutions were telegraphed to the White House.[16]

The rally furthered other goals of the Chicago White Committee chapter as well. Not only did the meeting show that the "aid short of war" policy commanded wide support in the Windy City, but it served as a valuable advertisement for the local CDAAA. Such mass assemblies, addressed by nationally known speakers, were taking place around the country. They renewed interest in the White Committee's cause and stimulated vital financial support. All the local press, even hostile papers like the *Tribune*, were obliged to cover events of this magnitude. Undaunted, *Tribune* people photographed some peace demonstrators outside the hall and featured them in its coverage of the rally. McCormick kept the story off the front page and portrayed the gathering as an eccentric assembly of emotional anglophiles. The *Daily News* put the rally on the front page and stressed CDAAA's concern with keeping America out of war. Only six weeks before, the *Defender* had denounced the White Committee as a group of rich men scheming to protect their investments in England. But the "World's Greatest Weekly" had evidently reconsidered its stance, for it ran a very favorable story on the rally. Only "a sprinkling" of blacks attended, however, although Stevenson had made certain Bronzeville was represented on the dais, but CDAAA had better luck with other local ethnic communities.[17]

Ethnics provided the obvious avenue along which to expand the committee beyond a small, elitist group. The Eastern Europeans were numerous and well organized, and they had reasons for opposing Nazism. Both the national White Committee leadership and the locals in Chicago recognized this opportunity. The pattern in the Windy City was to work through prominent ethnic leaders. Theodore Smith, sent by Eichelberger in July to help organize Chicago, made Polish groups an immediate priority. Smith talked with Karol Burke, city editor of the *Polish Daily Zgoda*, who reported that Polish sentiment favored CDAAA goals. Burke and Josef Martinek, executive secretary of the Czechoslovak National Council of America, each requested large amounts of White Committee literature for distribution among their groups. Lucy Mc-Coy's staff readily supplied them, and throughout CDAAA's life its leaders strove to cultivate and expand their connections with the ethnic communities.[18]

Ethnics played a vital, but distinctly secondary, role with the White Committee in Chicago. Key chapter leaders—Stevenson, Utley, Wright, Morrison, and Douglas—were Anglo-Saxon and Protestant to a man. They planned all local operations and, in conjunction with national headquarters, set policy. Their primary contacts were with the universities, a valuable but limited resource, and in the affluent northern suburbs, where many opposed CDAAA's program.

Stevenson and the other chapter leaders viewed their ethnic compatriots as both a strength and a liability. Ethnics provided an increasing proportion of the essential financial support and much of the mass audience needed to pack the Coliseum for the September rally. While Stevenson took care to apportion recognition among the representatives of various nationalities at the meeting, he also placed limits on their prominence in the committee's activities. No Eastern European frequented its inner councils, due more to circumstances than design in all probability. But Stevenson did exercise great care to attempt to prevent the committee from becoming publicly identified with Eastern European groups, especially the Jews. He tried to keep Jews from roles of public leadership in outlying chapters and to screen their large financial support from outside view. Fear of rousing anti-Semitism was the primary reason for this concealment. It also sprang from a larger desire to insure the committee's image as an organization primarily devoted to American self-interest. Knox and the *Daily News* shared an identical concern about their own position. Nevertheless, Stevenson had not completely outgrown the background of "country-club" prejudice in which he had been raised. His own biases may have subtly affected his handling of the issue. On the whole, however, the chapter retained enthusiastic support from Jewish groups.[19]

The most important agent linking the ethnic communities and the White group in Chicago was the Kelly-Nash machine. Kelly provided continual but quiet cooperation. Stevenson kept the mayor apprised of CDAAA's plans and activities; Kelly supplied contacts where needed, as with ethnic wards, and greased the wheels when impediments appeared in connection with committee activities. Like so much else concerning the machine, Kelly insisted that these operations be kept under wraps. His tacit peace with McCormick and the *Tribune* probably added to the mayor's concern that the CDAAA relationship remain covert. Kelly seldom commented in public on foreign affairs, a topic in any case largely irrelevant to the concerns of the machine. Moreover, he had no reason to aid the White Committee's leaders. Paul Douglas was perhaps the most important local critic of the Kelly-Nash organization. Stevenson, though a Democrat who kept his fences mended, was as yet a man of little political consequence. Kelly's cooperation stemmed instead from his avid loyalty to Franklin Roosevelt. For the Chicago chapter this type of relationship with city hall was ideal. The irreplaceable benefits of friendship with the machine came without the taint of an open association.[20]

If local politicians aided the committee's work, national politics interrupted it. Whatever momentum the September mass meeting had generated was lost as the committee curtailed its activities during the height of the 1940 campaign. CDAAA's avowedly nonpartisan stance was one factor militating against open activity. Although the group was sincere in its nonpartisanship, its program was by nature political and thus risked involving CDAAA in electoral rivalries. Identification with either party threatened to compromise the committee's integrity, alienate its sources of funding, and fracture its unity. Among the Chicago leadership, for example, John Morrison was a Republican; Douglas and Stevenson were Democrats. Additionally, the national political campaign absorbed the public's attention, energy, and money, and left the White Committee short of each. Both presidential candidates satisfied CDAAA on foreign policy issues, and no major developments arose on which it could base a drive. So the Chicago chapter avoided the political wars until election eve, when it placed identical advertisements in the *Tribune* and the *Daily News*. Commending the stance of both presidential contenders on the aid issue, the committee urged voters to give their support to those congressional candidates who favored increased assistance for Britain. Aside from this eleventh-hour appeal, the committee confined itself during October and November to informational activities in forums around Chicago.[21]

Two addresses given by Stevenson reveal the outlines of local CDAAA thinking at that time. By mid-October, the White Committee's opposite number, the America First Committee, had begun operations in the Chicago area. Representatives of the two groups met several times in joint public debates on foreign policy In part these appearances were designed to clarify the position of each committee, over which there was considerable public confusion. Stevenson rightly contended that the true measure of each committee's position was in the relative importance each placed on three considerations: aid to Britain, American defense, and the necessity of keeping the United States at peace. On this relationship America Firsters were vague and confused, for their committee had not yet faced the question squarely. Neither, however, had CDAAA or the nation at large. But in his first address Stevenson posed the question in terms favorable to the White Committee's position. He posited the choice as being between massive aid or none whatsoever. Stevenson emphasized that CDAAA viewed aid as a means of preserving peace by enabling Britain to stop Hitler's advance. The level of American material assistance had to be sufficient to accomplish this goal or the result would be worse than furnishing no aid at all. Token amounts of aid would weaken the United States and leave it to face the Nazis without major allies. While Stevenson opposed military intervention, he denied that the Neutrality Act represented any immutable formula for guiding national policy. He advocated retention of the law only so long as it suited American interests. The country need not worry about provoking Hitler. The German dictator would declare war on the United States if, and only if, he saw some advantage in doing so.

Stevenson outlined his views on the nature of the menace posed by Hitler in a mid-October meeting sponsored by the League of Women Voters. The heart of his case was that Nazism aimed at world revolution. He noted the possibility of a direct military threat to the United States, particularly if Germany captured Britain's Royal Navy. This theme, however, already was beginning to fade from CDAAA arguments. Lindbergh and others had demonstrated the extraordinary difficulties of an invasion attempt across the North Atlantic, and Hitler was having evident trouble in trying to cross even the English Channel. Stevenson placed more emphasis on the possibility of a Nazi incursion into South America. He noted that the bulge of Brazil lay closer to West Africa than to Florida. Although the United States could not afford to overlook the possibility of German military action in upcoming months, a greater concern was the potential long-term economic threat. Stevenson warned that German use of slave labor, harnessed ruthlessly to the combined productive capacity of the Continent, might drive American goods from world markets. Furthermore, with Hitler triumphant over all Europe, American industry would have to convert to military production on a massive scale, since the Nazi leader could in time manufacture the means to make a direct invasion of North America feasible. The results of such a conversion alone could well be disastrous to the current system of free enterprise and political democracy. Stevenson thus believed that a policy limited to domestic preparedness contained risks more serious than those of the aid-to-Britain program. The White Committee was advocating the "aid short of war" formula, he stated, out of consideration for American self-interest and, above all, from a desire to remain at peace.[22]

The tenor and circumspection of Stevenson's address were characteristic not only of the CDAAA in Chicago and throughout the United States, but also of most anti-Fascist activity during 1940 and early 1941. Speakers insisted that self-interest was the motive behind the aid program. Proponents consistently emphasized its advantages to the United States, and above all that aid offered the best chance for America to avoid active military participation in the fighting. Its advocates dealt in various ways with the element of risk involved in the policy. But seldom did they present it as a half-way measure, an interim step prior to full participation. The belief persisted that with luck American aid might enable Britain to defeat Hitler. At worst it would delay a Nazi onslaught against the Western Hemisphere and buy time for America to prepare its defenses. Aid proponents did not challenge the strength of peace sentiment among the public; they appealed to it. Many shared the desire for peace. Sometimes those who spoke in favor of aid were vague and couched their views in generalities, but caution was the keynote whenever their arguments became specific. There simply was no widespread public campaign for war in 1940. Americans saw an alternative to military participation. As late as February 1941 Gallup found that 70 percent of the public believed that aid contributed to keeping the United States out of the fighting.[23]

Were the proponents of "aid short of war" insincere in believing that aid might substitute for military participation? Often their opponents thought so. No doubt individuals varied in belief, expectation, and candor, but there is no compelling evidence to suggest that in general the proponents of aid were being disingenuous during 1940. The element of timing is important in this regard. In the context created by the fall of France, the aid policy satisfied the perceived need for serious and effective action against the growing power of Germany. Measured against American opinion and policy during the previous few years, the aid program was a major departure, a daring stroke. Preservation of peace remained a major goal of American policy, but the method of achieving it had gone from a rigid insistence on neutrality and nonintervention to an open effort to help one warring power achieve success. As to the effectiveness of American efforts to strengthen Britain, what contemporary—especially those who were not privy to secret government information—could judge this issue accurately amid the frantic events following Hitler's blitz westward? The urgency of the crisis encouraged a focus on imminent events. Until lend-lease, Roosevelt's pattern was to supply aid in discrete quantities and categories. No one did anything to dispel the perception that the British would put the material to almost immediate use. Nazi power appeared vast after the conquest of France, but Winston Churchill restored confidence in Britain on both sides of the Atlantic. The American public knew little about the worst aspects of Britain's situation, especially the war at sea. By year's end Britain had prevented invasion of the home islands and routed the Italians in North Africa. Because there was reason not to despair of Britain's ultimate success, a plausible case existed for the long-term prospects of "aid short of war."

Franklin D. Roosevelt revealed his own optimism concerning Britain's prospects when he unveiled the lend-lease program in December 1940. Wire-service coverage of his address emphasized four points: the president's intention to keep the United States at peace, his belief in the gravity of the international situation and the extreme danger it posed to the United States, his conviction that lend-lease was necessary to maintain the British war effort, and his confidence in Britain's ultimate success. The lend-lease proposal combined legal nonbelligerency with a projection of American productive power into the war. The policy also accorded with prevailing public opinion. Roosevelt believed that a sizable minority of Americans was still unwilling to admit that Fascist nations threatened the United States. One major goal of his speech was simply to convince people of the danger, and so to create a consensus that would justify the escalation of American aid. That the president believed such elaborate explanations were needed suggests that he considered more extreme actions politically impossible in the winter of 1940–41.[24]

Lend-lease represented the logical culmination of CDAAA's "aid short of war" policy. The committee had begun requesting some new initiative almost as soon as the election results were in. On November 11 William Allen White told a conference of midwestern CDAAA chapters that the organization no longer needed to create support for the aid policy. Ample public backing already existed, the chairman maintained. The task now was to channel it. White cautioned chapter leaders in private that he wanted them to adopt stances no more extreme than those the administration judged publicly acceptable. In an open appeal similar to that of the *Daily News*, White pointed to national unity as the nation's primary need. Stevenson issued a press release the following day which announced that the conference had resolved to "combat apathy . . . at this critical time." He echoed White's assertion that aid per se was no longer the question. Scale and pace were the real issues. Quoting war correspondent Vincent Sheehan, Stevenson contended that the next six months would be vital if Britain were to resist the Germans successfully. By the end of November, the Chicago chairman proclaimed that CDAAA's new goal was removal of all "restrictive legislation" hindering aid to Britain. Thus, over two weeks prior to Roosevelt's disclosure of the lend-lease proposal, the White Committee had given a broad endorsement to whatever move the president might make.[25]

Just as the lend-lease debate was about to begin, a serious internal dispute sidetracked the White Committee. An influential faction affiliated with the committee, known as the Century Club Group, had long advocated positions more militant than White was prepared to accept. Most members of the faction lived near New York City, and they were represented on CDAAA's executive committee in numbers sufficient to sway that group. The executive committee issued a statement on November 26 that reflected their views. Although ambiguously worded, the statement seemed to recommend a total repeal of the Neutrality Act and the use of American ships in convoys to Britain. Both positions reached further than any move contemplated by White—or Roosevelt. The statement followed a series of disputes between White and the Century Club Group, whose actions violated his dictum that the committee not adopt positions much more extreme than current administration policy. White not only disagreed with the New York faction's views, he feared they would undermine support for CDAAA throughout the country, especially in the midwest. Angered by the November 26 action, White wrote Roy Howard, chief of a newspaper chain unfriendly to the White Committee, repudiating the Century Club Group position in terms that suggested CDAAA's commitment to peace overrode every other aspect of its program. For whatever reasons, White so overstated his case that he provoked open warfare within the committee. Critical letters deluged CDAAA national headquarters. Faced with this uproar, on top of the ill health of both himself and his wife, the seventy-two-year-old White resigned his chairmanship on the day after Christmas.[26]

The committee delayed announcing White's resignation for eight days while it considered candidates to replace him and discussed how to present the affair to the public. During the interim, the Chicago chapter fought to have White reconsider his decision and continue as the national chairman. Both Stevenson and Morrison shared White's outlook. Since early December, Stevenson had been worried about the charge that CDAAA was coyly working for American military intervention. Like White, he blamed elements within the committee for lending credibility to such accusations. Still hoping that Britain could win with nothing more than economic aid and military supplies from the United States, Stevenson continued to fear the effects of military involvement on American society. Morrison had long been antagonistic toward the Century Club Group and the New York City chapter of CDAAA. He believed that they simply presumed their own leadership within the committee and understood neither public opinion nor majority attitudes within the lower echelons of CDAAA. White's resignation upset Morrison, who was quick to anger whenever the New Yorkers were involved. Morrison, Stevenson, and Utley joined Clark Eichelberger and William Emerson of the New England CDAAA office in a conference telephone call to White. Emerson and the Chicago leaders hoped to convince the Emporia editor to withdraw his resignation in the final hours prior to its public announcement. Their entreaties were unsuccessful.[27]

Morrison and Stevenson next sought to reduce the influence of the Century Club Group on CDAAA national policy. Emerson again cooperated, and together they asked that the committee relocate its headquarters from New York to a midwestern city, preferably Chicago. Stevenson also told Lewis Douglas, chairman of the CDAAA executive committee, that they did not want an easterner as White's successor. Midwestern chapter chairpersons met in Chicago on January 6 and formally endorsed these views. The conference named Wendell Willkie as its preferred choice for chairman. The national executive committee rejected the dissidents' wishes, despite the presence of Morrison and Stevenson at the decisive meeting. Former senator Ernest W. Gibson, a Vermont Republican, became the new national chairman. CDAAA headquarters remained in New York and thereafter Century Club Group influence over policy was probably greater than at any previous time. The Chicagoans found Gibson an acceptable choice, but they were angered by the continued ascendancy of the Century Club Group. The outcome prompted Morrison to resign from the committee. Partly for the same reason, Stevenson also contemplated leaving.[28]

Amid this organizational strife, the Chicago chapter attempted to encourage public support for the lend-lease program. With Morrison and Stevenson disgruntled, Clifton Utley delivered most of the chapter's major public addresses. He and America Firster Sterling Morton spoke to an audience of 500 at the Women's Athletic Club on January 10. Utley's arguments paralleled those Stevenson had used the previous autumn. Utley contended that Britain constituted America's first line of defense against Fascist aggression. He acknowledged that the lend-lease policy might provoke Nazi retaliation, but emphasized his belief that the Germans would ultimately endanger the United States anyway should their expansion continue unchecked. "It is better to take risks in offering aid to Great Britain than to wait passively," he said. Utley hoped that American aid could restore Britain to a position of mastery over Europe. Then London could bargain for peace from a position of strength. Ernest Gibson voiced similar views in an early February speech to an overflow crowd at a Chicago American Legion post. The former senator also told a University of Chicago rally that lend-lease was the policy that stood the best chance of enabling the nation to remain at peace. While they varied somewhat in emphasis, CDAAA spokespersons portrayed lend-lease in terms akin to those used by the *Daily News*, an approach similar to the one that the paper had employed in the fall of 1939 to support repeal of the arms embargo. Their arguments also mirrored those of the Roosevelt administration. In each case, committee representatives advocated the lend-lease proposal as the best means available to avoid war. The hope for continued peace, rather than exhortations about a moral duty to oppose fascism, was the main element in the Chicago chapter's argument.[29]

Yet the potent nature of the Axis menace was a major theme

employed by CDAAA leaders to develop opinion favorable to lend-lease. Appearing with Gibson at the University of Chicago rally, *Daily News* correspondent Edgar Ansell Mowrer dwelt upon the evils of the Nazi system and its fanatical hatred of democracy. The Chicago CDAAA produced a pamphlet called "The Atlantic Is Not 3000 Miles Wide Because –" which outlined the potential avenues along which the Germans could menace America. Employing maps to illustrate its points, the pamphlet contended that use of Atlantic islands and South American bases could enable Hitler to threaten the United States militarily. With the United States Navy concentrated in the Pacific against Japan, Britain and her fleet were the sole obstacles preventing this danger. Material aid from the United States would keep Britain in the war and thus sustain the Atlantic shield while America prepared her own defenses. In a more careful form, Chicago leaders had revived the specter of a direct military threat, an argument they had all but abandoned a few months before. So impressed was the CDAAA's national office that they ordered the booklet for mass distribution nationwide.[30]

Whatever their merits, CDAAA appeals met with a disappointing response in the Chicago area. A Gallup poll indicated that the midwest backed passage of the Lend-Lease Bill by a slim margin, but congressional mail from Chicago ran heavily against the measure. Through January, the city's congressmen reported receiving from three to twenty times more mail opposing lend-lease than favoring it. "The opposition has us on the run here," Stevenson confessed to Knox. In hopes of reversing this preponderance, the chapter organized a mailing of 500,000 letters to area residents, asking them to write their congressmen in support of the bill. The appeal was the costliest single project the chapter ever undertook, and it succeeded. By mid-February, all congressmen reported a more equal balance of opinion in their recent correspondence. Several noted that a majority of the mail they were receiving now favored lend-lease. Only late in February, as it became obvious that the bill would pass, did the volume of mail from both sides gradually decline.[31]

Along with widening public involvement in the debate, acrimony increased as well. The feud between Chicago's newspapers fueled this tendency in the Windy City, but it also reflected a national trend. Supporters of lend-lease often accused the bill's critics of aiding Hitler by accident or, more infrequently, by design. The *Louisville Courier-Journal*, for example, likened senate opponents of the bill to U-boat commanders, since both prevented aid from reaching Britain. Often the debate degenerated into name-calling. Real bitterness first surfaced during the 1940 elections and deepened during the lend-lease struggle. *New York Times* columnist Arthur Krock observed that Chicago had become a verbal cockpit despite the best efforts of responsible leaders on both sides. Stevenson and many others blamed the *Tribune*, citing the paper's insistence that the "aid short of war" formula masked a deliberate plot to maneuver the United States into war. The "World's Greatest Newspaper" indeed merited some of the blame for the burgeoning ill will, having for example labeled CDAAA members "cookie pushers," "warmongers," and "professional bleeding hearts." But *Tribune* opponents returned the fire with gusto. The Chicago chapter's lend-lease pamphlet queried, "Will YOU listen to the APPEASERS and wishful thinkers who tell us we have nothing to worry about . . . ?" The *Daily News* repeatedly accused its opponents of "playing Hitler's game," a stock phrase among aid proponents everywhere. Stevenson himself excoriated critics of administration policy. At one point he pledged that CDAAA would "refute the voices of appeasement" growing in Chicago. "Appeaser" became the favorite epithet employed by proaid forces, as "warmonger" was among their opponents. Each term revealed more about its user's fears than about the motive of those it supposedly described.[32]

Efforts by Stevenson and others to uplift the debate floundered. "Indeed, perhaps most Americans would agree that the importance of the controversy warrants more sobriety," Stevenson wrote to the *Tribune* in answer to its "cookie pusher" charge. Chapter leaders believed that any public attack on the *Tribune* would be "childish and undignified." At the outset of the lend-lease debate, Stevenson again issued an open appeal for moderation and tolerance. But the pressures against such a posture overwhelmed every call for decorum. The stakes—freedom or enslavement, peace or war—seemed too high to play the game with restraint. So the debate grew more hostile.[33]

Final congressional passage of the bill on March 11 left its proponents pleased, antiadministration forces despondent, and many participants sickened by the turn the debate had taken. Thoughtful elements within both CDAAA and the America First Committee pondered whether each group should disband. Many more people, regardless of whether they belonged to a committee, were relieved that the question was now settled and welcomed a respite.

The Chicago CDAAA chapter greeted the debate's cessation with special joy. For diverse reasons, the chapter was near the end of its tether. Lend-lease fulfilled CDAAA's original goal of all-out material aid to the Allies. Measured by this standard, the committee no longer needed to exist. Any continued action would require a reassessment of its purpose. Citing this reason, some elements within the Chicago outpost wished to conclude operations. Late in the lend-lease struggle, committee field workers reported lagging public interest. The familiar financial sources had gone dry, having been tapped repeatedly in the preceding months by both local and national requests. Committee activity had reached a virtual standstill by late March.[34]

Key members of the leadership bowed out at this time. Previously, Eichelberger had persuaded Morrison to withdraw his January resignation and to continue serving for the duration of the lend-lease debate. Having honored his commitment, Morrison announced his intention to leave. This time Eichelberger's entreaties failed. Morrison still resented the Century Club Group and he yearned for the increased money he could earn through lecturing. Largely for different reasons, Stevenson also wished to step down. He too bridled at what he considered the arrogance and self-centeredness of the New Yorkers. Committee work robbed so many hours from Stevenson's law practice that he doubted he was shouldering a fair share of the firm's caseload. Stevenson even feared that his CDAAA activities had damaged the firm's reputation and cost it business. If this problem existed, Stevenson's friend and law partner, James F. Oates, Jr., knew nothing of it. In any case, Stevenson's ambition focused on government service in Washington rather than a resumption of his Chicago law practice. He had entertained this idea since late summer at least and began extending feelers in the wake of White's resignation. These efforts bore fruit when Frank Knox brought Stevenson into the Navy Department as his legal aide. Stevenson did not depart for Washington until June, but his enthusiasm for CDAAA work had dissipated long before.[35]

Appeals for national unity on foreign policy issues resurfaced at the close of the lend-lease debate. Many within the Chicago CDAAA chapter viewed the unity appeal as a means to terminate the rivalry between America First and themselves and as a graceful way for CDAAA to retire. Clarence Randall, a member of the local CDAAA executive board, thought that America First was becoming stigmatized in the public mind as an obstructionist body. Realizing that a popular majority had turned against them, AFC leaders might now agree to dissolve. Other CDAAA members concurred with Randall's judgment, and Paul Douglas called publicly for both groups to disband. By now the two committees had developed a symbiotic relationship in Chicago. The CDAAA chapter saw itself as a listening post on the opposing committee's activities. Eichelberger's headquarters indeed relied on their reports concerning AFC strategy. So when the America Firsters chose not to disband, they helped decide CDAAA's future in Chicago as well. The bid for national unity failed when noninterventionists refused to yield. CDAAA's job was unfinished.[36]

The White Committee led the fight to focus popular attention on the administration's "aid short of war" program, but the committee's activities encompassed only a portion of the spectrum of public reaction to the crises across the oceans. Intense interest in the events abroad generated a desire to help the victims of aggression or to assist the United States in preparing for a possible threat. In ways both subtle and overt, the war colored daily life in America. Foreign policy issues crept into local politics, infiltrated movie theaters, and strained personal friendships. Seldom did the type of activity differ from the pattern previewed in the autumn of 1939. But now the tempo quickened and many outpourings reflected an intensified concern. After May 1940 the war refused to go away.

Public demand for war information soared. Throughout the city, librarians reported that they had never been busier. So heavy was the demand for former Nazi leader Hermann Rauschning's bestselling *The Revolution of Nihilism* that the *Daily News* summarized his arguments in a mid-June editorial. Chicagoans deluged the International Relations section of the John Crerar Library

with inquiries relating to the European war. Questions ranged
from the sophisticated to the simplistic. The Council on Foreign
Relations drew overflow audiences to hear such speakers as Wendell Willkie and former ambassador William C. Bullitt. Florida
Democrat Claude Pepper, perhaps the United States Senate's most
outspoken opponent of Hitler, attracted a large crowd to an out-
door rally on Flag Day in Chicago, one of many around the country during late spring. Despite rumors that the choice of so controversial a featured speaker had angered some of the rally's backers,
none of the sponsoring groups withdrew.[37]

Language provided one sign of how widely the war had pene-
trated the consciousness of Americans. The terms "blitzkrieg" or
"blitz" were appropriated to describe energetic movement, or the
hope of it, in all sorts of settings. A candidate for the office of
Grand Exalted Ruler of Elks saw his "blitz" fizzle. Distraught citizens of Chicago's Second Ward organized a "blitz" on rats. Other
people sought to capitalize on public loathing for the Nazi Führer.
Pickets in at least two Chicago labor disputes carried placards
reading, "Hitler must run this plant. They don't employ Negroes."
One of them was arrested on the grounds that the sign was too
inflammatory. Other Chicagoans plainly took the Nazis less seriously. The Willing Workers of the Cleveland Tabernacle Baptist
Church in Chicago divided into teams, designated as the "Americans" and the "Nazis," to compete in the church's 1940 fund-raising drive. Each team was in turn divided into "soldiers," "sailors,"
and "dive bombers." Such lightheartedness was rare in the summer of France's defeat.[38]

As the Allied debacle unfolded during the summer of 1940,
alarmed Chicagoans sought to "do their bit" in the emergency.
The British War Relief fund mushroomed in June and July. The
Daily News's society column predicted that the War Relief Ball
would be the height of the midsummer social season. Other organizations sought to prepare America for a possible foreign challenge. Through the National Rifle Association and local gun clubs,
area hunters formed the "Sportsman's Defense Reserve" and offered their services to protect the community. The Evanston-based
Women's Christian Temperance Union planned a "*Blitzkrieg* on
Booze." President Ida B. Smith declared that, "In this period of
world crisis, it should be evident to all who cherish the democratic

way of life that no nation, eaten at the core by self-indulgence, can long survive." Illinois schools also pledged to prepare citizens for the ordeal of modern warfare. Chicago public schools stressed the "inspired teaching of American History" to build morale. Boston schools offered to add extra night classes to train mechanics for national defense needs. The Lincoln Dental Society heard a brief talk on the defense situation in which the speaker reminded blacks that good oral hygiene was an important part of preparedness. Regardless of the importance or success of any of these efforts, collectively they suggest that organizations detected an anxiety among many citizens about the war. Groups responded to this concern, sought to channel the resulting energy, and in some cases attempted to exploit the unease engendered by the foreign crisis.[39]

Internal security was an issue of major concern during the summer of 1940, in part due to the emphasis Roosevelt gave the matter in a radio address on May 26. The president's speech warned citizens to beware of efforts by agents of unfriendly powers to sow dissension and discord in the United States. The aim of this "fifth column," FDR said, was to create indecision in the public and to paralyze the political process. The speech played to very real anxieties. For years Americans had feared Nazi activity in the United States as a menace to national security. Over 70 percent believed that a German fifth column already existed in July of 1940, and almost half thought that Nazi agents were operating in their own communities. Such fears soon brought a variety of responses. In Los Angeles, District Attorney Burton Fitts received an overwhelming response from area civic leaders to his call for a local campaign against espionage and sabotage. The *Denver Post* thought that local communists represented the worst danger. Alleging that most radicals supported themselves on public relief, the paper urged Colorado officials to eliminate political undesirables from the relief rolls. Using a different approach, the American Federation of Labor distributed millions of posters purporting to show how a fifth columnist could be identified. They looked normal, but they contended that democracy was doomed and disliked organized labor. Governor E. D. Rivers of Georgia applied himself with special vigor to the security needs of his state. Responding to reports of fifth column activity, the governor ordered all aliens living in Georgia to report for fingerprinting. He was prepared to cancel the professional and occupational licenses of those who refused to comply. Even America's transient population became aroused over the danger of spies. Jeff Davis, the "king of the hobos," announced formation of a hobo police force, the "Jungle Bulls," to keep watch for "fifth column stuff" among the nation's tramps.[40]

However much the security jitters were exploited by various persons or groups for reasons of their own, the concern was real and led to a scattering of incidents. In Pekin, Illinois, for example, authorities jailed eleven communists to protect them from a mob. The incident began when the eleven tried to distribute leaflets accusing Roosevelt of moving the United States toward war. Local members of the American Legion and the Veterans of Foreign Wars constituted the bulk of the crowd, which set fire to the activists' auto and beat several of those who persisted in trying to pass out the leaflets. Such violence was rare, but the feelings that prompted it were not.[41]

The internal security issue was of special concern to Chicago's blacks. Having experienced intolerance throughout their history, American blacks were wary of what some perceived as a new wave of hysteria. One of John Segenstacke's first columns in the *Defender* predicted that the fear of "fifth column" activity that was sweeping the country would ultimately be directed against blacks. Rumors abounded. One report claimed that Berlin had placed agents in all the city's best hotels and restaurants where they could eavesdrop on the conversations of the white elite. When the pro-Nazi German-American Bund and the Ku Klux Klan held a joint rally in August at a camp in New Jersey, black leaders became thoroughly alarmed. The *Defender* ran a rare front-page editorial denouncing the rally and indicting Americans for tolerating such activity. Similar complacency, said the paper, had caused the fall of France.[42]

Once again, the actions of various ethnic groups, especially Eastern Europeans, reflected their special concern with the events abroad. A coalition of Chicago's Polish organizations staged a massive rally at Soldier's Field on June 23. Together the groups had mounted a fund drive resulting in the purchase of fifteen field ambulances for the Polish army-in-exile. Archbishop Samuel A.

Strich headed the list of dignitaries attending the event. The annual summer series of Roof Garden Forums at the Jewish Peoples' Institute adopted the topic "Labor's Position in the Present Crises" as its theme for the season. Speakers discussed the positions of the AFL, the CIO—and the CDAAA. In the fall, over two-thirds of the lectures at the Sinai Temple Forum concerned the foreign situation. On September 1, the first anniversary of the war's outbreak, more than seventy Polish churches held memorial masses to honor Polish dead. Special services the same day at one hundred area synagogues prayed for deliverance of the conquered populations of Europe. Italian-American organizations in Chicago avoided any public stance on foreign policy or defense issues, while activities of some local German-Americans were arousing controversy. Elsewhere, on the East Coast in particular, spokesmen for these nationalities took pains to affirm their loyalty to the United States, their willingness to fight on its behalf if called, and their opposition to fascism. These well-publicized affirmations of patriotism were efforts to prevent widespread fears of domestic subversion from developing into full-scale repression.[43]

Divisions over American foreign policy even appeared among the Eastern Europeans on rare occasions. The Slovak *People's Daily* supported an Emergency Peace Mobilization rally in August. The Czech National Council blasted the paper for this act of "appeasement," and accused it of favoring Nazism. Editor Paul Hodos denied the charges and maintained that the paper's only goal was to keep America at peace. His stance was a lonely one, however, for none of the other Eastern European papers joined the *People's Daily*. Opposition to Axis aggression so pervaded Eastern European groups that the *Tribune* all but ceased to cover their activities after the fall of France.[44]

Conflicting public views on international affairs induced caution and circumspection among Chicago-area Democrats. On the advice of Democratic National Chairman Jim Farley, local chieftains confined themselves to a blanket endorsement of Roosevelt's policies and presidential candidacy. They intentionally soft-pedaled foreign affairs issues. After Knox entered the cabinet, the Illinois GOP proclaimed itself the "peace party." Democrats adopted the "preparedness" label in response, and these vague terms established the ring boundaries for the season's political shadowboxing.

Mayor Kelly dismissed as "beneath contempt" state Republican charges that the Democrats were scheming to take the country into war. This was Kelly's only comment on the foreign situation during the 1940 campaign, and in general local Democratic leaders kept silent on foreign policy issues.[45]

Nevertheless, Republicans injected foreign policy into local races. On the west side, two GOP challengers lambasted the records of their incumbent opponents. Joseph Wagner criticized Sixth District congressman Anton F. Maciejewski for voting in favor of both the draft and repeal of the arms embargo. Over in the Fifth, Martin Dykema charged that Adolph J. Sabath had allowed the nation to drift towards war. Dykema promised that a Republican Congress would halt this movement. The GOP's candidate for state attorney general, George F. Barrett, blasted the new draft law as a measure to provide "unnecessary cannon fodder" in support of Roosevelt's "secret alliances with foreign powers." Retorted the *Daily News*, "Barrett's lies, insinuations and unsubstantiated charges . . . are contemptible and loathsome." Foreign policy issues also figured prominently in races for Illinois's two congressmen-at-large seats. Both GOP candidates, Stephen Day and William G. Stratton, were McCormick allies and both stressed the pledge in the GOP party platform to oppose an American expeditionary force. Their Democratic opponents, T. V. Smith and Walter Orlikoski, were Chicagoans who championed FDR's stance on aid.[46]

All this furor yielded inconclusive results. Most state and local Democratic candidates ran behind the national ticket in Illinois. These differences were the margin between defeat and victory in the statewide races. Roosevelt carried Illinois with less than 51 percent of the vote, but Barrett, Day, and Stratton each narrowly defeated their Democratic rivals. Republicans also captured the governor's mansion and a Democratic seat in the United States Senate. Only in Cook County did the Democrats sweep to victory. A CDAAA poll just prior to voting day found that all Democratic candidates lent FDR's aid program their unqualified support, but it was their attachment to the Kelly-Nash machine that in all probability reelected these men. As Samuel Lubell has long contended, foreign policy did influence voting in the 1940 election, though the voting in Illinois does not support Lubell's finding in all particulars. Both in the state and nationwide the Democratic vote fell by about 7 percent from the total in 1936. As Lubell demonstrated, one factor in the reduction was the defection of voters of German-American heritage in above average numbers. However, Lubell's finding that the Democrats were also deserted by Italian-Americans does not seem to be true for Illinois. For the Irish, the other major ethnic group that might be expected to dislike administration foreign policy, the evidence suggests that there was no strong groundswell against Roosevelt. Overall, while foreign policy, as expressed through ethnicity, affected voters in the 1940 election, it was only one factor among several and appears to have been decisive only among German-Americans in Illinois. (See Appendix.)[47]

Still, public sentiment aroused by the storms in Europe did occasionally impinge on local decision making. In September, for example, a squabble developed over the city Censor Board's banning of the motion picture *Pastor Hall*. The film was based on an actual case in which the German government had imprisoned a clergyman for protesting against Nazi interference with religion. The Censor Board cited a city statute that forbade the showing of films portraying "depravity, criminality, or lack of virtue [in] a class of citizens of any race," or that tended to produce a breach of the peace. *Pastor Hall* contained scenes of murder and torture, said the Board, and lacked a wholesome moral. As one member admitted, the Board feared that the film would inflame the city's German population. "There are two groups of Germans here in Chicago, both very active," said Police Lieutenant Harry Costello. "What is balm to one is poison to the other." The *Hall* banning continued a pattern of censorship applied to anti-Nazi movies. In the preceding two years, the Board had prohibited the showing of at least seven other such motion pictures.[48]

This time the decision set off immediate criticism. The Chicago Civil Liberties Committee and the American Jewish Congress protested on the grounds of free speech. The *Daily News* assailed what it labeled undue consideration for "Nazi sensibilities" on the part of the Censor Board, which was in fact controlled by the police department. The *News* alluded to the Board's recurrent censorship of anti-Nazi works, while allowing the official German documentary film *Blitzkrieg in Poland* to play in various Chicago theaters. This seeming inconsistency also bothered Earl B. Dickerson, the only black alderman in the city. The Civil Liberties Committee arranged for a private showing of *Pastor Hall*, to which it invited representatives from various Chicago civic organizations. Following the viewing, Dr. Eric von Schroetler, director of the German League of Culture and editor of the anti-Nazi newspaper *Volksbund*, testified to the accuracy of the film. The gathering then concluded that *Hall* did not deserve the ban. Dickerson attended and promised to introduce a resolution in the City Council demanding a reversal of the Censor Board's decision.[49]

The swelling chorus of criticism forced city hall to reassess its position. Mayor Kelly had agreed to review the *Hall* case even before the Civil Liberties Committee showing. Meanwhile, other organizations joined the protest. The support of Chicago's Women's Clubs carried particular weight. They cited the seeming inconsistency of banning *Pastor Hall* while approving *Blitzkrieg in Poland*. Following a viewing of *Hall* by a group of supervisory police personnel, the Board cleared the film for showing. This successful challenge to the Censor Board's two-year-old policy was only one indication of altered public attitudes. The shifting stances of various organizations provided another measure of the changes wrought by the fall of France.[50]

Veterans' groups typified the growing militancy of American opinion and the anxieties that attended it. "Without discussion or opposition," the American Legion's 1940 national convention passed resolutions urging "all practicable aid for Britain," an impregnable national defense, and an active campaign to combat domestic subversion. The vague wording of the aid statement allowed the Legion to dodge this crucial issue, but other actions were more revealing. For the first time a Legion convention refused to approve a resolution favoring strict neutrality. The Illinois delegation now mutely accepted the majority will at the national gathering, unlike in the previous year when it tried to prevent Legion endorsement of Roosevelt's program. By January 1941 the VFW had also endorsed FDR's foreign policy. The following month Alvin York, perhaps America's greatest living war hero, visited Chicago for a VFW convention and radio rally. In his address to the assembly York championed the concept of aid and denied that he favored American entry into the war. Other speakers concentrated on the topic of national defense. Many were local

VFW officials, a number of whom actively opposed administration foreign policy and supported organizations such as America First. The halls of many Chicago outposts in both the Legion and the VFW echoed with dissent over the national leadership's position.[51]

If the overall trend in American opinion was favorable to Roosevelt's policies, the movement was neither universal nor always smooth. The divergence of American attitudes toward lend-lease was revealed by the variety of positions that organizations adopted on the issue and by the greatly varying levels of ease with which groups arrived at their stances. Some organizations, such as the Association of American Historians, adopted resolutions of support with relatively little controversy. Other groups were unable to agree at all on a position. The Conference of Catholic Bishops split almost evenly on lend-lease. After a lengthy debate brought the conferees no closer to consensus, the chairman advised the bishops to act as their individual consciences directed. The CIO experienced a similar dispute. Sidney Hillman led supporters of the plan, while Joseph Curran of the Maritime Workers and Steven Mills of the Newspaper Guild directed the opposition. Reconciliation proved impossible, and the CIO took no formal stand on lend-lease.[52]

The National League of Women Voters was also racked by controversy, although in the League's case the uproar ensued after the group had endorsed the president's bill. When Roosevelt first broached the idea of lend lease, League leaders had been examining ways to accelerate production of defense materials. The new proposal was attractive because it promised to expand American productive capacity and because it seemed to indicate that FDR wanted to bring more urgency to the preparedness effort. League president Marguerite Wells was aware of divisions within the membership over foreign and defense issues, and she was soliciting advice from the board of directors on how best to proceed when Roosevelt's initiative forced the issue. Following the Christmas holidays, Wells wrote the board members and state presidents to apprise them of her views. She suggested that the situation with regard to public opinion was becoming more complex. Whereas a consensus on "aid short of war" appeared to have formed after the election, now two diametrically opposed groups of dissenters had

emerged. She alluded to positions represented by the America First Committee and the Century Club faction of the CDAAA. Her letter did not ask for direct authorization to endorse lend-lease. In fact she implied that the League program authorized the board to endorse any proposal under which America acted "as a non-belligerent." The term meant, she explained, any action not calculated to lead the country into war. In some ways Wells fell victim in the letter to the very strengths of the group she headed. She focused on long-range issues and clearly discerned the significance of the two emerging poles of opinion. Wells predicted to the members that the next critical choice facing Americans would be to decide between "aid short of war" and what she called "aid regardless of consequences." Wells seemed not to appreciate that for many Americans, including members of her own organization, lend-lease posed just such a choice. The first inkling that the League was headed for difficulty came when the board of directors took up the bill, docketed as H.R. 1776. Before the board consented to endorse the measure, considerable discussion of the scope of presidential powers issue and the possible risk of war ensued. Wells announced League support for lend-lease on January 16, in a statement interpreting the plan as a substitute for war.[53]

Once again state organizations swung into action on the administration's behalf. Wells requested that the boards of each local League hold special meetings to discuss H.R. 1776 and become familiar with the League's analysis of it. Then they were expected to contact their local representatives encouraging them to vote for the bill. Though the evidence on this point is somewhat unclear, it appears that the League made more of an effort to have members write as individuals than it had during the "cash and carry" struggle. If so, the approach may have been an effort to offset the deluge of mail Congress was receiving from opponents of the bill. It may also have reflected the lack of unanimity within the Illinois League over lend-lease. The Hyde Park chapter alone, where divisions on the issue ran deep, sent hundreds of letters. In the state office, President Bogert canvassed the Illinois congressional delegation and reported to Wells on how they were expected to vote. League spokeswomen sought radio time to discuss the bill, but often found stations reluctant to grant it. To help disseminate information on lend-lease, the League circulated a flyer prepared by the CDAAA. Entitled "The Truth about the Lend-Lease Bill," the flyer devoted as much space to defending the bill as to explaining it.[54]

The defensive tone was appropriate, for lend-lease created an uproar within the Illinois League. "[I]t has been most absorbing," wrote Bogert politely. What absorbed her was a virtual rebellion within League ranks. The scale and nature of the dissent indicate that the *Tribune* was being taken seriously. Late in January, Bogert issued a letter to all local chapters urging them not to fall prey to "the truly shameless misstatements that are being circulated" against lend-lease. "The opinions of experts (some self-styled) are interesting," she continued, "but valuable only to the extent that the person voicing them has previously established his credentials as a disinterested authority. We should weigh their views in forming ours, but not let them inflame our minds and paralyze our judgement, which is what propaganda words like 'dictator bill' and 'appeaser' seek to do." Her efforts to pour oil on troubled waters did not end the internal controversy. To Bogert's surprise, Cook County proved to be an even greater center of discontent than the Republican strongholds downstate.[55]

Criticism focused on the issues of expanded presidential powers and whether the League board had exceeded its authority by endorsing lend-lease before the local Leagues had studied the bill. Downstate locals were less upset over the second issue than Cook County chapters, largely because Bogert had toured downstate the previous spring explaining NLWV procedures in detail. The Cook County group inadvertently compounded its problems by holding an open forum on lend-lease. Kenneth Colegrove of the CDAAA angered many attending members with an intemperate attack on the bill's opponents. So many Illinoisans resigned over lend-lease, and there was so much internal turmoil, that Bogert felt compelled to assure Wells early in February that a majority of the Illinois League supported the board's action. One of the resignations was the president of the prestigious Lake Shore chapter. The *Tribune* lavished publicity on the dissidents and denied Bogert space to respond. In her view Chicagoans were unimpressed by the furor, having developed skepticism toward *Tribune* campaigns over the years. Bogert worried more about the impact elsewhere in the midwest. Reports were reaching her from Wisconsin, Indiana, and Missouri that news of the controversy was creating unrest in those areas. By mid-February she was indicating to Wells that local dissent was on the wane. As members studied the bill, and in particular the amendments limiting presidential authority, they were giving it their approval. But controversy never entirely subsided. Two weeks later Bogert faced another upheaval in Flossmoor, a suburb on the far south side. Dissidents insisted on their right to make public their opposition to H.R. 1776. The local president was able to contain matters, but Bogert was moved to hope the whole batch would resign—after a suitable interval. Elsewhere the "merry-go-round," as Bogert phrased it, continued until final passage of the aid bill.[56]

The lend-lease struggle seems to have inflicted moderate damage at most on the League in Illinois. The state office indicated that only a small proportion of members had resigned. Bogert attributed much of the dissention to Republicans giving vent to their frustrations over Roosevelt's reelection. The antipathy toward the board's decision stemmed from ignorance of League procedures. If nothing else, she suggested, members would pay much greater attention to designing the program at future conventions. Still, the weeks of meetings with irate locals had taken their toll on the Illinois president. In a personal letter to Marguerite Wells, Bogert confided what she felt unable to say to her membership. "If a majority of our people permit themselves to be blitzkrieged out of their convictions by a determined minority, there will be no need to speculate whether or not Fascism can invade this country. It will have come, from within." The bitterness that became so pronounced over the course of the lend-lease debate had made its mark even in an organization that prided itself on a tradition of considering issues dispassionately.[57]

College campuses were no more immune from bitterness than the League. At the University of Chicago, for example, the earlier split in the student body hardened, disputes within the faculty broke into public view, and the university administration also became involved. During April and early May of 1940, faculty members filled the *Daily Maroon* with articles probing the current status of American neutrality. Walter H. C. Laves stressed the differences from the situation in 1914. Now Americans were more attentive to the war than they had been before and more alive to the dangers of involvement. Also, the country had forfeited the traditional rights of neutrals when Congress passed the Neutrality Acts. Laves concluded that the danger of involvement was less than it had been in 1914. Other scholars pointed to a different future. A learned article by Quincy Wright demonstrated that impartiality had not always attended official American neutrality. Another of his essays asserted that all nations were inescapably interdependent. In a long article for the *Chicago Journal of Commerce,* Wright expostulated in detail about Nazi propaganda and military methods. He then assailed Charles Lindbergh for belittling the danger of an attack on the Western Hemisphere and contended that it was impossible for the United States to remain safe in a lawless world. Wright ended his article with a plea for aid to the Allies, which he justified on grounds of American self-interest.[58]

The Nazi invasion of France stimulated campus discussion rather than ending it and added political action to the existing war of words. Anton J. Carlson, a nationally known professor of physiology, prepared a petition urging the nation to remain at peace. Over five hundred scientists across the nation signed the document, which emphasized the futility of war and the dangers it posed to democracy and freedom of thought. At Northwestern, political scientist Kenneth Colegrove also sought to mobilize faculty, albeit on a local scale and on behalf of financial and economic aid to the Allies. Colegrove's petition even called for an easing of restrictions against volunteering to fight abroad under foreign flags. At the University of Chicago, the dissident faction of the American Student Union formed its "Aid to the Allies" club in late May. Leaders Robert Merriam, Adele Rose, and Hart Perry wrote to William Allen White, offering their group's services. The club later became the prototype for campus CDAAA chapters across the country. Just prior to the semester's end the "Aid to the Allies" group arranged a successful mass meeting attended by nearly 1,100 Hyde Park residents. Similar rallies and debates enlivened campuses from coast to coast, and only summer vacation interrupted open debate at the nation's universities.[59]

Controversy resumed with the beginning of the fall semester. The University of Chicago advertised twelve new courses for the fall, each tied to the theme of preparedness. In contrast to its predecessor's militant position, the new editorial staff of the *Daily Maroon* adopted a cautious stance on foreign policy issues. The student newspaper called for clear thinking to pierce the confusion surrounding current events. Aside from opposing military training on campus, the paper refrained from editorial comment on foreign policy issues. The *Maroon* continued to cover all sides of the debate with an evenhandedness that put the major Chicago newspapers to shame. The views of campus Trotskyites and the Youth Committee Against War appeared regularly, along with those of Wright and Douglas. When Nicholas Murray Butler, the president of Columbia University, delivered a speech advocating rigid adherence to a university's set policy, even on off-campus issues, the *Maroon* condemned Butler's position for suppressing basic academic freedoms. On similar grounds, the paper also defended three divinity school students whom local police had arrested for handing out antidraft leaflets.[60]

While articulate spokespersons attested to the existence of a variety of viewpoints, the distribution of campus opinion remained difficult to assess. The *Maroon* conducted a series of polls of both student and faculty opinion. While the unscientific method used to compile these surveys limits their value, the high percentage of response lends them some credence. A mid-October survey found that over 80 percent of the faculty members contacted thought that the United States would eventually enter the war, and 37 percent favored an immediate declaration of hostilities. Support for the draft and for all possible aid to the Allies, including loans, was overwhelming. Ten days later, a poll of students found that three-quarters of those responding agreed with the concept of "all out aid short of war." Only 11 percent wished for immediate American entry into the conflict however. A smaller poll taken in January 1941 revealed that 55 percent of the students surveyed opposed lend-lease. In sum, the poll data suggest that the student body was more evenly divided in its opinions than the faculty.[61]

The deepening bitterness that characterized the foreign policy debate in Chicago also emerged at the university. At a New York City conference on science and philosophy, Professor Mortimer Adler contended that "democracy has more to fear from the mentality of its teachers than from the nihilism of Hitler." Adler's statement elicited a cascade of criticism, led by a savage blast from philosopher Sydney Hook. The *Maroon* brought out an extra edition dealing solely with campus response to the affair. So widespread was city interest in the matter that downtown newsstands requested issues of the *Maroon* for sale. Late in November, the expatriate German novelist Thomas Mann condemned the "beastmen" of totalitarianism before an overflow campus audience. One student columnist divided the antiwar movement into two wings, legitimate pacifists and those who looked for a "New Order of things." He then wondered, "Who is going to come out on top when it's all over—Norman Thomas and the Divinity school boys or the flying colonel and the lying colonel?" Antiadministration forces responded in kind to these verbal blasts.[62]

The crescendo came during the lend-lease debate. Unhappy with the type of rhetoric appearing in its news columns, the editors of the *Daily Maroon* decided to end their policy of silence on international affairs. From early January onward, the paper published a series of commentaries in support of the lend-lease program. The *Maroon* was among the first to contend that the aid policy was a settled issue and to brand its opponents with the stigma of obstructionism. The real issue facing the American people, the paper discerned, was the level of risk that the country was prepared to accept to bring about the defeat of Hitler. On this crucial issue, however, the *Maroon* offered no prescription.[63]

The *Maroon*'s was not the only campus voice to break a policy of silence on foreign affairs. On the evening of January 23, university president Robert M. Hutchins delivered a nationally broadcast radio speech in which he opposed lend-lease and charged that Roosevelt intended to take the nation into war. Hutchins's address ignited the campus. The following day a petition supporting lend-lease received 125 faculty signatures. Prominent faculty members recorded their own reactions to the speech. Carlson and Krueger defended it; Douglas and sociologist Lewis Wirth attacked it; Mortimer Adler alleged that Hutchins was contradictory and dangerously proaid. The *Maroon*, whose attitude toward the university president alternated between hero-worship and bemused skepticism, followed a bland initial comment on his speech with a point by point refutation a few days later. An unscientific poll of student opinion found that, while virtually all students had heard the speech, few had changed their opinions because of its arguments. Fifty-seven percent of the students agreed with Hutchins's views.[64]

Following the intense controversy occasioned by the Hutchins broadcast, the debate at the university began to go stale. Speeches, rallies, and demonstrations continued into March, but the arguments grew repetitive. With the exhaustion came a growing pessimism in student ranks. A *Maroon* editorial late in February captured this mood. While affirming its support of lend-lease, the paper feared that war, depression, and sweeping internal changes might lie ahead for the country. When Roosevelt signed the aid bill on March 10, its proponents on campus welcomed an end to the debate with a mixture of relief and anxiety.[65]

Passage of the lend-lease bill left the administration's Chicago supporters facing an uncertain future. They had chosen to restrict their program to the "aid short of war" formula. Having achieved that goal, they now lacked direction. The terms in which advocates of aid had conducted the debate prevented their victory from generating the kind of momentum that they then could have used to extend the nature of American involvement. Most Chicagoans, even in CDAAA, expressed no desire for a deeper commitment, in public anyway. Moreover, the intense debates within so many organizations over lend-lease boded ill for the future. So did the overall rise in bitterness as the controversy wore on.

One other factor contributed to the unease of administration forces in the city. Their opponents in America First and similar groups, while slower to get off the mark, had marshalled impressive popular support around the Chicago area and elsewhere. By December, noninterventionists were matching their CDAAA opponents stride for stride, and in January America First seemed to pull ahead in the race to capture public opinion. Thus, despite CDAAA's many achievements, its campaign in Chicago was far from won.

FOUR

BLOCKING THE PATH TO WAR

he White Committee and like-minded citizens hoped that the administration's "aid short of war" program would allow the United States to avoid participation in the fighting. Other Americans predicted that Roosevelt's policy would produce the opposite effect—that it would lead straight to hostilities. Appalled by this prospect, many of these people strove to thwart the efforts of the president and his supporters. Through the latter half of 1940, the ranks of the administration's organized opposition swelled with recruits of divergent backgrounds and beliefs. Pacifists enlisted along with former military men, social reformers marched beside ex–Liberty Leaguers, labor activists showed unaccustomed solidarity with businessmen, and communists joined ranks with Christian fundamentalists.

Composed of such dissimilar elements, the noninterventionists could never achieve real unity. Whereas a single organization, the CDAAA, dominated the "aid short of war" cause into 1941, over a dozen groups fragmented the opposition. Many factions were mutually suspicious and some refused point blank to cooperate with the efforts of others. Their only common bond was a dislike of the president's program. Differences in viewpoints among the antiwar forces helped to preclude development of an affirmative alternative to "aid short of war" for the duration of the foreign policy debate. None of the various policies proposed by the opposition found much public favor. The opposition suffered from the additional liability of seeming to defend the status quo, at a time when Hitler's domination of Europe meant suffering for millions of conquered peoples, acute peril for Britain, and possible future danger for the United States. Administration backers exploited this vulnerability and charged that their opponents were appeasers and secret or unwitting friends of the Nazis. Such allegations gained credence from the unwelcome support that America First and kindred groups received from American Fascists and from communists, until the latter group switched sides following Hitler's invasion of Russia. Despite these many handicaps, noninterventionists labored to halt what they viewed as an ominous movement toward war and to preserve their own vision—though it came in various guises—of what America was, what it had been, and what they hoped it might become. Their numbers were large and their convictions were strong. These two factors sustained them through the defeat over lend-lease and the other setbacks which were to follow. To the end, they viewed war as the greatest of all menaces to American well-being.

The first Illinois organization to react to the German onslaught against France in May 1940 was the state Federation of Women's Clubs. This group was holding its convention in midmonth to prepare for the upcoming national gathering. The Federation's national leadership had endorsed resolutions stating that the American woman bore a responsibility to "help overcome the enemies of democracy" and "to assist in securing a just settlement of the current conflict, which would include the establishment of a new world organization." These proposals drove the Illinoisans into rebellion. A public declaration announced that their group "unalterably opposed . . . military participation by the United States in a foreign war." At the Federation's national convention in Milwaukee, the Illinois delegation, under the leadership of Mrs. W. T. Bruchner of Chicago, succeeded in watering down the national leadership's original proposal. The convention eliminated the sections that recommended American participation in peace negotiations and membership in a postwar world organization. The women did go on record as favoring a modernization of American defense forces and more vigorous efforts to uncover subversion. But the antiwar forces at the convention achieved only a partial victory, as delegates rejected, by a vote of 202 to 74, a resolution to place the Federation on record against American entry into the war.[1]

By forming new organizations, other women expressed their fear that America might join the fighting. Around the country, dozens and perhaps even hundreds of women's committees appeared during the foreign policy crisis. In most instances, little is known about their numbers, membership, or the precise nature of their programs. Few attained national status, garnered much publicity, or sustained themselves for long. Some, like the Women's National Committee to Keep the U.S. Out of War, emerged from existing anti–New Deal organizations. Others were sincerely nonpartisan. The frequency with which the word "mother" appeared in their names suggests that these groups often expressed very traditional attitudes toward the role of women. Peace was a means of safeguarding the family and children. Simple aversion to war was often the thrust of their message. The rapid proliferation of women's groups, their generally local compass, the evident earnestness of their convictions—all point to a spontaneous outpouring of mass opinion. Certainly this was the case in Chicago. Under the leadership of Harriet Vittum, head of the Northwestern University settlement house movement, a number of north side Chicagoans met early in June and inaugurated the Roll Call of American Women. This group asked citizens to write to members of both political parties demanding inclusion of a strong antiwar pledge in each party platform. Down on the south side, Blue Island women organized a chapter of the National Legion of American Mothers. The Legion favored a strong national defense, but opposed sending American troops abroad except in case of attack. By late July, the Roll Call of American Women had established a vigorous chapter on the south side as well, which dispatched an auto caravan to Washington to lobby against American involvement in the war. Women's groups would demonstrate actively in the capital throughout the foreign policy debate.[2]

The crisis in France also spurred established antiwar groups to increase their efforts. Memorial Day was the occasion for especially widespread activity. The most prominent of such groups in Chicago was the Keep America Out of War Congress (KAOWC), a national federation of six organizations which favored strict adherence to the neutrality legislation. To offset Senator Claude Pepper's 1940 Flag Day speech, KAOWC leaders planned a mass meeting of their own for June 30. The rally was but the largest of several KAOWC meetings held around the country in early summer. Addressing the rally were Burton K. Wheeler, a Montanan who was emerging as the United States Senate's most outspoken critic of administration foreign policy, and O. K. Armstrong, a member of the American Legion's foreign relations committee. The CBS network carried their addresses nationwide. Rally organizers announced a four-point program: retention intact of the neutrality legislation, opposition to conscription, definition of foreign policy goals prior to rearmament, and support for a continuous session of Congress to oversee the conduct of American policy. Wheeler denounced Wendell Willkie as an agent of Wall Street who had captured the Republican party to help lead the United States into war. Unless the Democrats pledged themselves to peace, Wheeler threatened, it might be necessary to form a third party. KAOWC representatives also presented their views directly to the political parties. In testimony before the Democratic Party Platform Committee, KAOWC representative Russell W. Lambert stressed the need for a "defined and declared" foreign policy. The language of Lambert's plea attested to the suspicions common among antiwar groups regarding Roosevelt's intentions. They sought an ironclad presidential commitment to the preservation of peace, which most of them probably interpreted as also implying a pledge to refrain from policies that might provoke attack by one of the warring powers. Whatever their specific hopes, the efforts of Lambert and others met with an evasive response from the Roosevelt forces at the Chicago convention. The platform preserved freedom of action for the president.[3]

Late in June, KAOWC leaders began to formulate plans for a huge rally to demonstrate the breadth of antiwar feeling in Chicago. The impetus for this meeting came from the Veterans of Foreign Wars, through former state commander William J. Grace. The head of one of the city's largest investment firms, Grace was active in local Republican politics and served as the current executive secretary of the KAOWC. Grace planned the affair along with Avery Brundage, a wealthy Chicago contractor best known for his activities with the United States Olympic Committee. They enlisted the support of over twenty Chicago-area churches and patriotic groups, of which only the VFW was known nationally. Grace and Brundage named the coalition the Citizen's Keep America

Out of War committee. The similarity of its acronym to that of the Keep America Out of War Congress was not accidental, for the new Chicago group drew much of its staff from the latter body. But where KAOWC was predominantly an alliance of pacifists, Grace's CKAOW committee drew its strength from veterans and ethnic groups. To attract a crowd sufficient to fill Soldier Field, CKAOW engaged as speakers Missouri Senator Bennett Champ Clark and the renowned aviator, Charles A. Lindbergh. The rally effort received extensive publicity and ringing editorial endorsement from the *Tribune*. Adlai Stevenson contended in private that the original idea for the project and much of its financing had come from Colonel McCormick, though there is no evidence to prove a connection. The *Daily News* attacked rally organizers, labeling them "appeasers, pacifists, and isolationists" even while it admitted their patriotism. The chief target of these charges, which were reprinted in the *New York Times*, was probably Avery Brundage. He had praised aspects of Nazi Germany in a 1936 speech at New York's Madison Square Garden. The *Daily News* also spotlighted endorsements given the rally by local German-American groups, such as the German-American National Alliance (Einheitsfront), with Nazi sympathies. Throughout the debate, favorable comments from organizations of this type were a liability to noninterventionists that their opponents were quick to exploit.[4]

Estimates of the rally's success varied according to the observer, and the program itself experienced some problems. Senator Pat McCarran of Nevada, who replaced Senator Clark, at first refused to deliver his speech upon learning that only Lindbergh would get radio coverage. Although Grace was able to soothe McCarran's feelings, other problems remained. Chief among them was the size of the turnout. The *Tribune* stated that between 35,000 and 45,000 persons had attended, while the *Daily News* reported estimates varying between 10,000 and 35,000 for the crowd. Whatever the true figure, the audience was dwarfed by massive Soldier Field. *Tribune* photographers disguised this fact by framing only the densely populated bleacher sections, but the *Daily News*'s cameramen spotlighted the empty vistas. Brundage and Grace had hoped to fill the stadium and thus were disappointed by the attendance. Their grand expectations reflected a confidence in the strength and extent of the public's desire for peace that was almost universal among noninterventionist leaders. If the turnout came as a disappointment, Lindbergh's speech did not. All agreed that it was the high point of the rally. Observers agreed that the "Lone Eagle" spoke with an earnestness that more than offset his amateurish delivery. The essence of Lindbergh's message was that the United States, once rearmed, would be safe in this hemisphere. Regardless of their moral opinions, Lindbergh continued, Americans might well have to resign themselves to dealing with a Nazi-dominated Europe. He wished to continue to avoid entanglement in European political disputes whatever the outcome of the current war. Lindbergh further contended that cooperation between this country and Germany was still possible, since it was in both nations' self-interest to do so. The local White Committee was sufficiently impressed by the power of Lindbergh's appeal, as manifested by the size of the rally, to begin plans for a mass meeting in response.[5]

Bronzeville saw activity of its own. Communists were active among Chicago's blacks, as was true in other northern cities, and in the summer of 1940 the party was emphatically antiwar. The state convention of the Illinois Communist party heard William L. Patterson, a black spokesman from Chicago, stress that the struggle for black liberation was inseparably linked to the fight against war. Any new conflict, Patterson insisted, would crush civil liberties and reduce the living standards of American negroes. Those attending an antiwar rally at the LaSalle Hotel encountered an identical message some weeks later. Sponsored by the Peace Coordinating Committee, one of many ephemeral organizations that mushroomed during the blitzkrieg summer, the meeting was addressed by Congressmen John DeBoar and Frank Fries. More established organizations also got involved in peace work. The National Youth Congress and the YWCA held a joint conference on the theme "How can we keep out of this war?" The executive committee of the group Negro Youth voted to include a pledge not to fight outside the hemisphere as part of their program for the upcoming year. The largest of Bronzeville's antiwar gatherings occurred in August, when Paul Robeson, the singer and political activist, packed a rally sponsored by the Emergency Peace Mobilization. The principal theme at the rally was that blacks had no reason to fight for America so long as their rights as citizens were denied.

Later in the year, the American Peace Mobilization drew a crowd of 2,000 to a rally at Orchestra Hall. Author Theodore Dreiser demanded that the United States stay out of the war. He won audience approval for a resolution to that effect, which was sent to the White House the next day.[6]

Of greatest concern to the CDAAA and other preparedness groups were the actions of Chicago's German-American population. After many months of quiet, local German groups erupted into activity during the summer of 1940. On July 1 a large picnic highlighted the celebration of "German Day" in Chicago. Undertones of Nazi sympathy marked the gathering. Cheers greeted German Consul E. L. Bear's comment that all Germans praised the achievements of the Wehrmacht. Mayor Kelly attended and told the crowd of his confidence in the patriotism and loyalty of German-Americans. The substance of his speech was lost when the mayor, in a lapse of political judgment, allowed himself to be photographed beside the Nazi flags adorning the speaker's platform. Letters blasting Kelly's appearance flooded the *Daily News*, though no mention of the incident appeared in the *Defender*. Most correspondents to the *News* labeled the gathering "un-American."[7]

Anti-German feeling ran high in Chicago that summer, just as fears of a fifth-column danger were emerging across the United States. Following a series of anti-Nazi demonstrations at the Haus Vaterland Club, a gathering place for members of the German-American Bund, a bomb destroyed the northwest side bar on July 18. The German-American National Alliance cancelled two scheduled Forest Park meetings because of local tensions owing to its reputation for pro-Nazism. Donald R. Grimes, president of the Civic League of Niles Center, attended an Alliance meeting and reported that the speakers had indicted the United States for oppressing Germans and other minority groups. Such allegations, said Grimes, reminded him of Hitler's speeches.[8]

The previous February the Alliance had begun sponsoring its own weekly radio program over station WHIP in nearby Hammond, Indiana. The program heavily promoted the August 4 CKAOW rally. The action fit the Einheitsfront's general support for an American foreign policy based on peace and nonentanglement in European political affairs. The Alliance's program also broadcast appeals for German War Relief and aired allegations of persecution against German-Americans similar to those which Grimes reported hearing. By early August the Hammond business community was pressuring WHIP to drop the show. The station's board of directors quickly cancelled the program, citing its controversial nature. Termination on such a basis was unprecedented in the station's history. Alliance leader Paul Warnholtz protested the decision. He noted that WHIP had received and cleared each of the programs in advance. The board of directors remained unmoved, however, and the ban continued.[9]

Despite such bad publicity, the Einheitsfront continued to speak out. Letters sent by the organization to the delegates of each national party convention urged them to select candidates who would "avoid international meddling and not aid the allies." Dr. Watke Silze assured the delegates that his group was loyal; they just did not want the United States to fight for Great Britain. Later in the year a serious split developed within the Alliance. Charles H. Weber, a Democratic committeeman for the heavily German forty-fifth ward, approached Alliance leaders in a bid to enlist their support for Roosevelt. Warnholtz refused, saying that the group was united behind Willkie. Not all Einheitsfront members agreed with their leader, as events were soon to demonstrate. At a stormy meeting on October 4, former Alliance president Ernst Ten Eicken led a walkout of members in support of FDR. The Daily News estimated that one-third of those present joined in Ten Eicken's exodus. Mayor Kelly met with the dissidents to cement their loyalty. The Warnholtz faction nevertheless continued to control the Einheitsfront organization, and later urged Alliance members to back the CKAOW and the America First Committee in their struggle against the Lend-Lease Bill. As has already been noted, disproportionate numbers of German-Americans deserted the Democratic party in the 1940 election, which suggests that Warnholtz reflected sentiments among the wider ethnic community to at least some degree.[10]

Foreign policy issues also caused dissension among veterans' groups in the Chicago area and elsewhere. Illinois posts of the American Legion endorsed the Roosevelt administration's defense policy at their convention in August, but the leadership decided to block a floor resolution supporting conscription. Official Legion policy had always favored universal military service, but leaders confessed the draft measure had so divided the Illinois rank and file that any formal motion on the question would tear the state convention apart. Similar problems beset the Veterans of Foreign Wars. That organization stripped Otto Schwark of his honorary membership upon learning that Schwark had been elected president of the Einheitsfront. Overall, veterans' groups spoke out during the summer in favor of defense preparedness and against military involvement. Otis N. Brown, national commander of the VFW, told one meeting that "all Europe is not worth the blood of another American boy." But veterans did not escape the turmoil that was rising throughout the country. During the lend-lease debate, a few Chicago VFW chapters broke with the national organization's policy of support for the bill. Such open dissension was rare in either veterans' group, and its existence reflected the seriousness of the divisions occasioned by the foreign policy debate within both the Legion and the VFW.[11]

Divisions among American clergy and other church activists were more extensive still. The summer crisis prompted leading Protestant clergy to circulate petitions declaring their positions on foreign policy. At the same time that some were calling for aid to the Allies, others urged the United States to concentrate on preserving peace. The Northeast Conference of the Methodist church met at Atlantic City late in June and reversed an earlier decision to support aid for the Allies. Although there were important interventionist clergy, like Reinhold Niebuhr and Episcopal bishop Henry Hobson of Cincinnati, church leaders were more prominent in the ranks of the antiaid forces. They too held disparate views, ranging from Father Charles Coughlin's anglophobia and anti-Semitism to the idealistic pacifism of the American Peace Mobilization. Diverse opinions gave rise to numerous debates within church organizations. At a symposium arranged by the National Conference of Christians and Jews, for example, Congregationalist Moses R. Lovell provoked spirited controversy when he proposed an interfaith effort to counsel a negotiated peace for Europe. Here, and at countless other forums, religious leaders showed particular anguish over the dilemma created by their abhorrence of Nazism and their revulsion against war. These feelings were not easy for women and men of principle to reconcile.[12]

Leaders of business were also confused and inclined toward different paths. Despite allegations by Coughlin, Wheeler, and others that Wall Street viewed war as an unequaled opportunity for profit, the business sector was far from united over foreign policy. If some businessmen did dwell on the potential profits to be made in a war boom, others forecast that another war would bring a ruinous enlargement of the national debt and a drastic increase in the powers of the federal government. *Fortune* polled business executives about the economic consequences of a Nazi victory and found wide disagreement as to the probable effects. The executives split almost evenly on the question of whether it might prove necessary to reorganize the economy in order to compete with occupied Europe. The president of the United States Chamber of Commerce, James S. Kemper, was one of many who stressed the gloomier view and favored retention of the existing neutrality system. At a convention held just prior to Roosevelt's unveiling of lend-lease, the Congress of American Industry heard speeches from both Lewis Douglas of the White Committee and Robert Wood of America First. The heartiest applause of the evening went to Wood when he called for a negotiated peace in Europe. Thomas Watson of IBM had been advocating the same course for months, while Eugene P. Thomas of the National Foreign Trade Association had been recommending repeal of the Johnson Act and the extension of credits to the Allies. These diverse views attest that no single perception of self-interest was sufficiently compelling to create a consensus over foreign policy within the business community. Moreover, as Richard Lauderbaugh has shown for the steel industry, businessmen were no more immune from the impact of events abroad than any other segment of the population.[13]

The most powerful opposition to the administration's foreign policy came not from veterans, ethnics, or existing antiwar groups, but from a coalition of anti-Roosevelt Republicans, university people, and reform-minded businessmen who joined together to form the America First Committee. A handful of law students at Yale University first conceived the idea for such a committee in May 1940. Their plan took root slowly, and by midsummer the students had shifted the center of their organizing activities to Chicago. There they hoped to enlist a broader spectrum of public support.

The new committee announced its existence in September, but for months thereafter its chief undertaking was to sponsor a series of national radio addresses by prominent public figures. Former Wisconsin governor Philip La Follette and General Hugh Johnson, once the head of the National Recovery Administration, spoke under committee auspices. America First did not begin mass organizing until December, when the committee launched a major effort to defeat lend-lease. New chapters then mushroomed across the country. In the space of a few weeks, the committee went from being a small, special-interest group to an organization commanding a mass following.[14]

This was a far cry from the original thrust of the Yale activists. They had aspired to form a nationwide student antiwar organization in order to present their views at the major political conventions. To bring about this end, the Yale students wrote to colleagues throughout the country in hopes of enlisting their aid. Headed by R. Douglas Stuart, Jr., of Chicago, the Yale group emphasized the nonpartisan nature of the proposed committee and stressed that it would not endorse pacifism. Stuart and his friends believed instead "that the policy of the United States should be hemisphere [sic] defense rather than European intervention." An accompanying petition developed the students' position in greater detail. They contended that American democracy could survive only if the country kept out of war, demanded that Congress refrain from voting for war, and opposed any alteration of the "cash and carry" policy. Besides Stuart, three others members of the Yale group signed the original covering letter—Eugene Locke, Potter Stewart, and Gerald R. Ford. Two other active sympathizers who did not sign were Kingman Brewster and R. Sargent Shriver.[15]

Stuart proved to be the sparkplug of the effort. Only twenty-four in 1940, he was the son of the senior vice-president of the Quaker Oats Company, a firm which young Stuart himself would come to head. After graduation from Princeton in 1937, he had entered Yale Law School. Dogged, ambitious, articulate, and energetic, Stuart was unafraid to tackle important projects. With the antiwar committee, he had begun a campaign larger than he yet knew, one that would absorb his energies for over a year.[16]

The infant group sought as its initial goal to win a hearing at the national political conventions. Hoping for guidance and support, Stuart contacted several influential politicians with antiwar views. Senator Robert Taft of Ohio sympathized with the Yale students' aims but was unwilling to commit himself to their course. He advised them to secure a prestigious figure to head their effort, someone with experience and national contacts. In quest of such a figure, Stuart returned to Chicago and to the business circles familiar since his boyhood.[17]

The trail led eventually to General Robert E. Wood of Sears, Roebuck and Company. In early July Stuart met with two prominent Chicago businessmen, Thomas S. Hammond and Sterling Morton, both of whom were active in Republican politics. Together they drew up a list of choices to take charge of the new committee. Wood topped their list. The general was an old friend of Stuart's family and an outspoken advocate of a strict neutrality policy. He refused at first to accept the job out of concern that such a controversial public stance might redound against Sears. Repeated entreaties from Stuart and Morton finally persuaded Wood to take the matter up with his board of directors. After obtaining their approval, Wood agreed to assume the job on a temporary basis. The "temporary basis" was to last for seventeen months, from July 15, 1940, until AFC dissolved following the Japanese attack on Pearl Harbor.[18]

The sixty-one-year-old Wood brought a distinguished career in business and the military to the fledgling committee. After graduation from West Point in 1900, he began a meteoric rise in the army. Wood served in the Philippines and in Panama, where he became chief quartermaster for the Canal project. He quit the service in 1915 to enter business with the DuPont Company. After America entered World War I, Wood rejoined the army and was sent to France with Douglas MacArthur's Forty-second Division. He soon returned to the United States and served as quartermaster general for the entire United States Army, at the rank of brigadier general.

Following the armistice, Wood resumed his business career. He began as a vice president of Montgomery Ward, but switched in 1924 to its archrival, Sears, where the top management was more receptive to the types of innovations he wished to institute in retail merchandising. Mindful of population and economic trends,

Wood pushed Sears into a rapid expansion along three lines. He first shifted emphasis from the mail-order trade to retail outlets. Then he insisted that these outlets were to be dispersed around the suburban sections of cities. Finally, Wood pressed for an aggressive expansion into the South. Spectacular success resulted. Sears soon outdistanced Ward and became the nation's largest retail store. Even the Depression set back the charge only temporarily. Sears earned a profit in every year of Wood's tenure except 1932, and maintained its explosive rate of growth in the face of the continuing hard times.

Wood's devotion to capitalism did not blind him to the faults of the American economic system. Rather he sought to ameliorate many of its worst shortcomings in order to preserve the essentials of the private enterprise system. At Sears he pioneered such measures as wage rates that did not vary by season, allowances for sickness and vacations, an employee savings program, and a profit-sharing plan that became a model for the nation. Wood championed Roosevelt's candidacy in 1932 and he favored such New Deal efforts as the Agricultural Adjustment Act, the Federal Deposit Insurance Corporation, and the decision to abandon the gold standard. He served for a time as an advisor to the National Recovery Administration. Deficit spending disturbed Wood, but he supported Roosevelt again in 1936 and remained on the whole a friendly critic of the New Deal into 1939. When he then broke with FDR over foreign policy, Wood enjoyed widespread respect in reform circles for his record as an enlightened corporate leader. His prestige among businessmen was enormous. According to many estimates, Wood was the single most admired businessman in Chicago.[19]

With so formidable a figure at its head, the new committee began to take shape. For the remainder of the summer, Wood and Stuart worked to amass a group of distinguished citizens who subscribed to the original set of principles formulated by the Yale law students. Following the example of the White Committee, they sought to avoid partisan affiliations and to appeal to a broad spectrum of viewpoints. They wrote to persons as diverse as Herbert Hoover, Charles A. Beard, Henry Ford, and John L. Lewis. The committee's purpose, avowed Wood, was "to organize public sentiment against some of the unsound propaganda that is being dis-

tributed among the American people, notably that being put out
by the Committee to Defend America by aiding the Allies." In
addition to offsetting the activities of the White group, the new
committee would attempt to "give sane national leadership to the
desire of the majority of American people to keep out of the European War" and to "register this opinion with Congress." The pro-
visional name for the new organization was the "Emergency Committee to Defend America First."[20]

The call issued by Stuart and Wood met with an uneven and
disheartening response. Many businessmen, especially in the midwest, welcomed the proposed committee with enthusiasm. But labor leaders and intellectuals hung back. Two academics whom Stuart most prized, Charles Beard and Robert Hutchins, sympathized
with the goals of the new committee but refused to surrender their
independence by affiliating themselves with it. As the national
committee of America First finally emerged in September 1940,
three often overlapping elements predominated—midwesterners,
businessmen, and anti–New Deal Republicans. This preponderance persisted throughout the life of the committee, despite un-
ceasing efforts by Stuart and others to redress the imbalance. As
Stuart realized, the composition of its top leadership made America First vulnerable to charges that it was nothing more than another vehicle for Republican criticism of Roosevelt, thus hindering
the committee's ability to gain acceptance for its message.[21]

Hardcore anti–New Dealers did not control the central policy
apparatus of America First, however. The three key members of
the executive committee were Wood, Stuart, and Clay Judson, a
Chicago lawyer. Like Wood and Stuart, Judson was a political moderate. He had been president of the Council on Foreign Relations
and maintained close friendships with Adlai Stevenson and
Quincy Wright. Stuart also conferred frequently with William
Benton, then vice-president of the University of Chicago, who
represented the views of Robert Hutchins as well as his own. Others members of the executive committee—Hanford MacNider, Janet Ayer Fairbank, and John T. Flynn—were indeed confirmed
opponents of the New Deal. But their influence was never as great
as that of the three Chicagoans.[22]

The leadership of America First sought from the outset to
screen committee members in hopes of keeping the group free of

elements they judged undesirable. Their public appeals excluded Fascists, communists, and pacifists from participation, while welcoming all other viewpoints. In the course of all its operations, the committee strove to keep a distance between itself and other antiwar groups. This applied to such reputable organizations as the Women's International League for Peace and Freedom and the KAOWC no less than to the various American Nazi groups like the German-American Bund. AFC's strong emphasis on defense preparedness offended most pacifists and prompted them to lend only tacit cooperation to America First. A few members of AFC's national committee, Oswald Garrison Villard and Dr. Albert W. Palmer among them, resigned because of the committee's militancy on defense. American Fascists posed a greater problem. The committee had no difficulty keeping them out of leadership positions, but preventing their attendance at meetings, especially mass rallies, proved an impossible task. The presence of Fascists at AFC gatherings plagued the group throughout its existence and lent superficial credence to charges that America Firsters harbored secret pro-Nazi sympathies.[23]

The America First Committee in fact bore a far closer resemblance to the CDAAA than to the Bund. Some AFCers placed greater stress on preparedness, even on aid to Britain, than on an intent to keep America out of war. Out in Iowa, Hanford MacNider considered the committee's central purpose to be promotion of American defense. Other leaders agreed. "I am distinctly not an isolationist," declared Edward L. Ryerson, Jr., the president of Inland Steel. "As I understand, myself and the other members are in favor of all possible aid to England within legal bounds." A third member of the AFC national committee, Janet Fairbank, added that the committee platform "provides that the United States give all possible aid to England under the Cash and Carry amendment to the Neutrality Law." These claims came despite the fact that the official announcement of America First principles declared that " 'aid-short-of-war' weakened national defense." Thus from birth AFC shared another White Committee trait, internal division and confusion over the precise meaning of its program.[24]

The two groups did differ in their initial approach to organizing public opinion. The White Committee always saw itself as a grassroots organization and began forming chapters nationwide from the moment it was announced. America First eschewed a mass membership at the outset and limited its efforts to the radio broadcasts and a score of advertisements in major newspapers around the country. A barrage of mail arrived at AFC headquarters in Chicago as a result. The single most common feature of the correspondence was a request for leadership. Respondents sought a means by which to assert control over government policy and the international situation. Countless Americans were evidently searching for a vehicle to safeguard the peace they so prized. The massive outpouring of feeling caught the AFC leadership flat-footed. The committee lacked the organizational structure and the strategic design needed to exploit popular sentiment. Like the CDAAA, America First declined involvement in electoral politics, the traditional means by which public opinion influenced government policy. The committee sat out the 1940 campaign, a decision AFC leaders came to regret.[25]

In the waning months of 1940, America First began to present its viewpoint at local gatherings. From the standpoint of establishing the committee's policy, the most important of these talks occurred on October 10, when General Wood addressed the Chicago Council on Foreign Relations. His speech represented the most complete and authoritative statement of AFC's position to date.

Wood began by acknowledging that honest differences divided Americans on current foreign policy issues. The general perceived three major lines of argument that proponents of "aid short of war" used to justify their position: that totalitarianism was ideologically repugnant to Americans, that Britain merited this country's support as its first line of defense, and that a Nazi victory would leave the United States unable to survive economically. Wood attempted to refute each point. He shared the interventionists' abhorrence of dictatorship, but contended that the Versailles Treaty had demonstrated that war did not destroy ideology. Instead it left basic problems untouched. Dislike for a nation's ideology was, said Wood, an insufficient reason for waging war. The United States deplored the political system of the Soviet Union, but the two nations had lived in peace. America and Nazi Germany could do the same. Wood believed that sentimentality was clouding American policy toward Great Britain. In troubled times, the nation needed to root its position firmly in self-interest. To him this meant no aid beyond the bounds of the "cash and carry" formula. The Chicagoan further contended that many people had lost control of their emotions and were overestimating German power. He doubted that bombing alone would break British morale or that the Nazis could mount a successful invasion across the English Channel. How much safer was the United States, behind 3,000 miles of water rather than twenty-six? The Nazi economic threat did not seem compelling to the AFC chairman either. Wood believed that trade would flow whenever mutual advantage could be gained. Europe and Japan required American goods far more than this nation needed theirs. A similar relationship of economic advantage pertained to Latin America, where he believed the United States could also compete with success. This was one region where Wood sanctioned the unlimited use of American military power. He was prepared to use force if necessary to insure the existence of governments friendly to the United States and to resist incursion from outside the hemisphere. This willingness separated the general and America First from doctrinaire pacifists, and was one reason why the committee found many allies in Congress. During the battle of France, columnist Arthur Krock reported that most congressional noninterventionists had come to believe that defense of the hemisphere was a responsibility of the United States and to acknowledge Germany as a potential threat to regional security. America First and these congressmen shared a determination to keep war away from the United States, if necessary by resorting to arms.

Wood concluded his remarks with an assessment of the domestic political situation. He believed that elements both in and out of the government were confusing and manipulating the public on foreign policy. The vast majority of people did not want to fight in Europe. They supported "aid short of war," a misnomer in his eyes, only because they were not being told the full truth about the risks involved. Wood was certain the policy would lead to war, the results of which would be ruinous whatever the outcome on the battlefield. He pointed with alarm to the current scale of government indebtedness and forecast that the cost of modern war would enlarge it catastrophically. Worse still, a lengthy conflict would endanger Western civilization itself. "Competent observers believe that if the war is prolonged in Europe over one or two years, it will result in Communism in all Europe, with a form of National Socialism in England. If we are involved, it probably spells the end of capitalism all over the world."[26]

Holding such views as those, America Firsters were incensed by the lend-lease proposal. Roosevelt's plan supplied the missing catalyst for the committee to begin organizing a mass following. The bill overbore whatever divisions remained within AFC on the issue of acceptable levels of aid to Britain. All agreed that lend-lease fell outside the pale. The plain unneutrality of the new measure seemed a dangerous step toward war to most committee members. "The next three or four months will decide if we are going into a shooting war or not," declared General Thomas S. Hammond to an America First gathering in mid-December. But the lend-lease proposal also afforded its opponents an opportunity. At last the president had moved into the open, into Congress, where an aroused public opinion could meet and master the movement to involve the nation in the European conflict. America First rushed now to lead this struggle. The conclusion of the political campaign had freed leaders to devote their time to committee work. Its leadership had become convinced by then of the value of organizing masses of citizens into a nationwide network of chapters. The goal was to demonstrate the prevalence and vehemence of the public desire to remain at peace, to construct a barrier of opinion so strong that even Roosevelt would be unable to breach it. Committee leaders gave scant attention to how that opinion should be expressed. "Our job is to see that the people get the facts and that there are no more 'smart tricks' put over on them," explained General Hammond.[27]

The meeting that Hammond addressed took place on December 13 and heralded a major drive to organize the Chicago area. "This should be an offensive proposition, I think, rather than a defensive one," said Hammond. "We must have finances, headquarters, [and] a speakers' bureau." Another AFC organizer added that "the viewpoint of the committee should be represented at every meeting where war or peace is discussed." With a near desperate urgency, committee workers sought to create an efficient structure in time to influence the lend-lease debate.[28]

America First again followed patterns established by the CDA-AA. Members of the national committee recruited the key leaders for the parent AFC chapter in Chicago from among their networks of friends. Thomas Hammond became formal head of the Chicago outpost at the urging of Edward L. Ryerson, Jr., a close friend of both Wood and Stuart. Ryerson also recruited Janet Ayer Fairbank, who assumed operational control of AFC activities in the Chicago area.[29]

Mrs. Fairbank brought formidable qualifications to her new post. Unlike Ryerson and Hammond, her background was not primarily in business. Her experience as an organizer spanned three decades. She began as a leader of the women's wing of the Progressive party in Illinois before World War I. When the Progressives collapsed she became a Wilson Democrat. Fairbank stumped the midwest for the party in 1920, endorsing the League of Nations and vice-presidential candidate Franklin D. Roosevelt. Fairbank was the first woman to sit on the Democratic National Committee and served for eight years. Alarmed by the expansion of federal government power, she had broken with the Democratic party by 1936. For much of the decade she concentrated on writing novels. America First seems to have been her vehicle back into public life. Fairbank was bright, articulate, and a good administrator, but some coworkers believed that she was overly independent and inclined to be feisty. As de facto head of the Chicago AFC chapter, Fairbank sought to run operations down to the last detail. Since the national headquarters was also in Chicago, lines of authority could easily become crossed. The rapid proliferation of America First chapters during the lend-lease debate almost assured that the group would experience organizational snarls, and the urgency with which many members viewed the committee's task compounded matters. Confusion and friction resulted.[30]

Lend-lease supplied a stimulus for America First similar to that which the fall of France had given the White Committee. America Firsters interpreted their mission and the perils of failure in terms virtually identical to those CDAAA had employed during the previous summer. Both groups supported large increases in military preparedness. Both sought to avert the threat of war to the United States. Each feared for the future of democracy if its respective policy failed. Each perceived itself as defending an embattled way of life. The vital difference, of course, lay in where the rival committees located the source of the threat—Berlin or Washington.[31]

The parallels between the crisis committees recurred in their patterns of organization. The "America First Club Plan" could also have served as a blueprint for the White Committee. The building block in each case was the local chapter, whose initial organization developed out of personal acquaintance. The Club Plan emphasized that a small group of dedicated activists would be of greater use than an unwieldy mass of dilettantes. The chapters should cultivate contacts with local media in an effort to solicit a hearing for their views. Members should write frequent letters to their congressional representatives and to the media. The Club Plan advised local chapters to inquire about obtaining space in nearby storefront windows for a display of America First literature. Neighborhood schools or churches might agree to hold "Preparedness—But No War" meetings, for which the national or regional headquarters would furnish a "speaker of reputation." Chapters in various major cities would act as unofficial regional headquarters. The regional chapters were to sponsor mass rallies, where members from the surrounding area could come to hear speakers of national stature. The urban chapters would also supply speakers to local rallies in smaller communities. At the top of the AFC structure was the national headquarters in Chicago. There Stuart and his staff originated policy guidelines, issued most committee literature, coordinated national speaking tours, and tried to provide supervision for the entire operation.[32]

The care that America First gave to organization, the capabilities of the local leaders it was often able to recruit, and the wide appeal of its "preparedness, but no war" policy combined to make the committee a far more formidable unit than other noninterventionist bodies. Such groups continued to proliferate, but almost all were small and ephemeral. One of the most prominent was the No Foreign War Committee (NFWC), which received massive publicity for a few weeks during the winter of 1940–41. Its policies resembled those of America First, and in fact AFC leaders had a major influence in shaping the new committee's platform. Both groups favored preparedness, accepted aid to Britain within the confines of "cash and carry," and believed that elements within

American society were plotting to take the country into war. Despite these similarities, the NFWC faded from public view almost as swiftly as it appeared. The primary reason was that its chairman, Iowa newspaperman Verne Marshall, was as inept at running a workable organization as he was adept at attracting publicity. Charles Lindbergh, for one, at first entertained high hopes for the NFWC. Lindbergh soon gave up on Marshall as hopeless, and he was not alone in this opinion. By February of 1941, the NFWC was a dead letter.[33]

Meanwhile, America First prospered as a decentralized organization. Chapters numbered in the hundreds and varied widely in quality. Of the 648 branches officially claimed by AFC early in 1941, the executive committee regarded fewer than 150 as full-fledged chapters. Limited resources prevented either the national or regional offices from supervising local operations on anything more than an infrequent basis. Necessity threw most chapters back on their own resources. In northern Illinois, two elements emerged as vital for a chapter's success: its core of leadership and the cooperation of at least some elements of the local media. Where AFC attracted willing workers in leadership roles—Hyde Park, Evanston, Aurora, Rockford—chapters flourished. Other chapters existed in little more than name. The Belmont group, for example, laid plans for various public activities but never put them into effect. Throughout its existence the Belmont chapter never moved beyond being a small discussion group that gathered in a beauty shop. Besides effective leadership, successful chapters needed cooperation from local media. Each of the vigorous AFC outlets around suburban Chicago cited favorable publicity from a community newspaper or radio station as a major ingredient in its success. Where the media were hostile, AFC efforts withered.[34]

Despite this uneven pattern of development, the aggregate growth of America First around the Chicago area was little short of spectacular during the lend-lease debate. One enormous increase came when the Roll Call of American Women affiliated with the committee early in January 1941. The Roll Call claimed 10,000 members in and around Chicago. By this time, America First itself boasted 8,000 members in the city and its suburbs. Besides the downtown group, seven subsidiary chapters existed, four on the north side alone. Fairbank's office staff rose to seven by mid-February, supplemented by an average of ten volunteer office workers per day. America First sent speakers to over fifty gatherings around Chicago during February. Most of these meetings were small, but crowds as large as 1,200 came to hear major speakers. On February 20 Fairbank reported to General Wood that over 82,000 Chicagoans had authorized the use of their names on AFC petitions, and she expected that figure to swell by half before the lend-lease struggle ended. So high were AFC expectations that Mrs. Fairbank labeled even this figure "disappointing." While far below the *Tribune*'s claim of half a million, a total Mrs. Fairbank dismissed as "purely fictitious," the numbers represented an impressive total for a neophyte organization, composed of volunteers, to compile in the depths of a midwestern winter.[35]

Elsewhere the committee was less strong. Its appeals met with the best response in the midwest and in major cities everywhere outside the South. Florida was the only state in the Deep South where AFC took root, and its presence in the border state area was weak. Opinion polls showed that interventionist support was greater in Dixie than in any other region, but this does not explain the near total failure of AFC to attract support there. The issue remains unresolved. Success in other regions was better, although the pattern was erratic.[36]

Two special targets of America First appeals in the Chicago area were organized labor and veterans' groups. Official AFC literature described its constituency as "simple 100% Americans," but in private the committee's leaders appreciated the advantages of appealing to special interests. The campaign to win support among veterans made some progress, but the effort to woo labor floundered. To head its veterans' division, the Chicago chapter recruited Edward F. McGinnis, past commander of the Cook County Council of the American Legion. McGinnis possessed both prestige and extensive personal contacts within the Legion, but he labored at a severe disadvantage. The authoritarian nature of policymaking in both major veterans' groups limited the possibility of winning an open endorsement at the local level.[37]

The problem facing America First in its relations with labor rested not with national union leadership but with the hostility of local union officials. AFC was unable to convince a figure with stature comparable to McGinnis to head this sphere of their operations. The man whom the Chicago chapter appointed was known chiefly for his open opposition to Franklin Roosevelt. He faced an unpromising task. Already on record in favor of lend-lease were the regional director of the CIO, the president of the Chicago Federation of Labor, the secretary of the Illinois Federation of Labor, the regional director of the Steel Workers Organizing Committee, the business manager of the AFL, and another half dozen of Chicago's most important labor barons. The inaugural AFC labor rally failed to draw more than a tenth of the anticipated crowd of 5,000 to Carmen's Hall. With the president of Inland Steel Company as one of the principal speakers and no major labor leader willing to make an address, the poor attendance was not surprising. America First did collect the endorsement of a score of lower-echelon union leaders from around the city. A handful of maverick locals also pledged support, but the bulk of organized labor in Chicago gave its loyalty to the Roosevelt administration. The committee fared little better at the national level. Opposition to war and even to the aid policy was fairly widespread within union ranks, but it tended to come from unions or locals in which communist influence was strong. A CIO local in Chicago, for example, sponsored an antidraft rally in August aimed specifically at the city's black population. America First would have nothing to do with communists in this instance or any other, and surely that feeling was reciprocated to a large degree.[38]

The committee did try to enlist black support, but without much success. The Chicago chapter announced the formation of an Abe Lincoln chapter early in February. Val J. Washington, the general manager of the *Defender*, headed the group. The chapter received favorable publicity in the *Defender* and opened an office on South State Street. Soon it claimed 5,000 members, but it appears never to have been very active. The one photograph of a Lincoln chapter gathering to be printed in the *Defender* shows a group entirely composed of women. America First emulated CDAAA by including blacks on the dais at its rallies. But as with the White Committee, it may be that this is about as far as black participation extended.[39]

The marked growth in the size of the America First Committee was not attended by a similar development in its arguments. The stands taken by its leading Chicago area spokespersons, including such influential members of the national committee as Judson and Wood, remained almost static. In conjunction with CDAAA chief Ernest Gibson, Wood delivered a major speech to Chicago's largest America Legion Post on February 3, 1941. Little had changed since his message to the Council on Foreign Relations over four months before. Europe's conflict, in his view, was based on issues of slight concern to the United States; the rivalries sprang more from power than principle. Wood asserted that this country would be in a position to deal with any military or economic threat from Germany by the time Hitler could mount one. Two new elements did appear in Wood's speech. He presented a detailed case against any serious Nazi military threat in South America. The general also unleashed a denunciation of American interventionists. Wood condemned their "defeatist" doubts about this nation's ability to weather the international crisis and he deplored their efforts to create a "fear complex" among the people. Judson's addresses revealed that he shared General Wood's conviction that the argument for aid to Britain rested on emotionalism and violated American self-interest, and also his belief that Germany would only ruin herself should Hitler attempt to invade the Western Hemisphere.[40]

A different approach surfaced in a speech by another nationally prominent Chicagoan. In January 1941 University of Chicago president Robert Maynard Hutchins broke a nine-year policy of public silence on political issues when he delivered a nationwide radio broadcast on the topic "America and the War." Speaking as a private citizen, Hutchins lent his voice to the diverse chorus decrying the Lend-Lease Bill. America, he said, represented the last refuge of freedom on earth. It was imperative for the nation to remain at peace. All-out participation in the fighting would destroy democracy at home. Roosevelt was asking the American people to underwrite a British victory without apprising them of the implications such a policy would have. If lend-lease failed to turn the tide, military involvement would have to follow. Hutchins handled the question of the moral issues involved in the European struggle by drawing attention to the unsolved domestic problems of America, many of which he viewed as urgent. Americans ought to consider their values carefully and put them into practice at home before trying to spread them to other peoples. In any case,

Hutchins judged war a poor means to export American values. Entry into the war would more likely risk a century of gains toward justice and freedom. Hutchins concluded his speech with a call for both military and moral preparedness in order to deal in a more effective fashion with contemporary troubles.[41]

The Hutchins radio address provoked a diverse and powerful reaction. Most of the thousands of letters that poured into his office were favorable. Hutchins's views excited key elements within the leadership of America First as well. Stuart had admired the university president for years and pressed him repeatedly to join the AFC executive committee. Hutchins refused to surrender his independence or risk embarrassment to the university by affiliating with the committee. The two parties kept in close touch nevertheless through the quiet liaison efforts of William B. Benton. A classmate of Hutchins at Yale, Benton too was something of a *wunderkind*. After amassing a sizable personal fortune in advertising, Benton, as planned, retired at age thirty-five to devote his life to public service. In 1941 he was serving as a University of Chicago vice-president. Passionate antiwar views led him into early contacts with America First. Their relationship remained informal, though of great benefit to the committee. Benton helped to design much of AFC's advertising, acted as an unofficial advisor to the group, and served as a go-between for Hutchins and the committee.[42]

The substance of Hutchins's message tantalized America First, or at least many of its younger leaders. Close enough in content to AFC's platform that the committee could accept it, the speech was sufficiently different to make them yearn for Hutchins's participation in order to broaden their image. Hutchins, Benton, Wood, and Stuart shared an aversion to the European war and a suspicion that the "aid short of war" formula would lead to involvement. They agreed that a new war might consume American democratic institutions. But in Wood's speeches the central concern was for the survival of capitalism, for the basic structure of the economic system as it existed in 1941. To Hutchins, the real danger lay in the intolerance, brutalization, and exhaustion that he feared a war effort would breed. These forces might well extinguish all hopes for economic and political reforms. The extent to which General Wood and other businessmen on the committee approved of Hutchins's outlook remains unknown. Stuart, Fairbank, Judson, and many of the younger AFC staffers applauded Hutchins's stance however. Judson, for one, employed very similar arguments in private correspondence. Stuart urged Hutchins to speak out at least once more before the lend-lease issue was decided. The educator refused because he doubted his ability to say anything original.[43]

The committee's relationship with Hutchins further illustrated its frustrations. Despite widespread public perceptions to the contrary, America First was not dominated by reactionary business titans who yearned above all to turn back the clock to the days of Grover Cleveland. It was not the Liberty League reborn in a different guise. Yet the committee was unable to recruit the very figures it needed to dispel such an image. Without such leaders, America First experienced increasing difficulty in diversifying its popular support and in developing a positive program to present as an alternative to the administration's "aid short of war" policy.

The successful passage of lend-lease came as a devastating defeat to America First and other opponents of the bill. For them, it was a proving ground, the desired opportunity to use the power of public opinion to arrest the drive toward war. Against the administration they had waged a massive effort. Chicagoans alone had sent Congress tens of thousands of letters attacking the proposal. Resolutions at scores of rallies around the city, the metropolitan area, and the state decried lend-lease. Hundreds of speeches criticized the bill's alleged shortcomings. Even administration supporters were impressed by the outpouring of opinion against the measure.

The very size of the demonstrations against lend-lease made the bill's subsequent passage all the more painful. America Firsters were convinced that public opinion did indeed side with their cause. Poll after poll revealed the public's opposition to war. How then could such a dangerous measure receive popular approval? Roosevelt had won, they said, by misleading the public as to the true consequences of the bill. People who supported lend-lease had accepted the administration's ruse that the bill would not lead to war. Administration opponents thus believed that they had been outmaneuvered rather than outmanned. Nor would America Firsters accept that their beliefs had been discredited. They remained, many of them, convinced of the essential strength and righteousness of their cause.

Others were filled with doubt, or despaired of ever coming to grips with the wily FDR. Sterling Morton was one of those troubled by the outcome. A Republican to his marrow, heir to the fortune made by his family's salt company, Morton epitomized the sort of anti-Roosevelt, business-oriented viewpoint with which America First was supposed to be infused. In April 1941 Morton wrote to some of his fellow committeemen. Was national policy now settled, he wondered? Had events developed beyond the point where loyal Americans could oppose their government honorably? Was it time to ignore all misgivings about American policy and close ranks behind the president?[44]

His musings received a tart reply from Robert Wood. Himself weary of the struggle and under considerable pressure from officials at Sears to quit the committee, the general refused to abandon his current campaign. Wood reminded Morton that administration forces had sold lend-lease as a measure for peace. America First should see that they kept their promise. Wood was not one to retire in the middle of a fight. Neither was Janet Fairbank, nor Douglas Stuart. In the end they quieted the doubts of most of those like Morton, and America First resolved to continue. By so doing, they assured that divisions over foreign policy would widen rather than narrow during the remaining months of peace.[45]

FIVE

BEYOND LEND-LEASE

For the remainder of 1941 the foreign policy debate revolved around the issue of whether or not the United States should go to war. Following the enactment of lend-lease, General Wood tried to reassure Sterling Morton that the America First Committee had valuable work left to do. "True," he told Morton, "in a sense we are in the war now, but there is a vast difference in the position of being a friendly nonbelligerent and in the position of an active belligerent." This condition, of being only partway into the war and reluctant to proceed further, charged the final phase of the debate with a peculiar tension. Americans had invested great amounts of wealth and hope in the Allied cause. For a large popular majority the aversion remained compelling nonetheless. Those in favor of an immediate declaration of war never comprised more than a third of the public. Pollster Hadley Cantril dissected American opinion early in May and described the divisions he found. A popular majority was willing to accept war if necessary to save Great Britain. But one-fifth of Cantril's sample were committed to peace whatever happened abroad, and a further 15 percent denied that Germany posed any danger to the United States. A tenth of those Cantril surveyed either knew or cared nothing about foreign affairs. Of those expressing some opinion, 50 percent favored aid to Britain regardless of the dangers involved. They accepted such risks because they foresaw dire consequences to American security if Nazi Germany won. About 15 percent favored aid for various other reasons. Based on these findings, Cantril suggested that the crucial question in the coming months would be whether Great Britain would be able to win the war without American military participation.[1]

The course of events abroad suggested with increasing clarity that the desire for victory and the desire for peace were incompatible. Few of the momentous events that crowded upon one another in 1941 offered much comfort to the Allied cause. Britain suffered defeat wherever her armies met the Germans. In North Africa, London lost the fruits of spectacular victories over the Italians when a handful of newly-arrived German troops threw back the exhausted Britons. Almost simultaneously, Hitler added the Balkans to his domain. An expeditionary force dispatched by Churchill to Greece arrived just in time to be chased out by onrushing Nazi tank columns. The Royal Navy managed to evacuate many of the men to nearby Crete, only to pull them out again a month later when Hitler's paratroops seized the island by storm. The Germans thus had wrested control of the eastern Mediterranean from the British and seemed poised to deliver a knockout blow toward the Suez Canal and the oil fields of the Middle East.

Other events confirmed that the axis of land warfare had shifted to the east in 1941. Hitler surprised most observers by making no serious effort to invade England. Instead he prepared in secret to attack the Soviet Union. The assault exceeded all his previous efforts in scale and seemed certain to match them in success. The Soviets suffered huge losses in men, equipment, and territory. Britain received a much-needed ally and a welcome breathing space. Most observers believed that little permanent value would come from either of these gifts, however. Many Americans, among them the chiefs of staff, were convinced that the Nazis would conquer Russia without much difficulty. A victorious Germany could again turn on her enemies in the west, with her power strengthened still further by additional resources and slave labor.

Britain's most worrisome problem was located neither in the Mediterranean nor on the Russian steppes. Her vital lifeline for food and material stretched across the Atlantic. By 1941 the British were losing the struggle to keep their lifeline open. Hitler's U-boats ravaged one convoy after another, sinking ships faster than they could be replaced. Of all his many military concerns, this one weighed most heavily on Prime Minister Churchill.[2]

British officials hungered for American entry, of course, but at Churchill's insistence they were circumspect in how they sought to achieve it. The prime minister dispatched overt appeals to Roosevelt only twice. The first had come as France began to crumble back in June 1940. Now in early May, as the disaster in the eastern Mediterranean took shape, Churchill again appealed to Roosevelt for American belligerency. It was a sign that British fortunes were at their lowest ebb. Each overture was made in secret, with the consequence that Americans in general knew nothing of either one. Throughout the lend-lease controversy, Churchill had insisted in public that aid would be sufficient. Some evidence to the contrary nevertheless did appear in the American media. During a broadcast from London in December 1940, Edward R. Murrow revealed that most officials in His Majesty's Government admitted that Britain could not win without American entry. The following July Archibald Wavell, the outgoing British commander in the Middle East, and his successor, Claude Auchinleck, stated in separate interviews that a new American expeditionary force would be needed in order to achieve victory. These declarations were isolated exceptions to the pattern of British circumspection, however, and the press gave them only modest attention. They were far overshadowed by the innumerable assurances from the Roosevelt administration and its supporters that neither the plans, the desire, nor the need to bring America into the war existed.[3]

Aware as Washington was of the seriousness of the Atlantic situation and Britain's general plight, caution nonetheless characterized Roosevelt's actions throughout the remaining months of peace. Despite the public and private urging of such key lieutenants as Stimson, Knox, Hopkins, and Ickes, the president refused until autumn to ask Congress for permission to send American vessels by convoy direct to Britain. All intervening moves—the extension of American neutrality patrols deeper into the Atlantic, the dispatch of troops to Greenland and later to Iceland, the inclusion of Russia in the lend-lease program, the convoying of ships to Iceland, and the "shoot on sight" order to attack German U-boats—Roosevelt undertook with great circumspection and some reluctance. In each case top aides had pleaded with him to do more. Pressure on Roosevelt for some sort of decisive action reached its peak in May. Over two months had elapsed since the lend-lease vote, Britain's situation was worsening, and senior government officials knew that the Germans were massing against the Soviet Union. In addition to Churchill's overt request for American belligerency, Roosevelt received repeated urging from his cabinet to initiate convoying at least. Frank Knox delivered a speech to the American Newspaper Publishers Association that contained a barely concealed call for convoying. The tenor of Knox's address is suggested by the headline of the *New York Times*'s account, "This Is Our Fight." Soon thereafter the navy secretary reiterated his views before the Society of American Military Engineers. Administration opponents braced themselves for the worst when Roosevelt delivered a fireside chat on May 27. As the date neared, mail poured into Congress and the White House. Just before the speech the volume approached the level attained at the height of the lend-lease debate. Much of the country evidently anticipated dramatic developments, for the speech drew a larger radio audience than any previous presidential talk. Roosevelt's words were tough, but once again his actions were limited. While proclaiming an unlimited national emergency, he undertook no more than an expansion of patrolling in the Atlantic. There is some suggestion that FDR had decided that war would indeed be necessary, but if so, he disclosed nothing in public. To the press he was still describing convoys as a "last resort" and indicating that they were something he wished to avoid. Whatever his inner convictions, Roosevelt was well aware of the Allies' desperate circumstances. But he could not bring himself to ask an unwilling and unprepared nation to join the battle.[4]

Finally there was Asia, where Japanese expansion became ever more alarming to officials in London and Washington. From the spring of 1940 until the autumn of 1941, events in Europe all but eclipsed the Pacific situation in the media. The president was preoccupied by Europe for most of the period as well. Given the concentration on Germany and the shortage of military resources, a principal goal of American policy in the Pacific was to avoid war with Japan. Neither the White House nor the State Department, however, were willing to allow the Japanese a free hand. The re-

gion supplied certain essential raw materials and Washington believed that these sources had to be safeguarded. China also had a
claim on American support, to which Roosevelt was especially sensitive. In addition, the government refused to condone aggression,
especially by a partner of Germany. So Washington sought peaceful means to contain or even roll back Japanese expansion. Roosevelt left the burden of negotiating with the Japanese to Secretary
of State Cordell Hull, an unmistakable sign that the president's
priorities lay elsewhere. Hull sought in vain to reach a settlement.
The United States misjudged Tokyo's position from the start and
believed that American economic pressure could compel the Japanese to modify or renounce their program of expansion. Some of
Hull's senior deputies were determined to bring pressure on Japan. In July, when Roosevelt froze Japanese assets in the United
States, State Department officials applied the order in such a
harsh fashion that in essence they shut off the supplies of American oil upon which the Japanese economy depended. The action
brought about the very confrontation with the Empire that the
senior leaders had hoped to avoid. By mid-November, knowledgeable insiders expected war to come at any moment in the Pacific.
They did not expect it to begin at Pearl Harbor.[5]

By the spring of 1941 consciousness of the war had become
imbedded in the daily lives of Americans. Those who read newspapers encountered reminders of the war on almost every page.
Often the purposes behind the allusions to the struggle were
openly manipulative. In Chicago the *Tribune* ran a series of photo-
graphic essays on disabled World War I veterans to remind its
readers of the human costs of war. Over at the *Daily News*, critic
Sterling North continued to inject his foreign policy views into his
book review columns. "A leading bookseller has confided the as-
tonishing information," North once exclaimed, "that our local appeasers and Quislings buy none of the excellent books now available on the war in Europe." Using somewhat greater restraint, the
Tribune's movie reviewer, Mae Tinee, alerted her readers to alleged
propagandizing in films such as *Major Barbara* and *That Hamilton
Woman*.[6]

War themes became commonplace in the entertainment sections
of newspapers during 1941. This was as true for the antiwar *Tri-*

bune as it was for the more militant *Daily News.* The Sunday
Tribune's "Graphic" section ran dozens of pieces on the war, both
journalistic and fictional. The issue of November 23, for example,
contained an account of the German parachute attack on Crete, a
short dramatic play set amid the Norwegian campaign of 1940,
and an excerpt from Hans Habe's current bestseller on the battle
of France, *A Thousand Shall Fall.* In both Chicago dailies, the comics often touched on topics relating to the war. *Smilin' Jack,* a *Tribune* strip whose hero was a free-lance pilot, ran a long sequence
dealing with an unnamed foreign power's attempts to sabotage
American business in South America. In the *Daily News, Don Winslow of the Navy* uncovered an enemy weather station in Greenland
and later obtained a convoy-protecting device, which solved "democracy's chief problem." Another popular strip revealed that a
"certain European power" was plotting (under a deluge of explod-
ing bombs) a secret test "blitzkrieg" on an American town. The
target turned out to be Dogpatch and the invaders met stiffer
resistance from local citizens than they had expected.[7]

While no comic strip ever named a specific nation, the cartoon-
ists left small room for doubt about who their fictitious enemies
were meant to represent. In most cases, readers needed little insight or information to identify the Axis nations. Al Capp drew
Dogpatch's invaders as obvious caricatures of Nazi leaders, and his
use of the codeword "blitzkrieg" removed whatever slight doubt
remained as to his intent. *Don Winslow* chanced to capture the
Greenland weather station on the same day that headlines announced the U.S. Navy's discovery of a real German counterpart
on the same island. Regardless of whether or not readers identified specific countries, the strips reinforced the idea that hostile
powers threatened the safety of the United States.

How widely consciousness of war had spread by the spring of
1941 was revealed by two exhibitions of children's art that took
place in New York City. Schools from throughout the metropolitan
area participated. The child artists ranged in age from ten to fifteen years old. Alongside drawings of baseball, Superman, and
Mickey Mouse were scenes of air and sea battles, concentration
camps, and defense production. Regardless of whether individual
pupils had chosen these subjects or used them at the prompting

of teachers or parents, the appearance of such material suggests that the conflict had become an almost inescapable presence in America.[8]

The war appeared often in the feature sections of the newspapers, but it dominated their news and editorial columns. Coverage shrank during a brief lull after the passage of lend-lease, which coincided with a period of relative inactivity on the European battlefronts and the domestic political scene. The spring round of Allied reversals rekindled pressure at home and abroad to step up American involvement. Accordingly, efforts to prevent any new initiative also increased. In Chicago and around the country editorial policies seldom changed. The *Tribune* and the *Daily News*, for example, resumed their feud. The general thrust of each paper's position continued along the path each had followed since the fall of France. The *Tribune* maintained its adamant opposition to administration policy and repeatedly invoked the specter of war. Defeating Axis expansion remained the constant theme of the *Daily News*, although the paper never issued a public call for the United States to assume full belligerency.

Both papers acknowledged that the passage of lend-lease had altered America's relationship to the war, but each drew an opposite lesson from this fact. Readers received interpretations of events, indeed accounts of events, which differed in fundamental ways. Yet on the critical issue of whether or not American military participation was necessary, the two Chicago dailies, unlike papers elsewhere, did not disagree. Each reflected the prevailing popular view that the Allies could succeed without American manpower.

The *Tribune* viewed the course of American policy since the Nazi invasion of Poland as a series of deceptions by the Roosevelt administration. Under the guise of strengthening American neutrality, the president had manipulated the nation into a tacit alliance with Britain. But the *Tribune* was confident that Roosevelt had run out of room to maneuver. Further action would have to be military and could not be cloaked by the rhetoric of peace. The American people, alerted by lend-lease to the administration's designs, would refuse to take the logical remaining step—join the war. In believing it possible and proper for America to avoid further involvement in the European conflict, the *Tribune* did no more than take the administration at its word that lend-lease implied nothing about deeper American involvement. The paper approved of measures it considered beneficial to American defense, like the occupation of Greenland, and condemned as "provocative" any sortie beyond hemispheric bounds. Roosevelt's methods of operation were also objectionable. McCormick complained that the occupation of Iceland was too important a decision to undertake without consulting Congress or the public. As always, Roosevelt's motive for bringing the country into the war was to impose a dictatorship upon the United States. "[T]he Democratic party, like the Nazi party in Germany, is the expression of one man's will," declared one editorial. Throughout 1941 these and similar accusations appeared in the news columns as well as the editorial page with numbing regularity.[9]

If Roosevelt had brought the United States to the brink of war, *Tribune* readers could at least take comfort that the final plunge was by no means inevitable. On the contrary, McCormick insisted that circumstances better enabled Americans to steer an independent course. "The United States has never been in a better position to avoid involvement than it is now," affirmed an editorial in May. "It really is less involved than it ever was before." Despite local jokes about McCormick's supposedly medieval mentality, he was not blind to current conditions. His newspaper well realized that the distribution of power among nations was far different in the mid-twentieth century than it had been previously. Where McCormick differed from someone like Henry Luce was in his assessment that America's enhanced power did not have to function in a world of unprecedented interdependence. As evidence, the *Tribune* cited such events as the British sinking of the German battleship *Bismarck*. Readers were told that sea and air power continued to control the oceans and were assured that America possessed ample means to insure the safety of her Atlantic approaches and keep outsiders at bay. In its zeal to demonstrate that the United States was safe from attack, and thereby to undercut one argument for American intervention, the paper in effect contradicted its earlier judgments on the lack of preparedness. This unwillingness to concede even a limited vulnerability represented a narrowing of viewpoint. It was further evidence of the polarization of attitudes that was occurring on all sides in 1941.[10]

There was a similar lack of development in the *Tribune*'s positions on other important aspects of the international situation. As it had since the outbreak of hostilities, the *Tribune* refused to acknowledge that a moral basis for the conflict existed. "It is a war to preserve empire," the paper asserted, "to gain it, to extend it. It is a war for the domination of lands and resources of peoples who have never been able to defend themselves." None of this was the rightful concern of any American. The Nazi invasion of Russia on June 22 further reinforced this conviction. A front page cartoon in the *Tribune* pictured an almost noble-looking Nazi tiger leaping on a scrawny Stalinist buzzard. McCormick himself hoped that "the two villains of this new war would destroy themselves and each get his just dues in the fight." Thus the war between Berlin and Moscow also offered a solution to the problem of how to bring about a satisfactory conclusion to the struggle in Europe. Administration supporters often challenged their opponents to develop a positive alternative to the aid policy. Thoroughgoing isolationists could have responded by denying that the United States had any interest in European events, thus dismissing the problem as irrelevant. That this happened so seldom is noteworthy, as it suggests how few of the opponents of aid were completely indifferent to the outcome of the war. The only alternative open to them was to urge a diplomatic settlement of the conflict, as some did on occasion. It was never a major theme with McCormick, however, perhaps because he realized that the possibilities for successful negotiations were remote. Instead, his paper reminded its readers repeatedly of the potential dangers of trying to police a world indifferent at best to American values and resentful of outside attempts to interfere in regional or internal affairs.[11]

Where the *Tribune* emphasized long-term risks, immediacy characterized the perspective of the *Daily News*. To a degree unusual among the proaid forces, the paper seldom ventured beyond prescriptions for specific problems and avoided discussion of eventual results. When columnist Raymond Clapper noted that many business journals were worried about the ultimate effects of the massive defense buildup on American society, the *Daily News* responded that every particle of effort was needed to meet the immediate challenge posed by the Axis. As late as April 1941 the paper would insist that the United States had committed itself to material aid and nothing more. Although the *Daily News* believed

that America should insure the delivery of aid to its intended re-
cipients, the paper did not view the current situation as parallel to
that of 1917. Nor did it acknowledge the existence of a duty to
enter the war. This denial of an ulterior motive for the aid policy
came in response not to a jibe from McCormick, but to a call for
American intervention from Walter Lippmann. Thereafter, the
Daily News remained silent on the war issue for the remaining
months before Pearl Harbor. The paper confined itself to editorial
support for each new Roosevelt initiative and became, in effect, an
administration mouthpiece. Typical was its reaction to the presidential announcement of a "shoot on sight" order in September,
authorizing the navy to fire at German U-boats whenever encountered. The *Daily News* portrayed the escalation as a proper response to the Nazi aggression and sided with the administration in
a subsequent controversy surrounding the incident that had
prompted the new order. Item by item the paper went down the
line with Roosevelt, in the news column as well as on the editorial
page. This was bipartisanship, or "national unity" in the contemporary phrase, in a thoroughgoing way.[12]

The only flashes of militancy found in the *News* came from its
foreign staff. At least twice in the spring of 1941, the paper ran
dispatches on the front page that openly advocated American military intervention. William Stoneman wrote from London that
American experts on the scene "are now agreed that the immediate participation of the U.S. in the war is a matter of desperate
emergency." Stoneman's sources believed that a German victory
was possible unless Britain received important reinforcements.
The United States could furnish immediate help in the Atlantic,
American entry would be a tonic to Allied morale, and war would
spur the United States to the herculean production efforts needed
to bring victory. From Italy, John Whitaker also urged American
entry. But the furthest Chicago editors were prepared to go was a
comment by Carroll Binder, in one of his last columns as head of
the foreign staff, that the trend of events "suggests that the contribution of American materials to Britain may not prove sufficient
to free the United States from the totalitarian menace." As specu-
lation rose in mid-May about FDR's upcoming fireside chat, an
editorial declared "This is our war" and affirmed that the country
would follow presidential leadership. Roosevelt balked at belliger-

ency, and the *News* never repeated its hint. Measured against the paper's continued outpouring of support for "aid short of war," these promptings were insignificant. None appeared after May 1941. Perhaps the silence was due to Knox's position in the cabinet. Mowrer, Binder, and the other editors may not have wanted to risk compromising him. If so, it is testimony to their perceptions of public opinion. Perhaps too they left advocacy to Knox himself, behind closed doors. The entry of the Soviet Union into the war against Hitler certainly complicated matters. The *News* made no effort to conceal its distaste for the Soviet system and justified aid to Stalin solely on the basis of expediency. Moreover, the invasion made American intervention seem less necessary. Whatever the reasons for its reticence, the *News* declined to prod the administration openly. As a consequence, the paper failed to bring before its readers a full and accurate picture of the challenges facing American policy.[13]

Other journals were less circumspect about the war question. *Editor and Publisher* magazine surveyed the opinions of American newspapers in July of 1941. It found that about 250 favored active military and naval participation in the war. These ranks grew as the United States began to take losses in its undeclared naval war with German U-boats. At the end of September, the *San Francisco Chronicle* subtitled one of its very rare front-page editorials, "Now Is the Time for the U.S. to Act." The piece contained no direct call for war, but the way it invoked memories of 1861 and 1917 left no doubt about its meaning. Columnist Frank R. Kent, appearing in the *Louisville Courier-Journal* and elsewhere, was direct. He criticized Congress and the public for failing to understand that America should enter the fight. In November the *Cleveland Plain Dealer* and the *Atlanta Constitution* joined those calling for a declaration of war, and the *Denver Post* predicted, without comment, imminent hostilities with Germany.[14]

This degree of militancy was exceptional. Like the *Daily News*, most newspapers did not call for war and many continued to hope into the final days of peace that the "aid short of war" strategy would accomplish the defeat of Nazi Germany. The *Editor and Publisher* survey revealed that 615 papers, out of a total of 867 responding, opposed active military involvement. Into September, sources as informed as the *New York Times* and Walter Lippmann affirmed their confidence in the adequacy of America's current policy. Lippmann's "Today and Tomorrow" column of September 12 forecast that the Axis would not win and challenged the Allies to find the ways and means to achieve victory. A few days before, the *Times* had editorialized that lend-lease remained a viable alternative to full participation so long as aid was sent in sufficient quantities and on schedule. As late as November, following the sinking of the American destroyer *Reuben James* by a U-boat, the *Times* was campaigning for nothing more extreme than public recognition that a basic conflict of interest existed between Nazi Germany and the United States. The paper used the incident to plead for a consensus on behalf of "aid short of war" rather than to develop a case for an outright declaration of hostilities.[15]

The black press continued to speak to the special needs of its readership. The *Chicago Defender* had relatively little to say about the foreign situation, but hammered away ceaselessly at continuing discrimination in the defense effort. Beginning in March a column devoted exclusively to foreign affairs appeared on the editorial page at irregular intervals. Ethiopia remained the principal focus overseas. British efforts on behalf of Emperor Selassie's country helped win London a more favorable hearing in the paper. But suspicion endured. The *Defender* doubted, for example, that Africans would see much improvement from the ringing words of the Atlantic Charter. Columnist Lucius Harper had been sympathetic to the Soviet Union throughout the foreign policy debate. He continued to insist the struggle was nothing more than a "money war," however, long after Hitler's invasion of the U.S.S.R. had set American communists on their heads. Editorial commentary on foreign affairs was rare, but individual pieces matched the insight, and usually exceeded the balance, of those in Chicago's dailies.[16]

The persistence of discrimination in the military and in hiring for defense work infuriated the *Defender*, as was true of black papers around the country. One editorial sarcastically noted that even Hitler used slave labor in his factories, while America denied its blacks a place in war-related work. Another piece noted the rising incidence of suspected sabotage in defense plants and suggested that the remedy was to hire blacks, whose record of patriotism was "spotless." The *Defender* gave support and extensive coverage to the March on Washington movement that led Roosevelt to issue Executive Order 8802. The "World's Greatest Weekly" in fact attributed the rising militancy of American blacks to the climate created by the war.[17]

Regardless of their particular slant, newspapers contributed to the division of opinion in 1941 by presenting contrasting accounts of national and international events in their news columns and editorial pages. They helped create the polarization of the public in more overt ways. The papers fueled bitterness by featuring attacks on various participants in the foreign policy debate.

Repeatedly, the *Daily News* lashed out at critics of the administration, often going beyond a refutation of their arguments to attack the legitimacy of the opposition itself. America First was a favorite target. An editorial in late July implied that many recent AFC policy positions had given aid and comfort to the enemy. This, the paper reminded its readers, was the constitutional definition of treason. The *Daily News* also employed the tactic of guilt by association against the AFCers. "They have provided, however unintentionally, a rallying point for every fifth columnist in the land," the paper charged. Hitler counted on such groups to immobilize American public opinion so that he could complete his conquest of potential American allies. Other attacks were more responsible. In early August the paper speculated about what the country's situation would have been had the nation rejected lend-lease. Not only had that policy succeeded in keeping friendly nations in the fight, noted the *News*, but the dire warnings made by administration critics had proven untrue. The United States was still a republic and still at peace. Senatorial opponents, whom the *Daily News* variously referred to as "a willful group of little men" or "the monkey wrench gang," had offered nothing in the way of constructive alternatives to the president's program. Early in the year the *News* had defended the right of administration opponents to speak out. By October the paper was dismissing their complaints about denial of access to public media and assembly halls as a ploy. Nye and Lindbergh sought martyr's status for themselves to elicit support for a course discredited across the nation. If administration supporters obtained a preponderance of radio time, it was because they outnumbered the opposition, not because of any conspiracy.[18]

The *Tribune* responded in kind. While the *Daily News* spotlighted the activities of the German-American Bund, the *Tribune* concentrated its attacks on the more extreme elements among the forces working to defeat Hitler, such as the Fight For Freedom Committee and Clarence Streit's Federal Union movement. The *Tribune* belittled their popular support, but sought to portray their positions as typical of all of Roosevelt's backers. The drive toward war, maintained the paper, was led by a clique of wealthy socialites and financiers concentrated around New York City. The attitudes of this group were "colonial," so strong was their affection for Britain. Reporter William Fulton contended that the eastern clique controlled the airwaves and filled them with propaganda. Scarcely a hint of anti-Semitism emerged in the countless *Tribune* diatribes against the "war promoters," although how readers interpreted the often ambiguous attacks is unknown.[19]

Seldom did either newspaper mention its rival. The few obvious allusions appeared in the *Daily News*. On April 8 one of its editorials denounced an item in "the Chicago mouthpiece for the American Cliveden set." A July editorial chided McCormick for his alleged hypocrisy. The *Tribune* decried the Democrats as a boss-ridden party, observed the *Daily News*, while it remained on good terms with the Kelly-Nash machine. McCormick railed against the eastern warmongers, yet his current Republican favorite was New York's Thomas Dewey. The increasing stridency of the "World's Greatest Newspaper," said the *Daily News*, stemmed from its frustration at being ignored. The *Tribune* also ran afoul of the evening paper's penchant for assigning guilt by association. In July the *Daily News* noted that both the *Tribune* and the Nazi press opposed extending the terms of service for American draftees. A November cartoon returned to the theme of hypocrisy. It pictured a man, whose pockets contained a Lindbergh speech and a copy of the "Daily Appeaser," smearing both the government and the army while simultaneously soliciting cigarettes to send to soldiers. The *Tribune* was conducting a "Smokes for Yanks" campaign at the time.[20]

All this the "World's Greatest Newspaper" suffered without reply. Only once in the two years prior to Pearl Harbor did the paper confront its critics. An editorial in the *Chicago Times*, written by former *Tribune* business editor S. E. Thomason, accused the *Tribune* of conveying German propaganda. Under the title "These

Jackals Grow Too Bold," an editorial lashed back. "Up to now . . .
the *Tribune* has treated the nagging by two little evening contemporaries with silence born of contempt," the response began. But
imputations against its patriotism could not be tolerated. The *Tribune* denounced Hitler's regime and denied that it had ever
spoken in favor of the Nazi system. Hatred of dictatorship, the
editorial continued, was the very reason for the *Tribune*'s strong
opposition to American intervention, since most thinking people
realized that war would breed dictatorship in this country. The
reply concluded with a blast at the financial weakness, editorial
dependence, and misguided zeal of Chicago's evening newspapers. With that, the *Tribune* lion settled down once more.[21]

Everywhere across America the level of bitterness rose—in the
press, in Congress, in the statements of leaders on all sides of the
debate. Spokesmen for the crisis committees led the way. In a letter to the *New York Times*, Robert Sherwood, a playwright active in
the CDAAA, suggested that the America First Committee was refusing to reveal the identities of all its financial backers because
some of them had Nazi sympathies. Amos Pinchot countered for
the committee by stressing the integrity of leading members like
General Wood. Pinchot then accused the CDAAA of hypocrisy for
claiming to desire peace while secretly working for war. Wood himself employed a similar rebuttal in response to a comment by Interior Secretary Harold Ickes that AFC leaders were Nazi "fellow
travelers." It was an old trick, said Wood, "for a war party to claim
a monopoly on patriotism." Congress was also affected by the
worsening tenor of the debate. House Speaker Sam Rayburn
noted in May that there was more direct criticism of members by
their colleagues than at any previous time during his twenty-eight
years in Washington. A decline in decorum by volunteer public
committees was perhaps not surprising, and acrimony in Congress
was hardly unprecedented, but the bitterness infused the press as
well and was not confined to its more sensationalist elements. The
San Francisco Chronicle ran a cartoon showing Senator Gerald Nye,
a leading administration critic, waving an America First banner
aboard a Nazi caboose. By November the *Chronicle* was referring
to the AFC as "Amerika Fuehrst," and this in an editorial defending the group's right to freedom of speech. The *New York Times*
also colored its coverage of certain events in ways that accorded

with its editorial viewpoints on foreign policy. Minor gaffes by opponents of aid received prominent coverage. Accounts of crowds at America First meetings suggested that disloyalty and pro-Nazi sentiments were prevalent among them. On one occasion the *Times* ended a story about the views of Charles Lindbergh by reporting that the flyer's statements were being quoted in Rome and Berlin. The *Tribune* may have been unusually blatant about editorializing in its news columns, but it was not unique.[22]

The doldrums of late summer muted the foreign policy controversy in Chicago and across the country. Roosevelt's August meeting with Winston Churchill, which produced the Atlantic Charter, occasioned only modest and predictable comment from the *Tribune* and the *Daily News*. Not until autumn, when naval skirmishing increased in the Atlantic, when the administration proposed a virtual repeal of the Neutrality Act, and when events in Asia took on a sudden and ominous prominence, did a final outburst of debate erupt.

The central thrust of the proposed revisions in the Neutrality Act was to end the ban on the use of American merchant shipping in war zones and to arm the merchantmen thus employed. But the United States was already deeply involved in the battle of the Atlantic. Using executive authority, Roosevelt in July had authorized the use of American shipping in convoys as far east as Iceland and directed the navy to escort those vessels. Ships of other nations, including Britain, were allowed to join the convoys. Since April, moreover, the navy had conducted an expanded antisubmarine campaign in the western Atlantic. What began as observation patrolling evolved into a shadow war kept hidden from the public until September.[23]

Roosevelt unveiled his policy of undeclared naval war in a speech on September 11, one week after a skirmish between a U-boat and the American destroyer *Greer*. In general, the press welcomed his "shoot on sight" order. Most papers accepted the president's interpretation of the incident as yet another example of German aggression. The *Los Angeles Times*, the *St. Louis Post-Dispatch*, the *Atlanta Constitution*, the *Denver Post*, the *Cleveland Plain Dealer*, and many others agreed that the Nazis had provoked the United States. There was less of a consensus on the impact Roosevelt's move would have. Both the *Times* and the *Constitution* stressed that only Hitler would determine if the order would bring war, though the *Times* expressed the hope that American toughness would force Germany to back down. The *Post-Dispatch* praised the calculation and restraint of Roosevelt's action. The *Denver Post* emphasized America's continuing determination to stay out of the war and interpreted the "shoot on sight" order as a necessary move for hemispheric defense. Only the *Plain Dealer* expressed disappointment that the president had not gone farther. The Cleveland daily commented that the order was "rather ineffectual" and called on Roosevelt to ask for repeal of the Neutrality Act. A few papers, like the *Chicago Journal of Commerce*, believed the president had gone too far already. The "shoot on sight" order meant to them that FDR had taken the country into war, usurping the prerogative of Congress just as he had done so often before in domestic policy.[24]

The *Cleveland Plain Dealer* proved to be an accurate prophet, for on October 9 Roosevelt asked Congress to alter the Neutrality Act. His strategy was to request at first only the authority to arm merchant shipping, and then, if the situation seemed promising, to seek approval for convoying as well. The armed ship bill passed the House on October 16 by an overwhelming margin. Administration forces in the Senate thereupon added a provision to include convoying when they took up the measure.

As issues, neutrality revision and the undeclared naval war held the potential for another national debate as searching as the earlier lend-lease contest had been. In fact, the new dispute never came alive. Administration critics, with the *Tribune* assuming its usual place in the vanguard, attacked each new move with their customary heat. But they had diminished their public credibility by the repeated use of apocalyptic forecasts that never seemed to come true. Roosevelt's supporters, in Chicago at least, were so certain of victory that their arguments seemed to spring more from habit than from a sense that the public really required convincing. They too had little to say that was original and defended the new revisions as the latest manifestations of an accepted policy. Thus administration forces were relying on the "aid short of war" argument down through the final weeks of peace.

The *Tribune* considered the proposed neutrality revisions to be "The Climax of Hypocrisy." Since April the paper had been predicting that Roosevelt would ask for convoys. Now McCormick reminded his readers of the president's earlier pledges to keep the nation at peace. Were not the proposed arming of merchantmen and the direct delivery of military goods to belligerents each hostile and provocative acts? Secretary Hull described this policy as one of self-defense, but the *Tribune* noted that such an excuse could be used to justify any manner of action. The Japanese, for example, had pleaded self-defense when they invaded Manchuria in 1931. McCormick insisted that the present proposals were just another Rooseveltian dodge to avoid giving the people an honest choice between peace and war.[25]

Tribune arguments, as well as its reporting of the Atlantic sparring, contained more substance than most of the paper's previous critiques. However worthy his motives were, Roosevelt had initiated a shooting war at sea, moving aggressively against a foreign power with whom the United States was not formally at war. An American president, not a German dictator, had begun this policy without consulting the legislature or the public. Now the president was asking for congressional approval to conduct further hostile acts, without inviting the nation to go to war. Roosevelt's position was at least inconsistent, and perhaps even hypocritical, but his vulnerability on this account was much reduced by the nature of modern war. The magnitude of Hitler's success and his methods for achieving it had altered American perceptions of what represented acceptable ways of protecting the United States. Harsh opponents appeared to justify harsh means to deal with them. Nazi ruthlessness, decisiveness, and lack of regard for conventional diplomatic and military practice inclined many Americans to endorse a similar approach, suitably amended, in response. The previous excesses of FDR's domestic opponents prevented them from exploiting whatever potential vulnerability remained in the president's position. The text of *Tribune* charges followed the same shopworn litany that had been a fixture of the preceding twenty-five months—"conspiracy," "warmonger," "dictatorship." Who but the faithful could still believe?

Firmer ground on which to argue was no substitute for respectability or big battalions. The *Daily News* avoided direct rebuttals to *Tribune* positions and sought instead to discredit their source. Charges that the United States had waged an aggressive and illegal naval war prior to the "shoot on sight" order, said the *Daily News*, had originated in Berlin. The *Tribune* charged, correctly as it happened, that the *Greer* had acted as the aggressor in its duel with the U-boat. In its reply, the *Daily News* again chose to ignore the substance of the issue and instead to attack its morning rival, chiding McCormick for coming to Berlin's defense before the Nazis had done so themselves. The colonel's attacks, the paper alleged, stemmed from his intense desire to spite the administration. Therefore they could be dismissed. As for neutrality revision, the *Daily News* based its support on the same reasoning it had used to advocate "cash and carry" two years before. The proper posture for the United States was to return to America's traditional insistence on freedom of the seas.[26]

The overall tendency among newspapers supporting revision, as most did, was similar to the approach appearing in the *Daily News*. The papers interpreted both convoying and the arming of ships as extensions of the policy that the United States had pursued since hostilities broke out in 1939. The *Los Angles Times* believed that it had long been clear that the Neutrality Act was a hindrance to American security rather than a benefit. Concurring, the *San Francisco Chronicle* condemned the law as a fake that invited danger to American shores rather than keeping it away. Roosevelt's proposals offered a better chance to preserve the peace. The *New York Times* also stressed the continuities with the intent of administration policy, evident since "cash and carry," to avoid war by aiding the Allies. As the United Press syndicate reported, most congressional backers of revision defended the modifications on the grounds that they "would stave off American participation in the conflict."[27]

Congress approved the administration's convoy bill in November by much smaller majorities than it had given to lend-lease. Did the diminished margins indicate that Roosevelt's policies were becoming too militant for the country to accept? The *Tribune* had predicted this would happen and the administration's foes took heart from the vote. FDR also seems to have believed that he had pushed public opinion to the limit. These perceptions are important in themselves, but in fact the congressional vote was influenced by more than just the members' judgments of the bill's intrinsic merits or its implications for war. Most importantly, the

administration lost votes from influential Democrats who were disgruntled by its failure to curb strikes in defense industries. Congressional anger over the activities of certain unions, notably the
United Mine Workers, had been growing for months. Some legislators also condemned lagging defense production and feared that
the navy was insufficiently equipped to handle added responsibili-
ties. Nevertheless, the administration mustered sufficient votes to
effect passage, in part by promising to deal with the strike issue.
American ships now sailed all the way to Britain, through a gaunt-
let of U-boats then nearing peak effectiveness. On the Atlantic,
the United States had come to the brink of war and a bit beyond.
A policy of "aid short of war" had become one of "aid short of all-
out war." The choice predicted by Marguerite Wells of the League
of Women Voters had been made. Americans had decided in favor
of "aid regardless of consequences." How long the precarious balance would endure, and what would follow it, became the paramount questions.[28]

The sea lanes east absorbed public concern. Would they bring
war, as they had in 1917? Polls showed that public opinion approved of convoying by overwhelming majorities. Yet the familiar
dichotomy persisted; in late November 1941 only one American in
four favored an immediate declaration of war. Neither the public
nor their president were willing to seize the initiative and take the
final step into full belligerency. McCormick, of course, believed
otherwise about Roosevelt, and the *Tribune*'s opposition to such a
move was known nationwide. Throughout the autumn the *Daily
News* kept mute on the question of war. Its period of most outspoken militancy had occurred during the previous spring, the nadir
of Allied fortunes. Then the paper had proclaimed "This is our
war" and had thrown the door open for Roosevelt to lead the
nation as far as he wished to go. This martial ardor wilted under
the summer sun. By August, "our war" had come to mean a maximum effort to supply the British with material, a position no more
advanced than that taken the previous winter. The paper gave no
clue as to the reasons for its backsliding. For the remaining
months of peace the *Daily News* rested content with the administration's policy of "half-way" war. White House caution and an indeci-
sive public left Hitler with control of the tempo and flow of action,
still in command of center stage.[29]

This was so despite the sudden and acute intrusion of the crisis in Asia. One of the most striking aspects of the years before Pearl Harbor is how little attention much of the press, in Chicago and elsewhere, paid to relations between America and Japan. The two Chicago newspapers, each with a large, independent foreign staff of high caliber, almost ignored this subject and in general tended to slight events in the Pacific. From the fall of France until the Pacific situation became critical around October 1941, Asia seldom received front page attention. The *Tribune* and the *Daily News* of course covered major stories, such as the Japanese occupation of Indochina, and the rare analytical pieces that each paper presented were often very insightful. Prominence and frequency of coverage represented as great a problem as content. Stories on Japanese-American relations were few in number and seldom appeared on the front page. As a result, the coverage failed to convey a sense of continuity and context that could emerge from repeated exposure.[30]

Considerable variation existed in the scope, prominence, and quality of the treatment given Asia by different newspapers. A few, like the *New York Times* and the *San Francisco Chronicle*, regularly contained solid reporting on east Asia. Others, like the *Boston Globe*, the *Los Angeles Times*, and the *Denver Post*, devoted less attention to the area, but still ran quality articles on occasion. Most papers, most radio commentators, and the *March of Time* as well, resembled the Chicago dailies. They largely ignored the Pacific until the latter half of 1941. Even then, reports concerning Japan received less prominent positions in papers like the *Atlanta Constitution* than did articles dealing with Europe. In effect, Nazi success all but pushed the Pacific situation out of most newspapers until the autumn of 1941.[31]

Coverage of Europe dominated that of Asia in a different sense as well. Their respective stances toward Europe conditioned the way in which each Chicago paper, and many elsewhere, interpreted Japanese expansion. The war in Europe was indeed a vital element in the interplay of forces around the Pacific. By curtailing the ability of the Western powers to oppose Japanese designs, German success opened avenues of opportunity that Tokyo might not otherwise have found. Both Chicago newspapers properly noted these links. But the *Daily News* went further, basing its interpretation of Japanese policy on the pattern established by Germany. Japan's decision to join the Axis alliance in September 1940 seemed to confirm the soundness of this outlook. Formation of the Axis was one of the few stories relating to Asia that would hit the front page before the autumn of 1941. Nazi aggression had dominated the foreign news for months. Now Japan thrust herself into the headlines and into public consciousness by the very act of aligning with Hitler and Mussolini. From the perspective of a reader, Japan had become, perhaps indelibly, the Nazi Germany of the Pacific. Subsequent news and editorial treatment in the *Daily News* reinforced this impression. One *Daily News* cartoon pictured Uncle Sam with his eyes fixed on Europe, while a Japanese rattlesnake coiled behind his ankle. The cartoon intended to spur public opinion to a greater awareness of Asia, but it captured the paper's own unconscious attitude as well. A series of reports by A. T. Steele, appearing in January 1941, analyzed Japan's "unique brand of fascism" and described Tokyo's ambition to conquer all of Asia. Japan differed from her German partners only in that her military machine was much less formidable and her economy more vulnerable to outside pressure. In psychology and ambition the Axis partners were alike. All they understood, or responded to, was force applied with toughness. The *Daily News* believed that a firm American stance in the Pacific would force the Japanese to retrench.[32]

The tendency to use contemporary European history to interpret events in Asia was common in the press. Columnist Chester Rowell labeled Thailand the "Poland of the Asiatic" when it appeared that Japan intended to attack that neutral nation. The extensive coverage in the *New York Times* often focused on the connections between East Asia and Europe. Sometimes this provided valuable insight, as when the *Times* analyzed the effects that France's collapse was likely to produce in Southeast Asia. Other articles, however, seemed determined to portray Japan as an Oriental adjunct to Germany. This theme predominated in many papers. The *Louisville Courier-Journal* even coined a term, "Bertok"—an amalgam of Berlin and Tokyo—to suggest how closely the methods of the two Axis nations coincided. Each employed threats in hopes of gaining concessions. Americans, said the *Courier-Journal*, now knew what response to make to such tactics. The paper insisted that the United States must not be intimidated by the threat of war into granting any Japanese demand. Like most American media, the *Courier-Journal* evidenced little sympathy or respect for Japan. The *Cleveland Plain Dealer* took this attitude even farther. It insisted that Japan had long been overrated as a military power and declared that the United States ought to "stamp out the Oriental pest."[33]

Europe cast a different sort of shadow over Asia in the *Tribune*. Only once did the paper suggest that the Japanese sought to dominate the Pacific in the way that Hitler bestrode Europe. Much of the *Tribune*'s response to the Pacific situation and the administration's Asia policy represented a straightforward transferral of the paper's position regarding Europe. Roosevelt again emerged as the chief obstacle to peace. Readers who disagreed with McCormick on the subject of Hitler would likely have dismissed the colonel's opinions toward Asia as being cut from the same cloth.[34]

Such a view was not wholly warranted. Bombast and prejudice aplenty existed in the *Tribune*'s treatment of American policy, but McCormick showed far greater insight into the situation in the Pacific than he did when dealing with Europe. The *Tribune* issued repeated warnings concerning the danger that the United States might become a front for Western imperialism in Asia. From Syria to Java, the *Tribune* observed, the realities of imperial control bore little resemblance to the ideals enunciated in Roosevelt's Four Freedoms. American intervention in Asia would help the native peoples not at all and benefit only their masters in Western Europe. But misguided altruism and an abiding fondness for European royalty were not the only reasons why Washington desired to plunge the United States into war. The *Tribune* discerned an additional motivation:

> Are we not only to police the four freedoms in all parts of the world, but as an economic effect of that to say who is to have the resources of the world? The job grows bigger and bigger.
>
> The four freedoms are not in a particularly healthy state in any of the vast region to which Singapore is the key; but that is not so important as the very heavy investments of capital in

profitable enterprises, which are not less profitable because of their proximity of abundant and cheap native labor.

So the *Tribune*, for all its partisan Republicanism and championing of private enterprise, did not believe that commercial interests in the Pacific justified risking war with Japan.[35]

The *Tribune* sought to avoid a clash with Japan, believing that peace would best serve American self-interest. Tokyo did not desire war with America, the paper contended. Japan's primary concern was to bring an end to her inconclusive war with China. McCormick maintained that these affairs and the general balance of power in Asia made little difference to the welfare of Americans. Our chief interests in the region were economic. Along with Robert Wood of America First, McCormick believed that mutual economic advantage would overcome political differences. While it was true that the United States would prefer to obtain strategic materials in Asia from Western sources, the Japanese had proven to be good business partners in the past and were likely to remain so in the future unless angered by the administration. In advocating a policy of accommodation toward Japan, the *Tribune* once again had come out against strong opposition to Axis expansion.[36]

Deteriorating Japanese-American relations during October and November of 1941 made the East Asian situation front-page news at last. Both Chicago papers noted that hard-liners, led by the new premier, Hideki Tojo, had taken control of the government in Tokyo. By early November each paper was forecasting an imminent showdown in the western Pacific. Such predictions were so widespread that the serious reader of almost any major metropolitan newspaper must have seen them. The *Daily News* ascribed the increased tension to the designs of German policy, while the *Tribune* believed that the crisis represented a triumph of British diplomacy. By the third week of November, they, along with many other observers, had developed a fatalistic conviction that war was inevitable. Prevailing opinion expected Japan to launch the initial attack toward Thailand and Singapore. Neither the *Daily News*, the *Tribune*, nor anyone else considered Hawaii a target.[37]

In a fundamental sense, there was no foreign policy debate after lend-lease. Having established their profound disagreement on several key premises pertaining to the national and international situation, the two sides had little to say to one another. Events confirmed each one's conviction of the soundness of its own stance and the mistakenness of its opponent. Neither Chicago paper added much to its essential position, which each extended to Asia as friction with Japan became more ominous. Instead they repeated old arguments endlessly and sniped at the motivations of their opponents. Because neither side seemed able to make its case more compelling, each tried to advance its cause by undermining the other. Often the method was to discredit the opposition's integrity rather than to undermine its arguments.

Both sides ignored the major flaws in their respective positions. For the *Tribune* this was its refusal to accept Hitlerian Germany as a menace of uncommon magnitude. Public opinion and the government had already rejected such complaceny by 1941, and the *Tribune* became an almost irrelevant critic on foreign policy. The weakness in the *Daily News*'s position was exposed after lend-lease, as it became clear that "aid short of war" was not turning the tide of battle in 1941. Great Britain was no nearer to defeating Germany in May than she had been ten months earlier. No one could be certain what ultimate effect the invasion of Russia would have on the course of the war. The dilemma between the goals of peace and victory thus emerged. To the last, the *Daily News* declined to declare its choice, in effect refusing to lead opinion. Elsewhere, some papers or commentators encouraged American to choose war, but such promptings were exceptional. Far more prevalent was the continued belief that the "aid short of war" policy would prove sufficient to bring about Hitler's defeat.

Along with other observers, the *Tribune* and the *Daily News* glimpsed the approach of war. Despite their disparate viewpoints, each paper acknowledged impending hostilities without enthusiasm. By December 1941 the newspapers had ceased trying to influence policy or arouse opinion. They settled back uneasily to await events. It did not prove to be a long wait.

SIX

THE LAST MILE?

ollowing the successful outcome of the lend-lease debate, administration supporters
lapsed into relative inactivity for almost three months. Their lack
of initiative paralleled the lassitude that gripped the White House
during the spring of 1941. The pause was especially pronounced
in Chicago, where it further undermined the strength of the local
chapter of the Committee to Defend America (CDA), as the old
White Committee now called itself. CDA in Chicago never fully
recovered its previous vigor and the chapter suffered defections
of key personnel to a newer and more militant organization, the
Fight For Freedom Committee. Nationally, Fight For Freedom advocated outright military intervention by the United States, but its
message never caught fire in Chicago. The city's remaining
CDAers followed their national organization in prodding Roosevelt to begin convoying, but the Chicagoans continued to emphasize cautious "short of war" arguments similar to those they had
stressed from the outset of the foreign policy debate. Whatever
their banner, administration forces in Chicago, and to a great extent elsewhere as well, concentrated as much on discrediting such
opponents as the America First Committee and the *Chicago Tribune*
as on furthering American involvement in the war.[1]

The only significant action undertaken by the Chicago chapter
of the CDA during the spring of 1941 was to outline a new set of
goals. On March 18, Paul Douglas announced that the committee
now advocated the use of American ships in the convoys bound
for Britain. Other facets of CDA's program included support for a

firm Asian policy, centering around an embargo of goods to Japan, and a pledge of vigorous efforts to combat Axis propaganda in this country. Each point reflected CDA national policy. One month later, John Morrison elaborated upon the original announcement. Morrison's statement made no specific mention of convoys, but it emphasized that CDA's new slogan was "Deliver the Goods." The choice facing America, according to Morrison, was not between peace or war but between a British or a Nazi victory. Because the "aid short of war" formula still promised to accomplish the goals of American policy, it would continue to form the basis of CDA's program. Morrison explained that the committee had been quiescent out of hope that its opposition would abide by national policy. Recent America First activity had shown this hope to be futile, said Morrison, and CDA was preparing to respond. Yet the only immediate action came not from the Chicago office, but from the chapter in Hyde Park, where members began a letter campaign that urged Roosevelt to authorize convoys.[2]

Morrison's account of the committee's recent hibernation told only part of the story. Chicago leaders had indeed hoped that keeping a low profile might discourage America First from continuing its efforts. But other factors overshadowed this consideration. Factionalism and disagreement within CDA's upper echelons in Chicago, continuing friction between their office and the Century Club Group in New York, and a general weariness with foreign policy debates all contributed to their inactivity. The Chicagoans disagreed about what policy goals to pursue subsequent to lend-lease. A February strategy session had not even raised convoying as a potential consideration. All seven midwestern delegates to a March meeting of CDA's national executive committee had urged the organization to underplay the convoy issue. Their views did not prevail. Chapter leaders in Chicago later argued among themselves over whether they should endorse the new program. After extended debate, Paul Douglas and Quincy Wright persuaded a majority to vote in favor of the national committee's position. The chapter then decided upon a sharp reduction in local activity pending new developments in Washington and abroad.[3]

Important changes were occurring within the leadership of the Chicago chapter. Adlai Stevenson had grown tired of CDA work and yearned for a job in the Roosevelt administration. In late April Stevenson resigned as chairman, although he continued to serve on the chapter's executive committee. His successor was Harland H. Allen, a local investment counselor and economist. The fifty-three-year-old Allen had left a long career as a college teacher to head his own investment firm. Despite his occupation, Allen lacked the ready access to large contributors that Stevenson had provided through his social connections. The new chairman also did not possess his predecessor's close links to the *Daily News*. Of the two losses, the drop in financial support represented the more serious handicap. By early June, the Chicago chapter had only eighty-nine dollars in the bank and faced the prospect of drastic cuts in office staff and facilities.[4]

Allen's accession to the chapter leadership was part of a larger overhaul. A *CDA News Bulletin* announced on June 23 that a thorough reorganization had taken place. Paul Douglas now headed the chapter's policy committee, Clifton Utley and Louis Wirth directed the production of local publicity, and Lloyd Warner supervised its distribution. Douglas, Wirth, and Warner were all professors at the University of Chicago, and their accession to key leadership positions indicated how heavily the chapter had come to rely on the university.[5]

No change in philosophy accompanied the turnover in personnel. Allen believed that American productive capacity would be the decisive element in an eventual Allied victory. CDA rhetoric did grow more bellicose, but not more precise. One *News Bulletin* declared that the committee's mission was to insure "that full wartime participation shall not be too late." Despite the militant implications of such a statement, the bulk of CDA pronouncements reiterated the familiar theme that America's task was to furnish the material for other nations to use in beating Hitler. Use of the slogan "Deliver the Goods" sometimes seemed to refer as much to all-out production as to convoying. Through April, chapter spokespersons still emphasized the utility of backing Britain in order to buy time to prepare American defenses—the same rationale behind the destroyer deal eight months earlier.[6]

A belief that material aid alone would enable Great Britain to achieve victory continued to be widely held in 1941, even among informed circles and by some proponents of military intervention.

Just after lend-lease became law, correspondent Leland Stowe of the *Daily News* delivered an optimistic report on Britain's prospects to members of the Contemporary Club in St. Louis. A lengthy letter by writer and editor Max Eastman, appearing in the *New York Times* on May 11, also expressed confidence that time favored the British. Eastman's example is especially intriguing because his letter included a call for American belligerency, which he justified on the grounds that it would better position the United States to shape the peace. In general the public rejected such belligerency, but it did share the expectation that Britain would win the war. Confidence in Britain's ultimate success actually grew in 1941, despite Hitler's string of successes. Gallup surveys found in April that 57 percent of the public believed that victory would come to the British. By August the figure had risen twelve points. As Eastman's case demonstrates, confidence in a British victory did not preclude advocacy of full American belligerency, but it did undercut the argument that Britain's fate depended on American military involvement. Since a majority of the public believed it more important to assure British survival than to remain at peace, and most Americans expressed a willingness to accept war if they could be persuaded it was necessary to insure a Nazi defeat, Americans could therefore continue to postpone belligerency only so long as they perceived Great Britain's prospects as satisfactory.[7]

Max Eastman was not alone in thinking about the postwar world. Additions to the Committee to Defend America's policy during the summer of 1941 showed that its members too had begun to consider the future shape of international relations. Beginning in July, the "Deliver the Goods" slogan gave way to "Total Production for Total Victory . . . Then Peace Through Justice." This was the first evidence of CDA concern with postwar conditions. The committee saw itself as an instrument by which to "discuss the plans and prepare the minds of people for a post-war international organization that will live and preserve peace." Thus CDA had again taken up the original purpose of its parent committee, the League of Nations Association, and of the man who directed both organizations, Clark M. Eichelberger. Roosevelt and Churchill endorsed this concept in the Atlantic Charter, issued on August 14, but the problems of peace never became an important priority in the Committee to Defend America's agenda. For CDA, like Roosevelt, immediate concerns overshadowed all else.[8]

Chief among the more pressing problems was the lack of national unity. CDA's implicit definition of "unity" excluded opposition to national—meaning the administration's—foreign policy. The committee aimed to curb partisan political resistance and to undermine the effectivenss of America First and other organized opposition. Early in June administration supporters in Chicago staged their supreme bid to demonstrate the public's desire to close ranks in the present emergency.[9]

Their device was a massive "Unity Day" rally. The "All Chicago Citizen's Committee on America's Crisis" sponsored the event. Although he did not chair the new group, Adlai Stevenson was its moving force. Several other prominent members of CDA also served on the Citizen's Committee, and CDA's Chicago chapter provided most of the staff work necessary to arrange the rally. The Citizen's Committee included a sufficient number of persons free of CDA ties, including R. Douglas Stuart's uncle, to lend at least a veneer of authenticity to its claims of independence. The facade of an independent sponsor served two purposes. It lessened the chance that the affair would appear as just another CDA demonstration, and it enabled Stevenson to snare a long-sought quarry, Wendell Willkie.[10]

The strident antiwar candidate of the closing weeks of the 1940 campaign had long since become a vocal proponent of Roosevelt's European policy. His support of lend-lease earned Willkie a string of virulent denunciations in the *Tribune*. Since December Stevenson had been trying to convince Willkie to speak in Chicago and to join the Committee to Defend America. Willkie refused to become associated with the committee or even to address the public under its auspices. Stevenson finally secured his consent to appear at a mass meeting so long as it was not a CDA function.[11]

Rally backers strove to build upon the contacts forged by the CDA among various interest groups within Chicago. Stevenson's initial idea had been to stage the mass meeting on Memorial Day at Soldier Field. One motive behind such an audacious move was to preclude use of the facility by America First. Stevenson also hoped to use the traditional holiday parade as a precursor to the rally by ending the parade route at Soldier's Field. The whole idea of using the facility collapsed when parade organizers, principally veterans' groups, rejected Stevenson's plan. Undeterred by this setback, the Citizen's Committee rescheduled the meeting for early June at the Chicago Arena. They then looked to familiar sources for support. Stevenson convinced Mayor Kelly to issue a proclamation in support of the unity rally. Kelly also offered financial help, although whether directly or through recommendations to donors remains unclear. To help fill the arena, Stevenson again relied upon the Eastern European groups. He contacted the various ethnic newspapers and organizations, asking them to publicize the rally and encourage their fellow nationals to attend. As usual, each major group received recognition on the dais. The national headquarters of the Committee to Defend America used its contacts with the motion picture industry to arrange for the appearance of such stars as Judy Garland, Don Ameche, Linda Darnell, and Dennis Morgan. Rally organizers also engaged the poet and biographer Carl Sandburg to deliver an address.[12]

The result was, by several measures, the most successful interventionist mass meeting to be held in Chicago during the prewar period. Perhaps 24,000 Chicagoans jammed the arena to capacity on the evening of June 6, with hundreds more outside. Sandburg received wild applause when he denounced Charles Lindbergh's indifference to the outcome of the struggle in Europe. Willkie's address, which received national attention, stressed the urgency of Great Britain's plight and underscored the dangers posed by German U-boat attacks on Atlantic convoys. He urged President Roosevelt to dispatch American troops to Iceland and American shipping to the Home Islands. With the exception of a handful of hecklers from a women's antiwar group, the crowd responded warmly to Willkie's remarks. Paul Douglas wrote a glowing report of the meeting to Secretary of the Interior Ickes, a former Chicagoan who served as an unofficial liaison between the administration and reform elements in the city. The size and enthusiasm of the crowd, wrote Douglas, demonstrated that Chicago was by no means as "isolationist" as its reputation indicated. The alderman cited as evidence the unanimous support for the administration's foreign policy among the local Eastern European population.

Douglas went so far as to state his conviction that a majority of Chicagoans favored strong action against Hitler.[13]

For the rally's covert organizers, the Committee to Defend America, the meeting amounted to a swan song. Within weeks Stevenson had departed for Washington to work for Knox. He left behind a chapter dissolving into contention and insolvency. Early in July Clark Eichelberger queried the Chicagoans about the reasons for their lack of cooperation with the national organization. He received a blistering reply from the new chairman, Harland Allen, who denounced Morrison and his staff for "burying the Chicago Committee alive." Allen cited staff cuts, an exhausted treasury, and a general lack of cooperation by Morrison as proof of his charges.[14]

The decline soon spread to other area chapters. "Our poor old committee here seems done in," wrote one Winnetka volunteer to Stevenson. Efforts by Allen and his assistant, Paul Lyness, to revitalize moribund chapters proved unsuccessful. The Hyde Park group, for example, accomplished little during the summer and disbanded near the end of August. The Chicago office tried to keep up the flow of news bulletins and petitions to area outposts, but some chapters complained that they no longer received CDA literature. Throughout the summer, committee forces around Chicago lacked strong leadership and any clear strategic direction. By August the CDA had become all but invisible in the Windy City.[15]

Elsewhere the committee's health was much better. In Cleveland, for example, the local chapter sponsored a large and successful rally in September. The decentralized structure of the CDA meant that the virtual collapse of even so major an element as Chicago had no effect on other regions, although satellite outposts in surrounding communities were likely to be crippled. As it happened, however, interventionists never lacked a vehicle through which to express their views.[16]

Already a new organization had arisen which hoped to supplant CDA as the catalyst for interventionist sentiment. Fight For Freedom Incorporated, as its name suggested, embodied a more militant position than that of its established counterpart. The new committee's original press release, issued in April 1941, stressed however that its immediate aim was the same as CDA's, to promote delivery of supplies to Great Britain. The statement made no mention of an American expeditionary force. Fight For Freedom originated as an outgrowth of the Century Club Group in New York City and its Chicago staff also split off from the declining ranks of the local CDA. Fourteen of the twenty-four members of FFF's executive committee in Chicago had been members of the White Committee. Their ranks included such important figures as Clifton Utley, Clarence Randall, W. Lloyd Warner, and Louis Wirth. The three key members of the new group—its chairman, Denison B. Hull, its director, Courtenay Barber, Jr., and its assistant director, Dr. Albert Parry—were CDA alumni. Hull was a prominent Chicago architect, Barber was an insurance executive, and Parry was a freelance writer with a recent doctoral degree in history from the University of Chicago. By the spring of 1941 each man had decided that full American participation in the fighting would be necessary if the Allies were to defeat Hitler.[17]

Barber and Parry sparked the new effort. In June, Fight For Freedom headquarters dispatched Herbert Agar to Chicago. An editor of the *Louisville Courier-Journal*, Agar was one of FFF's most influential members. His purpose was to advise Barber and Parry as they sought to organize a chapter. The three encountered a mixture of sympathy and reticence among many of those whom they met. Both Hull and Clarence Randall agreed to give money toward the formation of a chapter, but neither man wished to have his name connected in public with so radical a cause as military intervention. After weeks of discussion, Hull and Laird Bell, a wealthy Chicago lawyer and a member of CDA, overcame their misgivings and consented to lend their names to a chapter. Along with Parry and Barber, these men formed the backbone of the Chicago operation.[18]

This reluctance was not unique to Chicago. Nowhere did Fight For Freedom grow with the same explosive speed as CDA or America First had shown. Nor did it rival either of them in mass membership. So major a city as Cleveland lacked an FFF chapter until four days before Pearl Harbor, perhaps because CDA continued to be active there throughout 1941. The experience of Chicago and Cleveland suggests that the relative strength or weakness of the local CDA chapter influenced the prospects of FFF taking root. In fact, however, the relationship between the two groups defies simple categorization, as one would expect in decentralized and locally oriented operations. The Committee to Defend America remained vigorous in New York City, where Fight For Freedom was also very active, and often the two cooperated. While in general FFF activity rose as that of CDA waned, local conditions allowed for great variations in the overall pattern.[19]

Measured by the standards of the debate in Chicago up to July of 1941, the objectives of the new organization were extreme. Barber circulated an introductory letter listing five immediate goals. Fight For Freedom urged that the navy be allowed to shoot German submarines on sight and called for the occupation of all strategically valuable Atlantic islands. Accordingly, the committee wanted congressional authorization for the use of American troops outside the Western Hemisphere. Fight For Freedom also advocated the complete repeal of "the so-called Neutrality act" and demanded severance of diplomatic relations with the Axis nations. The statement did not call for a declaration of war, noting instead that "no just peace is possible unless this nation fulfills its responsibility" at home and abroad. Lest there be any doubt as to the chapter's intent, Barber stated bluntly, "we mean fight and we mean freedom." Fight For Freedom planned to carry its message to the people by furnishing speakers to meetings of various local groups, staging gatherings of its own, organizing street parades, and conducting motorcades. Because Fight For Freedom commanded such limited resources in Chicago, the chapter began its public activities with a number of street meetings. These generated sufficient public interest and financing to embolden the committee to plan a mass rally for the end of July. In keeping with the bitter tenor of the debate in 1941, the theme of the upcoming meeting was neither preparedness nor the need to make war on Hitler; it was an attack on the *Chicago Tribune.*[20]

The choice thus reflected the increasing tendency among administration supporters in 1941 to underplay their own foreign policy program and instead to concentrate their efforts on discrediting their remaining opposition. In various cities around the nation, local officials tried to deny the America First Committee access to meeting places. One baseball fan was so incensed by Brooklyn Dodger president Larry MacPhail's refusal to allow

America First to use Ebbets Field that he promised to boycott Cubs games whenever the Dodgers visited Chicago. President Roosevelt labeled Charles Lindbergh a "copperhead," prompting the aviator to protest by resigning his reserve commission in the Army Air Corps. The same trend was evident within the ranks of the opposition. As 1941 wore on, what had been a debate began to degenerate into a shouting match.[21]

Innuendo and name-calling had always been a part of the debate, as they have of political discourse in general. But the pervasiveness of their use was much greater in 1941 than in previous stages of the debate and these elements assumed a larger place in the rhetoric of each side. Administration supporters, cabinet members, congresspersons, newspapers, and unofficial spokespersons all resorted to the use of invective. The trend extended beyond such normally vituperative types as Harold Ickes, Dorothy Thompson, and Claude Pepper. The president of the New York City Council, for example, declared that 60 percent of the crowd at one mammoth AFC rally were Bund members or Nazi sympathizers. The Columbia Broadcasting System, bowing to pressure from the major Hollywood studios, dropped gossip columnist Jimmy Fidler due to his outspoken antiwar views. The studios also pressed the *Los Angeles Times* to discontinue Fidler's column, but the paper refused.[22]

No one shouted louder in Chicago, with fewer inhibitions, than Robert McCormick's *Tribune*. The paper thus made an irresistible target, and perhaps a worthwhile one as well. How much influence the *Tribune* actually wielded over its readers on political and policy matters is an unanswerable question. But the sheer size of its circulation and its position as Chicago's sole morning newspaper gave the *Tribune* the image of power.

Quiet efforts had long been underway in a number of quarters to damage the *Tribune* or embarrass its publisher. Back in November 1940 Carroll Binder of the *Daily News* had been in contact with Francis P. Miller, director of the Council on Foreign Relations in New York City and a central figure in the Century Club Group. During World War I, Miller had served in an artillery unit adjacent to Robert McCormick's battalion. Miller sent the *Daily News* copies of notes he had written in 1923. They recorded the substance of conversations with enlisted men under McCormick's command. They charged McCormick with mental instability and implied that he had deserted under fire. The men alleged that McCormick arranged for a bogus medical leave of absence just as the battalion was about to go into action at Cantigny. Miller admitted that all of his evidence was hearsay, that none of the enlisted men were in a position to prove their allegations, and that many of their comments reflected a dislike of a pompous and eccentric commanding officer. Nevertheless Miller allowed Binder to do whatever he wished with the material and authorized the use of his name as its source. Binder forwarded a copy of the document to Harold Ickes, requesting advice on how best to use the allegations. For reasons which remain unclear, the *Daily News* never printed any of Miller's charges.[23]

The volatile secretary of the interior had welcomed Miller's information. Ickes detested McCormick and his newspaper for their opposition to the New Deal, for their hostility to social welfare reforms, and for the *Tribune*'s tacit alliance with the Kelly-Nash machine. In his personal correspondence, Ickes generally referred to the *Tribune* as the "World's Gutter Newspaper." In April 1941 a *Tribune* editorial ignited the secretary's seldom dormant temper by hinting that Ickes had accepted graft in order to pay for his farm in Maryland. Stung in his valued integrity, Ickes drafted a scalding nine-page reply. The letter impugned McCormick's business, military, personal, and sexual life, as well as his mental health. Ickes concluded by challenging the colonel to a public debate on all aspects of the two men's careers. Cooler heads probably sanitized the final draft, if it was ever sent, for no records exist of a public or private reply from McCormick.[24]

Others among McCormick's opponents were initiating steps to cause him more long-term concern. Their goal was to create a new morning newspaper in Chicago of sufficient power to rival the *Tribune*. The key figure in this effort was Marshall Field III, heir to a huge retail fortune and a leading Chicago philanthropist. Field had recently acquired a liking for the newspaper business and had founded *PM*, a daily in New York City. One of Field's principal reasons for beginning *PM* was to voice his support for a determinedly anti-Fascist American foreign policy. Now Field wished to do the same in Chicago. In several important respects Field was McCormick's opposite. They supported different political parties and disagreed on the merits of Roosevelt as a leader. McCormick criticized Britain far more often than he extended praise. Field was a consistent anglophile. The *Tribune*'s antiwar position especially infuriated Field, who supported the Century Club Group. Early in 1941, Field confided to his friend William Benton that he intended to contest the *Tribune*'s morning monopoly in Chicago. Benton urged Field to purchase the *Chicago Times*, a languishing afternoon tabloid, or the *Daily News*, which Benton believed Knox might be willing to sell. Field instead decided to create a new full-sized paper and began the enormous task of supervising its development.[25]

The Chicago chapter of Fight For Freedom played a significant role in the birth of the new morning daily. Courtenay Barber learned of Field's intentions through FFF headquarters in New York and greeted the news with enthusiasm. Chapter leaders sensed an opportunity to reap wide publicity by hitching the fledgling outpost to the anti-*Tribune* movement. As a result, the theme of Fight For Freedom's first major Chicago rally was "What's Wrong With the Chicago *Tribune*?"

Planning for the meeting revealed the inexperience of the local staff and the formidable dimensions of the task facing the chapter. Local radio stations refused to broadcast the address of the featured speaker, former *Tribune* correspondent Edmund R. Taylor. On July 27, two days before the rally, Barber dispatched a frantic telegram to Harold Ickes, pleading with the secretary of the interior to use his influence to secure radio time. Ickes attempted to help, but his belated efforts failed to persuade station managers.[26]

The rally itself encountered several difficulties and met with a mixed response. A crowd of 3,000 filled Orchestra Hall. Building attendants, some of whom wore America First buttons, turned away hundreds of other would-be listeners. The air conditioning system had broken down that afternoon, leaving the audience to swelter in torrid July heat. The meeting was late in starting and seemed to drag along due to an over-abundance of preliminary ceremony and the verbosity of introductory speakers. Stifling conditions within the building steadily eroded the crowd, and the choice seats left empty by absent dignitaries caused resentment among the throngs packed into the galleries. Episcopal bishop Henry Hobson, Fight For Freedom's national chairman, delivered a lively speech in which he urged the convoying of goods to Britain and occupation of strategic Atlantic islands. Many observers considered Edmund Taylor's featured address to be a disappointment. Instead of a *Tribune*-style denunciation of his former employer, Taylor presented a balanced and almost genial assessment of the paper's performance. Before adjourning, those who remained in Orchestra Hall passed resolutions condemning isolationism and pledging support for a new morning newspaper.[27]

Action following the meeting was less restrained. Pickets from a strident antiwar group, known as We, the Mothers, Mobilized for America, harassed the crowd as it was exiting the hall. A few scuffles broke out and the police moved in to arrest a number of men. Small bands of citizens roamed the streets, smashing *Tribune* vending machines and burning several hundred copies of the paper. Gradually the crowd dispersed. FFF leaders had not anticipated this type of reaction and apologized to the police for the disorder.[28]

The rally and its aftermath brought the Chicago FFF chapter valuable publicity. Even the *Tribune* covered the meeting, in an article notable for fairness and balance. Encouraged by the general response, Barber and Parry stepped up the chapter's activities. Parry asked Ulric Bell in New York to contact President Roosevelt about appearing at a proposed FFF rally at Soldier's Field early in September. A number of Eastern European groups and the VFW had already agreed to cooperate if such an event could be arranged. Nothing came of this idea, but a meeting late in August drew 1,500 to hear the former mayor of Narvik, Norway, denounce Nazi aggression. Fight For Freedom received extensive cooperation from local Scandinavian organizations in staging this successful assembly. Parry also contemplated repeating the Orchestra Hall formula by using other ex-members of the *Tribune* staff, including William L. Shirer. Financial shortages forced postponement of the plan, and in fact no other alumnus of the *Tribune* ever spoke in Chicago under FFF auspices.[29]

McCormick and the *Tribune* remained the central target of Fight For Freedom's local efforts. On both sides, the campaign took on aspects of a vendetta. *Daily News* editor Paul Scott Mowrer declined to publish FFF attacks on the *Tribune*, noting that Knox never printed third party criticism of rival newspapers. Mowrer's refusal hardly mattered, so widespread was FFF's assault on McCormick. Its campaign drew nationwide attention and brought requests from many out-of-state newspapers for copies of the Taylor speech. Many Chicagoans wore FFF buttons reading, "Chicago Needs a Morning Newspaper." The group had distributed over 60,000 pieces of literature by mid-September, including handbills picturing a swastika atop the *Tribune* Tower and featuring the slogan "Billions for defense, but not 2 cents for the *Tribune*." The Chicago FFF chapter copied without authorization a *Daily News* cartoon that showed Hitler in Siberia staring across the Bering Strait at an isolationist. In the FFF version, the isolationist was reading the *Tribune*. Parry directed that the speakers at an October 3 rally emphasize personal attacks on Charles Lindbergh and Mc-Cormick. Author Rex Stout berated the *Tribune* for its alleged Nazi sympathies, while Augustus Lindbergh labeled his half-cousin "America's Number One Isolationist."[30]

The *Tribune* struck back hard. The target was Albert Parry, temporarily in charge of the Chicago chapter while Barber was on vacation. In an article entitled "Russian Born Writer Leads Pro War Group," the paper attempted to portray "the man who sits at the center of the Fight For Freedom Committee spider web" as a communist. Despite the suggestion of "New England and colonial ancestors" in Parry's name, he had been born "Albert Paretzky" in Russia. The *Tribune* professed to have records indicating that Parry, or Paretzky, had fought on both sides during the Russian Revolution. Parry had once described himself in the *American Mercury* as "a left pink" who entered the United States in 1921 expecting its imminent "sovietization." When confronted with the *Mercury* article, the paper stated, Parry had explained it as a "humorous caricature of Soviet attitudes towards America." The *Tribune* doubted Parry's word on this point, and noted that the Communist party in Chicago was active in the campaign against the paper. Parry wrote the *Tribune* to deny its various innuendos. He noted that FFF refused to cooperate with local communists under any circumstances. The paper refused to print his letter.[31]

Meanwhile the effort to create a rival morning daily continued. Fight For Freedom kept this their primary goal in Chicago. The committee helped to circulate petitions through which 100,000 persons eventually pledged their support for a new paper. Barber had at least one long discussion with Marshall Field, and came away hopeful that Field would produce a serious challenger to the *Tribune*. The October 3 rally passed a resolution damning the "World's Greatest Newspaper" and promising a warm welcome for the proposed competitor. When arrangements for the new daily neared completion, its editor, Silliman Evans, sponsored a contest to name the new challenger. Among more than 222,000 entries, an overwhelming majority of respondents chose the "*Sun*" as the title. Field accepted the verdict over his personal favorite, "The McCormick Reaper." After long months of effort, the *Sun* first appeared in Chicago on December 4, 1941.[32]

Fight For Freedom never attempted to become a mass membership organization in Chicago. The chapter instead sought to broaden its base of support by cultivating allies among established interest groups. To do so, FFF followed paths blazed by CDA and America First.

One obvious prospect was the Committee to Defend America. Beginning in June 1941 and continuing until Pearl Harbor, Barber made repeated overtures to merge the two chapters. All the local FFF leaders favored such a move, and Barber reported that a majority within CDA endorsed the idea as well. The stumbling block was Harland Allen. For unrecorded reasons he balked at a merger. Below the level of Allen's office, cooperation occurred anyway. The Rockford CDA chapter sent Barber its membership list and requested mailings of FFF literature. Former members of the defunct Hyde Park CDA suggested that Barber might wish to take over their former headquarters as an FFF outpost. Fight For Freedom enjoyed good relations with Paul Douglas and many of the other remaining CDA leaders. During the congressional debate over final modification of the Neutrality Act, as an example, Douglas telephoned a wavering congressman at Barber's request in an attempt to retain the man's vote.[33]

Fight For Freedom's solicitations to ethnic groups were more successful than its overtures to CDA. The Scandinavians of the Chicago Danish Committee and the Swedish Provincial Society of America helped FFF to stage the rally of August 25. Fight For Freedom sought cooperation from Eastern European organizations, blacks, and even some Italian groups. Their efforts brought mixed results. The staff of the *Chicago Defender* refused to look at

FFF literature. Parry obtained private funding to establish a Negro Division within the chapter, but the move fizzled when he was unable to locate a suitable person to run its operations. Fight For Freedom also tried to approach black groups through contacts in organized labor, only to meet with indifference and hostility once again. Other groups were more receptive. The local Eastern European press used FFF announcements, and Barber saw that advance word of upcoming rallies reached all their editors. Fight For Freedom soon went farther and began to design meetings around specific ethnic groups. For "Honor the Heroes" Day, October 23, they featured Greek and Yugoslav folk groups. The Chicago FFF chapter and the Czechoslovak National Alliance cosponsored a rally in mid-November, at which Dorothy Thompson and Jan Masaryk delivered speeches. This gathering drew 3,000 people to the International Amphitheater. Albert Parry had contacts with the Mazzini Society. He managed to convince this group to help sponsor a rally specifically aimed at Italian-Americans. They planned to hold it on December 7.[34]

The Italian community in Chicago had remained almost mute throughout the foreign policy debate. In April 1941, however, an incident interrupted their silence. John F. Arena, editor of a local Italian-language newspaper, *La Tribuna*, was killed in a style that indicated a professional job. Some months prior to the shooting, Arena had been ousted from another local newspaper, *L'Italia*. The *Daily News* identified *L'Italia*'s owner, Philip D'Andrea, as a former chieftain in the Capone mob. Arena's widow told of receiving threatening phone calls demanding that her husband cease a series of articles he was writing for *La Tribuna* on the activities of Italian Fascists in Chicago. Arena had charged that the Italian consulate was a center of subversive activities. Police officials stated that the consul, Dr. Ricardo Moscati, had refused to cooperate with an investigation of *La Tribuna*'s allegations, terming the matter "too small" to concern him. Arena had promised to name local firms that the consulate had pressured into running advertisements in *L'Italia*. Information supplied by the Federal Bureau of Investigation suggested that at one time Arena himself had been pro-Fascist, with direct connections to Italy. Only hours before his murder, the slain editor had consulted with aides from the Dies Committee about testifying on the activities of OVRA, the Italian secret police, in Chicago. Chairman Dies, a man much given to political conspiracy theories, endorsed the supposition that political subversives had assassinated Arena.[35]

Although the facts behind the Arena affair never came to light, the episode provided a tantalizing glimpse into the seldom-seen undercurrents of Chicago's Italian community. Anti-Fascist sources told *Daily News* reporter Frank Smothers that they believed Arena had always remained loyal to Mussolini. He had, however, fallen out with members of the consulate. The sources alleged that Dr. Moscati's office controlled most of the city's Italian societies but that popular opinion mistrusted and resented the consulate. As a result, the Italian War Relief Fund raised less than $3,000 from among Chicago's nearly 330,000 Italian-Americans. If feelings ran cool toward Il Duce, neither was there an outpouring of anti-Fascist sentiment. Elsewhere, in St. Louis and New York for example, anti-Fascist organizations were formed among Italians, but not in Chicago.[36]

Italian-Americans in other cities also kept whatever sympathy they had for fascism muted. Following the Arena killing, the Department of Justice began a national investigation into threats against prominent American anti-Fascists. Only one person, New Jersey writer Geofredo Pantaleoni, reported receiving threats. A study in New York by the American Council on Public Affairs found that only 5 percent of the city's Italian-Americans were Fascists, though 35 percent were described as either sympathetic or susceptible to Fascist views. A tenth of those surveyed were determinedly anti-Fascist, while 50 percent of the sample were classified as apolitical. Most Italian-Americans, the study reported, felt completely assimilated into American life. The Council did find evidence of extensive propaganda efforts by the Italian diplomatic corps, which controlled or influenced much of the Italian-language media.[37]

Chicago's German-Americans were only slightly more outspoken on both sides of the foreign policy debate than the city's Italians. Swastika flags once again adorned the speaker's platform at the German Day Picnic, prompting Mayor Kelly to avoid the affair this year. Some Chicagoans attempted to encourage anti-Nazi sentiment by starting a local chapter of the German-American Congress for Democracy. Organizers gave up in despair when only seventy-five persons, most of them elderly, attended the Congress's initial meeting at Turner Hall. The largest of such groups nationwide, the Loyal Americans of German Descent, seems not to have had a chapter in Chicago. Pro-Nazi groups also remained quiet, and the Einheitsfront succeeded in avoiding a repetition of the public controversy that had surrounded it during much of the previous year.[38]

Another group maintaining a low profile throughout 1941 was Chicago's Jewish community. Their heavy financial support of the Committee to Defend America did not extend to Fight For Freedom, at least in Chicago. The only time local Jewish leaders commented openly on their role in the debate came as a response to charges made by Charles Lindbergh, who asserted that Jews were a leading faction of the movement to push the United States into war with Germany. Spokesmen for the American Jewish Congress denied Lindbergh's accusations, explaining that their own goals were the same as those of President Roosevelt and most other Americans—to keep America at peace, to strengthen the national defense, and to oppose Hitler. They further insisted that American Jews were divided over foreign policy along lines similar to the public in general. Otherwise, prominent Jewish religious and secular leaders remained silent throughout the debate, more so than in other major American cities. The Rosenwalds of Sears, Roebuck had perhaps more reason than most to speak out, since their senior employee headed the America First Committee. The family not only kept silent, but there is no evidence that they ever brought pressure on Wood because of his actions.[39]

Black Chicagoans remained divided on the proper course to take in response to the ongoing foreign policy crisis. Churches played an especially active role in airing issues. At their annual conference, sixty-two local African Methodist Episcopal churches voted their support for the administration's preparedness policy, while opposing any plan to send American troops overseas to fight. Later the group sponsored a debate on whether the United States should enter the war. A. C. MacNeal, managing editor of the *Defender*, spoke in opposition to entry. Sidney Jones of the Labor Department took the affirmative. In an address to a Los Angeles forum on "War and the Ministry," William Braddan, a prominent Chicago Baptist, told the audience he would preach

war if the United States joined, because Baptists believed in an Old
Testament God. In contrast to the activism of the churches, Fight
For Freedom was invisible in Bronzeville. Local citizens did organize a Committee to Fight for Negro Freedom, but its purpose was
to protest the treatment black soldiers were receiving in the South.
Criticism of the discrimination blacks continued to face in all areas
of the national defense effort formed the most common single
theme in letters printed in the *Defender* throughout 1941. Writers
defended every possible response to the injustice. Amos Washington promised to be a conscientious objector until the military
ended Jim Crow policies. Others, like Ed Petersen and Robert
Higgenbotham, believed that racial progress justified support for
the defense effort, especially in light of Nazi racial attitudes.
Higgenbotham blasted a frequent contributor to the *Defender*'s letter column, calling him a communist and a fifth columnist. Bitterness cropped up everywhere by late 1941.[40]

Organized labor, by contrast, moved into the foreign policy debate to a degree unprecedented prior to 1941. On June 16, several
AFL locals sponsored an "Americanism Day" rally. Mayor Kelly
told the gathering that the welfare of American workers depended
on the defeat of Nazi aggression. The main speaker was Father
Edward J. Flanagan, head of the celebrated home for wayward
juveniles, Boys Town. Father Flanagan urged the nation to meet
the menace posed by fascism and international communism,
though by what means he did not say. Fight For Freedom came to
enjoy cordial relations with Chicago labor leaders, after an initial
period of coolness when CFL headquarters received FFF literature that did not bear the label of a union printer. Barber's office
established an active Labor Division under Abraham Rosenfield.
He worked closely with Arthur J. Goldberg, at that time a young
lawyer active in labor affairs, and Samuel Levin, an official of the
Amalgamated Clothing Workers of America. Levin arranged for
the distribution of FFF leaflets at union functions and Goldberg
provided contacts with various locals. The leadership of the CIO
in Chicago and of the Steel Workers Organizing Committee contained many Poles, who tended to be sympathetic to FFF goals.[41]

Union sentiment swung toward a bolder foreign policy stance
during the summer of 1941. In September the Illinois conventions
of both major labor organizations endorsed Roosevelt's program,

and the CIO issued a strong denunciation of Lindbergh and America First. Fight For Freedom sources indicated that the main factors inhibiting labor activism were a residue of antiwar feeling, virulent antagonism between the AFL and CIO, widespread suspicion of outside propaganda groups among union personnel, and a general predisposition to concentrate their efforts on industrial matters. Local CIO officials detested the *Tribune* and promised full support for the rival *Sun*. The situation with the AFL promised less. Top leaders of the Chicago Federation, many of them aging and parochial in outlook, were reluctant to move beyond their formal endorsements of administration foreign policy. Parry's contacts guessed that only political pressure from Washington or city hall would rouse the Chicago Federation of Labor. In the end, FFF decided to concentrate on the CIO, emphasizing the twin themes of all-out production and repeal of the Neutrality Act. Their efforts bore fruit on November 3, when the Cook County *CIO Newsletter* issued a strong endorsement of neutrality revision.[42]

Fight For Freedom had little specific success with veterans' groups in Chicago. Both major veterans' organizations underwent internal turmoil over foreign policy issues throughout much of 1941. The problem was familiar; some local outposts balked at the policy decrees of the national headquarters. Roosevelt received staunch backing from the national organizations of both the VFW and the American Legion. In April, well before most other groups, the Legion's national committee unanimously endorsed a policy of unlimited aid to Britain, including the idea of convoys. The Illinois state committee followed suit within hours. Dr. Joseph C. Menendez, commander-in-chief of the VFW, issued a similar call before the Cook County VFW Council one month later. But not all local veterans were in accord with official policy. The Cook County American Legion Council voted to decline participation in the Unity Day rally at which Wendell Willkie spoke. Ironically, given the theme of the rally, legionnaires avoided participating because they viewed the affair as too controversial. At the same meeting, the council tabled a resolution that applauded the interventionist stand of outgoing Legion commander, Milo J. Warner.[43]

Clashes within the VFW emerged into public view early in August, when newly elected Illinois commander Earl Southard was suspended by the national headquarters and faced court-martial

on charges brought by his own post. Southard was secretary of the
Citizen's Keep America Out of War committee, the Chicago-based
antiwar group led by William Grace and Avery Brundage. Members of Southard's post charged him with disloyalty to the United
States for distributing a CKAOW handbill that contained the message: "H.R. 1776 [the Lend-Lease Bill] is as viciously unconstitu-
tional as anything ever advocated by a tyrannical government or
king or legislature, either local or foreign. Like the Stamp Act and
other tyrannical acts, it calls for NO OBEDIENCE from free men and
women." The maximum penalty facing Southard was dishonorable
discharge from the organization. William J. Grace, a lawyer and
Southard's fellow member in both the VFW and CKAOW, served
as his attorney. With 400 uproarious spectators looking on, the
trial got underway on August 20. The court ignored Southard's
plea of innocence and summarily declared him guilty. He received
a reprimand and a suspension from the organization. But the case
was not yet settled. Friends appealed the decision on the floor of
the national convention, which took place just days after the trial.
Lengthy and heated debate finally ended when the convention
upheld, on a voice vote, the verdict against Southard. On the same
day antiwar forces succeeded in blocking a proposed resolution
that would have condemned groups opposed to administration
foreign policy. Menendez was evidently impressed by the strength
of antiadministration forces and worked to effect a compromise in
the Southard case, although he refused to appoint a committee to
investigate the court-martial. But he also allowed the convention to
reinstate Southard, so long as the reinstatement required acceptance of the reprimand. Finally, Menendez suppressed an effort
by Grace to present CKAOW views at the convention. There matters ended.[44]

Compared to the internecine warfare within the VFW, the
American Legion convention appeared tranquil. Well aware of the
divided sentiments among its membership, the state organization
tried to straddle foreign policy issues. Its official magazine, the
Illinois Legionnaire, acknowledged that no one could be certain
which policy could best provide for a sound national defense. But
government leaders possessed the most complete information on
the international situation, it said, and were thus in the best position to make a judgment. For that reason members should support

administration foreign policy. The state convention began on August 22, at about the same time as Southard's trial. Illinois leaders expected a bitter debate between Cook County legionnaires, who backed Roosevelt's foreign policy, and the downstate posts, most of whom opposed the president. Within hours after the opening gavel sounded, a dozen antiadministration resolutions clogged the convention's agenda. Roosevelt supporters controlled the organizational machinery and used it to blunt the opposing onslaught. Roland V. Libonati, a Democratic state assemblyman from Chicago, funneled each of the hostile motions to Chicago lawyer George Sugarman's resolutions committee. Sugarman at first combined and toned down the proposals. Then, growing bolder, his committee tabled the lot. Angry anti-Roosevelt forces renewed their drive on the convention floor, again without success. A sharp floor debate culminated in vigorous speeches by United States Senator Scott Lucas and Illinois Governor Dwight Green. Both emphasized the need for united action. The convention then passed a national unity resolution by a voice vote. The administration's friends had finessed their way to a major victory in Illinois.[45]

A similar pattern of events unfolded at the Legion's national convention in Milwaukee during the second week of September. The chief difference was that the national leadership was more firmly in control than state officials had been in Illinois. America First detected the adverse prospects and charged that the Legion chieftains were committed to convoys and to eventual war against Germany. Outgoing national commander Warner rejected these accusations, saying the Legion's only goal was to insure American security. Nevertheless, within a week headlines in the *Daily News* were declaring "Legion Shifts Towards War." Disgruntled Illinoisans charged that Warner had packed key committees with administration boosters. Whatever the truth, the convention reversed the recommendations of its foreign relations committee and approved a series of resolutions favorable to President Roosevelt. They urged repeal of the Neutrality Act, asked for an end to limitations on troop deployment, and pledged firm support for American foreign policy. Even the *Tribune* admitted that these resolutions had encountered only modest opposition, a fact it attributed to "duplicity." Many Illinois legionnaires seemed to agree that they had been hoodwinked. One month after the national convention, the state leadership felt compelled to announce that it would void any local resolution in conflict with the policy set forth at the national convention. The issue provoking this dispute was foreign policy. Legionnaires in Indiana were also disgruntled. One group of Hoosiers actually split off from the national organization in protest over the stance adopted in Milwaukee.[46]

In contrast to the veterans, the League of Women Voters somehow avoided serious controversy for the remainder of 1941. The League lent consistent support to the administration on foreign policy, while chafing at what the women considered inefficiency and ineffective management in the preparedness effort. "Win the Battle of Production" was the slogan attached to the major NLWV campaign of the summer, approved at the May meeting of its general council. In subsequent months, the League came increasingly to focus on the problem of strikes in defense industries. The organization endorsed collective bargaining and was by no means anti-union, but it was impatient with any activity that hindered defense production. This sense of priorities put the League in the position of being a sometime critic, however sympathetic, of the administration and the labor movement. Perhaps this posture helped assuage the feelings of those members who thought the League mistaken in its stance on lend-lease, thus contributing to the relative harmony in subsequent months. It seems more likely, however, that disgruntled members had simply quit or decided to keep silent on foreign policy. The NLWV endorsed repeal of the Neutrality Act, again on the basis of the group's avowed preference for a foreign policy that discriminated against aggressor nations. This time no furor erupted. Proposals to revise the national program regarding foreign policy all leaned toward greater belligerency, not a lessening of involvement.[47]

The University of Chicago campus was less harmonious, though the strength of administration advocates continued to wax. Many aspects of the national debate were reproduced there in microcosm. The campus witnessed the same hardening of attitudes on both sides, with an attendant lessening of tolerance, which had come to characterize the country at large. This was true despite a continued stress upon the principles of free speech by some elements of the university community.

One example of the grimmer resolve and the strains on free

speech was the editorial policy of the *Daily Maroon*. Late in March the paper reversed its earlier sympathies for striking workers in defense industries. The *Maroon* emphasized that on no account should war production be delayed, although it rejected antistrike legislation and worried that union disruption of the armament effort might provoke a wave of repression. The paper evidenced less sympathy for President Hutchins's foreign policy views than on previous occasions. Though still respectful and perhaps even susceptible to some of his arguments, the *Maroon* attacked Hutchins for oversimplifying the dilemma facing America. The choice was not a simple one between war and peace, but involved consideration of the quality of life to be led in the future. America might remain at peace and yet find her existence harsh and morally repugnant in a world dominated by Adolf Hitler. By April 1941 the *Maroon* had come out for American entry into the war. This stance was based on the goal of "democratic revolution," by which the paper meant a resolve to combat both the forces of totalitarianism and those who wished for a return to traditional modes of power politics and imperialism. Later editorials elaborated on this implied criticism of Britain and France and called for an open elaboration of their war aims.[48]

Relative to Chicago's two leading newspapers, the *Daily Maroon* mixed a large portion of balanced coverage and defense of free speech with its attacks on antiadministration forces. The radical left dominated antiwar organizations on campus through the spring of 1941 and received persistent criticism from the *Maroon*. One peace rally was labeled a "circus" and pronounced "barren of ideas." But the *Maroon* defended certain administration critics, such as Lindbergh and Hutchins, with whom it respectfully disagreed. An editorial decried Roosevelt's use of the term "copperhead" against Lindbergh as an unwarranted attempt to inhibit freedom of expression. The *Maroon*'s "Bull Session" column continued to air a variety of viewpoints on all issues. Trotskyites were as likely to appear as young Democrats.[49]

After classes resumed for the fall semester, signs again pointed to a wide awareness of the war on campus. Because many freshmen believed that they would soon be entering the armed forces, enrollments soared in courses with immediate practical value. Whether expectations of war were held as widely as at Fordham,

where 82 percent of the students expected imminent American
entry, is not recorded. However, a new round of campus rallies
and demonstrations took place. Now proadministration forces
were clearly ascendent, although a determined contingent of antiwar activists persisted in making themselves heard.[50]

Once again issues bearing on the war filled the pages of the
Daily Maroon. What remained of the American Student Union announced that it was continuing its policy of supporting all measures for the defeat of fascism. The *Maroon* dated this attitude
from June 22, 1941—the German invasion of Russia—and doubted
that the left enjoyed much credibility on campus following its latest
abrupt reversal of policy. Other observers agreed with this assessment. On November 12 a coalition of pacifist organizations staged
the largest antiwar rally held at the university that semester, to
protest against the dispatch of any new American expeditionary
force to Europe. A crowd of 300 attended this "No AEF, No War"
demonstration and heard Professor Maynard Kreuger assail the
nation's fixation with Hitler. Krueger stressed that the sources of
the current conflict were more complex than popular opinion understood. The image of a madman set loose on a peaceful world
oversimplified the realities of international rivalries and competi-
tion for resources. Administration forces were active as well. Led
by Lloyd Warner, they grew more extreme in their program. At a
late October "V" rally, Warner drew cheers when he called for a
declaration of war on Germany. Other speakers denounced America First as a greater foe, albeit an unwitting one, than either the
communists or the Axis. The crusade against dissenters had come
to the university. Early in November, Warner called for a ban on
all those whose aim was to obstruct the defense effort and for the
arrest of their leaders. Among the targets of Warner's attack were
the German-American Bund, Gerald L. K. Smith, Father Charles
Coughlin, and "a large number of people using America First as a
cover."[51]

A series of editorials outlined the *Maroon*'s own position on the
international situation. The paper again declared itself in favor of
all-out aid to any nation fighting the Axis alliance. It acknowledged that this policy would probably result in full American participation in the European fighting. War with Germany was inevitable in any case, the paper believed, unless Hitler was defeated.

Furthermore, America could not take her rightful place in the eventual postwar reconstruction of the world unless she assumed a full role in bringing about the victory.[52]

The *Maroon* also addressed the major dilemma facing American policy in the autumn of 1941, whether victory or peace was the paramount goal. At the outset of its discussion, the *Maroon* noted that German actions had destroyed the belief that nations behaved according to the guidelines established by international law. Given the current state of anarchy, the question of whether or not America should be involved in the war was a separate one from whether or not to declare war. The *Maroon* then proceeded to laud both Roosevelt and the American public for their cleverness in discerning this distinction. The United States was wise to ignore anachronistic legalities while involving itself in the war. The paper's awareness of the American position, and its approving ascription of a rational design to the policy that helped to bring about that position, suggested that the *Maroon* was still wedded to peace rather than to victory. At least it was satisfied for the moment with a program of limited war. Like Roosevelt and many of his supporters, the *Maroon* was unwilling to engage in a vigorous campaign to alter public opinion by preaching the necessity for total war. The student paper had come closer to confronting the basic issue than either of Chicago's two principal newspapers, and its devotion to peace is therefore especially revealing.[53]

Neither the Committee to Defend America nor Fight For Freedom was even this bold. The CDA had all but ceased to exist. Its only major activity was an extended speaking tour downstate by Paul Douglas. While the subject of each of his addresses was the need to support administration foreign policy, in fact the Chicago alderman was testing the waters for a possible senatorial campaign in 1942. Douglas confined his speeches to the "aid short of war" formula, using arguments unchanged from the winter of 1940–41. The only difference was his inclusion of Japan as an enemy who had to be stopped.[54]

Fight For Freedom was a more vigorous organization, but its policy was little more venturesome than that of the essentially defunct CDA. Following the precedent set by Stevenson's old office, the Chicago chapter of FFF insisted on being treated as a semi-autonomous branch by the national headquarters in New York.

But the group never succeeded in establishing a sound financial base in the Windy City. A fund-raising visit by Herbert Agar in mid-November netted about $9,000, a tenth of what FFF had hoped to generate. Since Fight For Freedom rallies usually produced a deficit of around $5,000, the lack of funds curtailed the level of activity the group could sustain. Less apparent were the reasons for its restraint on policy matters. Fight For Freedom in Chicago was militant in little more than name. Perhaps older leaders such as Denison Hull and Clarence Randall were personally not inclined to advocate war. Perhaps they judged public opinion in Chicago unwilling to accept such a course. Whatever the cause, Fight For Freedom never mounted a major local campaign for full-scale military involvement. Administration supporters in Chicago lagged behind their cohorts elsewhere in the boldness and militancy of the policies they advocated. Coupled with a similar policy on the part of the *Daily News*, it meant that there was no prominent voice in Chicago calling for war. Harold Ickes did so at the Sinai Temple Forum in October, but his address received little attention from the local press and did not provoke a public debate.[55]

Elsewhere, especially in New York City, the situation was different. From the latter stages of the lend-lease debate onward, readers of the *New York Times* would frequently have come across calls for full participation. Among those making such a case were Rex Stout, James P. Warburg, the members of the Union for Democratic Action, Allen Dulles, Bishop William T. Manning, Harold Ickes, Frank Kingdom of the local CDA, Herbert Agar of FFF, and numerous authors of letters to the editor. The issue was debated by such groups as the American Academy of Political and Social Sciences and the Young Women's Republican Club. Informed New Yorkers could hardly have avoided encountering the issue at some point in 1941.[56]

A sampling of major metropolitan newspapers reveals that local citizens across the country had begun to raise the war issue by the autumn of 1941. Students entering UCLA heard its president, Robert G. Sproul, declare that the stakes involved in the current struggle justified going to war. In St. Louis, Dr. Frank M. Lahey, president of the American Medical Association, told a gathering of the Southern Medical Association that the United States should declare war. Cleveland hosted a prowar rally in early November. Later that month, Harvard professor Sidney Fay told a Boston audience that America should send an expeditionary force to Europe without delay. In upstate New York, thirty-eight members of the faculty of Syracuse University issued a similar call.[57]

Given the realities of the international situation, the question of whether the United States ought to enter the war surely deserved to be discussed. How much difference such forthright calls for involvement made is debatable, however. Support for full military participation remained very much a minority position. Furthermore, an October Gallup poll found that in New York City, where proponents of war were most outspoken, support for Roosevelt's foreign policy actually lagged behind the national average. Simultaneously, the Fight For Freedom Committee, whose top leadership had for months been urging Americans to analyze the international situation, discovered divisions within its own ranks over whether to endorse convoys. The need for discussion around the nation was evident. As late as mid-November, after eighteen months of intense debate over foreign policy, almost half the respondents of one survey indicated that they did not have a clear idea of what the war was about.[58]

In Chicago, the two crisis committees viewed themselves as championing administration policy rather than as prodding the policymakers. The committees were unwilling to go farther and faster than Roosevelt indicated, and the president himself refused to travel the last mile into war. As a result, most Chicago spokespersons approached the debate from the same perspective they had employed prior to, and during, the lend-lease controversy. Behind the proposals advocated by most American enemies of fascism was the continuing hope that victory could be won without full United States participation. Neither CDA nor FFF probed into the assumptions underlying government policy or encouraged the public to confront the possibility that defeat of the Axis might require American manpower. Only once did an interest group in Chicago get out ahead of public opinion and the White House, when CDA began advocating convoys in April. Otherwise, the administration's friends eschewed provocative analysis in favor of efforts to undermine their opposition, by fair means or foul, under the banner of national unity. Elsewhere, the voices raising the issue of war were stronger, but the trend toward the use of invective was just as great. Nowhere did the proponents of intervention achieve the unity they sought. They won every important domestic battle, but left the course of war abroad very much in doubt.

SEVEN

ATTACK AND COUNTERATTACK

The failings of leadership among interventionists were not apparent to their opponents in Chicago. Roosevelt enjoyed a series of tactical successes, from the occupation of Greenland to the final revision of the Neutrality Act, which screened the deeper flaws in his policy from the eyes of most contemporaries. Antiadministration forces remained convinced that Roosevelt and his supporters had determined long ago to take the United States into the fighting abroad. They believed that only the continuing public rejection of an immediate declaration of war had frustrated FDR. The opposition constantly cited opinion polls that attested to the widespread public wish for peace. Consistently high attendance at their own meetings reinforced the conviction among the leadership of America First and the other antiwar groups that their cause retained majority support. But time after time the president undertook actions which brought the country ever deeper into the spreading world conflict. Every step seemed to increase the likelihood that America would become a full belligerent. Many antiadministration leaders in Chicago believed that their fundamental task was to bring Roosevelt's supposed designs into direct confrontation with popular antiwar sentiment. In such a contest the antiwar forces were certain that the president would have to yield. Their inability to force such a confrontation, together with the succession of Roosevelt's accomplishments during 1941, alarmed, angered, and frustrated antiadministration forces.[1]

Repeated attacks on the integrity of many domestic critics further fueled their resentment. As befitted a diverse movement, their members reacted along a variety of lines. Many noninterventionists disparaged the honor and credibility of their opponents with a bitterness equal to anything they received in return. Others struggled to defend themselves on the grounds of free speech. An indeterminate number changed their opinions or were driven into silence. Some redoubled their efforts in the search for a winning strategy, while others gave way to hopelessness and despair. To the end, a core of leadership existed that commanded the energies of a sizable and resolute body of followers. Convinced that their cause was righteous and that it retained majority support, these people persisted in their efforts to prevent the administration from leading the nation into a war that they felt certain would be disastrous for the well-being of the United States.

Wherever they turned in 1941, noninterventionists seemed to encounter hostility and a desire to silence their viewpoint. The America First chapter in Santa Monica, California, was denied permission to use the local high school auditorium for a meeting. The school board explained that America First was so controversial that a gathering was likely to produce disorder. Supporters of the Roosevelt administration packed the Des Moines rally at which Charles Lindbergh made his controversial reference to Jews. Catcalls mingled with cheers as AFC leaders emerged on stage and occasional heckling interrupted the proceedings. In April, O. A. Whitehead, a young actor appearing in a Chicago production of "Life With Father," planned to address a local America First rally. The play's manager, Harry Kline, threatened to discharge Whitehead if he delivered the speech. Kline charged that by associating with "the AFC crowd" Whitehead would hurt business and thus violate a clause in the Actor's Equity contract. A spokesman for Actor's Equity rejected this interpretation. The parties appealed the dispute to the play's New York producers, who eventually sided with Whitehead. These and countless similar incidents were expressions of rising antagonism on both sides of the debate.[2]

Hostility toward administration critics surfaced at all levels. Illinois attorney general George F. Barrett resigned from the National Association of Attorneys General following a dispute over his right to speak. The NBC Blue network had agreed to broadcast his address to the association convention in Indianapolis.

Upon reading sharp criticism of "dictatorship both at home and abroad" in an advance text of Barrett's address, association president Earl Warren cancelled the radio arrangement. Warren suggested that Barrett deliver his message to the attorneys general behind closed doors. Barrett refused and issued a public resignation that combined blasts against Nazism, communism, and the New Deal. The Illinoisan then read his original address over a local radio station. Prior to initiating his cancellation of Barnett's national broadcast, Warren had held a number of conferences with U.S. attorney general Francis Biddle. Whether the two men discussed Barrett is not known, but already foreign policy issues had arisen at the conference. A number of speakers had championed Roosevelt's foreign policy. Under Secretary of War Robert Patterson had endorsed a further extension of aid to the Allies, and both Frank Knox and Senator Thomas Connally of Texas were scheduled to speak on behalf of the administration. With three such prominent spokesmen on hand, it is a mystery why convention leaders bothered to silence the much more obscure representative from Illinois.[3]

Other intimidation occurred even closer to Chicago. Senator Burton K. Wheeler received a threatening letter from "A Citizen's Committee of 100% Americans" following the announcement that the senator would address an America First rally in Rockford. "If you set foot anywhere near here," the letter warned, "well, you shall have no one to blame for what might happen to you—and other copperheads tailing you." Wheeler was granted extensive police protection and spoke without incident. Printed attacks in the *Daily News* on administration opponents were less violent but still malicious. Whenever the paper mentioned Avery Brundage, head of the Chicago-based Citizen's Keep America Out of War committee, it noted that Brundage had been cheered by the crowd at a German-American National Alliance gathering. The paper also referred repeatedly to a National Alliance endorsement of CKAOW. Thus the *Daily News* sought to taint the Chicago-based antiwar organization with disloyalty because of its alleged association with pro-Hitler groups.[4]

The CKAOW and its leaders were vulnerable to such charges. So virulent was the anticommunism of Brundage and William Grace that it all but blinded the two men to the evils of fascism.

Each man added to his anticommunism a pronounced anglophobia and an intense dislike of Roosevelt and the New Deal. Grace
described Great Britain as an enemy of the United States. His
repeated calls upon Americans "to resist presidential efforts to
function under H.R. 1776" represented the sort of frank obstructionism that other antiadministration leaders were desperate to
avoid. Its choice of speakers further underscored CKAOW's right-
wing bias. Featured at the organization's largest 1941 rally were
former senator Rush D. Holt and Gerald L. K. Smith, a lieutenant
of the late Louisiana demagogue, Huey Long. Holt had earned a
reputation as an intemperate critic of Roosevelt and a strident
anticommunist. Smith was an open anti-Semite and a Fascist sym-
pathizer. The general extremism of CKAOW assured that the organization could not become a major force in the debate, but the
committee was sufficiently prominent to embarrass the entire antiwar cause in Chicago.[5]

The most serious example of this type of vilification occurred
soon after the passage of lend-lease. The target was America First.
A St. Louis–based organization, the Friends of Democracy, Inc.,
issued a pamphlet entitled "America First—Nazi Transmission
Belt." The pamphlet contained lurid attacks on AFC. It noted that
both the German-American Bund and Father Charles Coughlin
had expressed foreign policy views similar to elements of the AFC
platform. Readers were told that Bundists had attended America
First meetings. Quotations by Senators Burton Wheeler and Gerald Nye, criticizing aspects of the British imperial system and decrying the influence of international financiers, appeared on the
pamphlet cover alongside excerpts from Adolf Hitler's Jew-baiting
and anti-British diatribes. The pamphlet characterized noninterventionist activity in America as "America First-Aid of the Nazis."[6]

Extreme as these charges were, they received wide publicity and
approval. On the national committee of the Friends of Democracy
were such respected national figures as Lee DeForest, Paul Douglas, Will Durant, and Thomas Mann. These names lent stature to
the group, but in fact none of them knew much about the operations of the Friends and none had seen the pamphlet before it was
issued. The Chicago chapters of Fight For Freedom and the Committee to Defend America received and distributed thousands of
copies of "Transmission Belt." Support for the allegations it con-

tained came from sources as prestigious as the *New York Herald-Tribune*. Angry America Firsters demanded a retraction from the Friends, but L. M. Birkhead, director of the group, defended every word. Birkhead, who styled himself a civil libertarian, contended that the pamphlet "merely stated what is a fact; the America First Committee meetings are being used as rallying places for enemies of democracy." A few Friends of Democracy national committeemen resigned over the affair, but most stood behind Birkhead's intentions even when they did not fully approve of his methods. The pamphlet angered America First leaders and may actually have helped to solidify their ranks. No important defections resulted from the Birkhead attack, but it may have damaged AFC nonetheless. The effects of such a campaign on undecided or ill-informed citizens are impossible to measure in the absence of survey data, but it seems likely that it cost America First potential support.[7]

The controversy that was coming to surround America First did make many of its friends wary of open association with the committee. One important example of such reluctance was University of Chicago president Robert Maynard Hutchins. Personal inclination and a sense of obligation to the university led him to keep his contacts with America First unofficial and discreet. In the wake of the "Transmission Belt" charges, Hutchins and university vice-president William Benton resolved to exercise even greater care in dealing with the committee. "Most certainly, you should avoid all tie-ups, even undercover, indirect ones, with the local chapters of America First," Benton advised in an April 4 memo. Their caution came at a time when Hutchins had reentered the foreign policy debate. Only a few days prior to Benton's memorandum, Hutchins had delivered his second nationally broadcast address on the international situation.[8]

Entitled "The Proposition Is Peace," the new speech reiterated and expanded upon the views Hutchins had introduced in his January broadcast. At the center of his new address were two suppositions. Hutchins rejected the moral legitimacy of limited American involvement in the European war, and he denied the contention that this nation's self-interest required an Axis defeat. If Roosevelt was sincere in his conviction that a "total victory" over Hitler should be the primary goal of United States foreign policy, then, said Hutchins, "we must fight." But he insisted that the country wished for peace above all else. Since the outbreak of hostilities Roosevelt had assured people of his devotion to peace. The Gallup poll indicated that an overwhelming majority of the American public still had no desire to fight. Popular support for the "aid at the risk of war" program, although sincere, rested primarily on the hope that aid lessened the likelihood America would enter the war and, hence, ultimately on the desire for peace. Hutchins affirmed that "the power to decide for peace or war" still rested within the borders of the United States. Therefore, "aid short of war" was not in the national interest.

Hutchins was convinced that public priorities were correct. He denied that the issues at stake in the present war warranted American entry. The Allies, even with Britain at their head, could not by American standards lay claim to the cause of democracy. Aside from the destruction of Hitlerism, their war aims were unknown. Hutchins questioned whether Roosevelt was prepared to insist that Britain observe the Four Freedoms throughout her empire. Did FDR intend a long and exhausting global struggle until his noble ideals were everywhere achieved? Hutchins judged such a prospect too terrible to contemplate.

Above all else Hutchins feared the effects of war on the United States. He forecast that the struggle to subdue the Axis would be long and absorbing. The costs, he predicted, would exceed even the terrible tally in money and men and might jeopardize the political system itself. "If the United States is to proceed through total war to total victory over totalitarian states, it will have to become totalitarian too," he warned. The basis for the organization of the state would have to shift from a means to promote the happiness of its members to a mechanism for waging war. The rights of every citizen would become subordinated to the demands of the machine. With victory would come debt, despair, intolerance, injustice, and a destruction of the capitalist underpinnings of American political freedom. The path Hutchins recommended as an alternative lay toward the realization of American ideals at home. Solving domestic problems would absorb all the country's energies. To fulfill their laudable desire to improve the world, Americans should begin by setting their own house in order, creating thereby an example for the rest of the world to emulate, and restoring the faith of peoples everywhere in the idea of democracy.[9]

The address elicited prompt and vigorous response. Vice-President Henry A. Wallace happened to be in Chicago for a brief visit. He dropped by campus to play tennis, where he was queried by an enterprising *Maroon* reporter. Wallace reaffirmed that peace did indeed remain the administration's principal goal. He evaded further questions on whether the government was willing to accept the defeat of Great Britain as the price for avoiding hostilities. Other commentators took on Hutchins more directly. A *Maroon* editorial contended that he overestimated the certainty that war would induce militarization and totalitarianism in the United States. The *Daily News* criticized his belief that the country could remain at peace via unilateral action. The course of the war abroad would have a decisive influence on the nation's future. The logic of Hutchins's position, said the *News*, suggested that he was pro-Nazi. Hutchins doubted that the Allies could win unless America joined the hostilities, but he did not wish the country to do so. Therefore, said the *Daily News*, he must wish for an Axis victory.[10]

Five members of the university faculty responded to the address a week after its delivery. The group included Paul Douglas and the deans of both the Business School and the Humanities Division. The most penetrating reply among the five came from associate professor of political science Jerome C. Kerwin. Like the *Daily News*, Kerwin disagreed with Hutchins concerning the degree to which America could remain unaffected by the impact of events in Europe. "Whether we get involved in the war or not," said the political scientist, "will be determined not by us, but by the man who sits on the seat of the mighty in Berlin—he will decide." Kerwin dismissed any idea that the problem facing America was a simple dichotomy between war and peace. The vital issue was aid and whether the free nations of the world could pool their resources before Germany overcame each one individually. Kerwin agreed with Hutchins that domestic problems merited attention, but the professor deemed the threat from fascism so real and pressing that it took precedence over all other considerations. Hitler, Kerwin believed, was unlikely to give the United States the opportunity to achieve "national perfection."[11]

The campus debate sparked by the Hutchins speech attracted wide attention beyond the confines of the university. In an effort to disseminate the views of Hutchins and his critics to all interested parties, the *Maroon* issued a special supplement containing the complete texts of both the president's address and the five faculty replies. It sold a record 16,900 copies, many of them in downtown Chicago. Most of the thousands of letters Hutchins received in response to his broadcast were favorable. After surveying the mail, Benton wrote to Ralph Ingersoll that it seemed as if "it's the poor and the great inarticulate mass of people who are against intervention. The word 'inarticulate' appears thousands of times in the mail Bob is receiving." Benton believed that Hutchins had evoked such a massive response because he had represented a viewpoint that countless people were unable to express for themselves.[12]

Students at the University of Chicago received Hutchins's views more favorably than the faculty. Spot interviews conducted by the *Daily Maroon* indicated that most students were impressed by his position. Despite its basic disagreement with Hutchins, the *Maroon* moved in the aftermath of his address to endorse a pair of proposals similar in spirit to points Hutchins had made. Americans, the paper declared, focused too much on the "archdevil" Hitler in their definition of the current world struggle. The United States should stand for "democratic revolution" throughout the world as an alternative to reactionaries as well as to totalitarians. Soon thereafter the *Maroon* called upon the British to detail the general principles and specific aims for which they fought. The terms of the editorial implied that the worthiness of these goals could influence the degree of American support for Britain. The *Maroon* did not reveal what contribution Hutchins's speech had made toward its new criticism of American and Allied policy, but in fact the tenor of its editorials in the weeks following his address was uncharacteristic of the paper's general position. Whatever effects Hutchins was able to produce on campus were of secondary importance, however, if the *Maroon* is any measure. He failed to alter its basic outlook on foreign policy and the war.[13]

Among the faculty Benton found wide dislike and misperception of Hutchins's position. Many were unclear as to how much aid for Britain he favored. A substantial number believed that Hutchins wished to curtail supplies altogether. His views on American military preparedness were also suspect. Other faculty members agreed with Dean William Spencer of the Business School, who considered Hutchins an impractical perfectionist whose preoccupation with achieving utopia ignored contemporary world realities. Benton believed that Hutchins had failed to convey his point on this matter. He actually expected that only a few modest reforms would be possible in the near future and desired above all else to avoid a retrogression from the New Deal. Finally, Benton found that Hutchins had not communicated to the faculty his awareness that the country must choose between evils. Hutchins himself detested Hitler, but feared the effects of war even more than the spreading sickness of totalitarian aggressions.[14]

Led by Quincy Wright, Roosevelt supporters among the faculty sought to arrange a debate with Hutchins. William Benton favored this idea, both because he believed that Hutchins could outshine any potential opponent and because he was searching for a means to promote noninterventionism on the "University of Chicago Round Table," the university's popular public affairs radio program. The debate never occurred, possibly because Hutchins refused to become tied down to the foreign policy controversy. Undaunted, Benton persisted in his quest to use the "Round Table" to explore "the problem of intervention." He was "not a bit satisfied" that administration critics had used the program to advantage and he hoped to provide opportunities to improve this record. He also viewed the foreign policy debate as an opportunity to advance the status of the "Round Table," and with it, the university as a national institution. To do so, Benton wished to undertake a series of broadcasts featuring Wheeler, Lindbergh, Hutchins, Knox, and other figures prominent in the controversy. Benton contacted the leading noninterventionists through Douglas Stuart and America First. But again he was unable to arrange the spectacular clashes which he had envisioned.[15]

Early in July, the "Round Table" became the scene of a major controversy of a different type. On the program's production staff was a young researcher, Richard M. Scammon, who was an ardent member of the Fight For Freedom Committee chapter then forming in Chicago. The army had drafted Scammon and he was due for induction in mid-August. After conferring with his fellow FFF members, probably Parry and Barber, Scammon decided to challenge General Robert Wood of the America First Committee to a public debate. The fledgling chapter hoped thereby to reap needed publicity and launch its Chicago activities with a major rally. Scammon informed his immediate superior at the "Round Table," Sherman Dryer, of his intention to leave the staff in order to speak on behalf of Fight For Freedom. Dryer agreed to let Scammon depart, although further details of their conversation soon became a subject of dispute.[16]

The problem developed because Scammon's intentions became public knowledge the same evening. Whether through misunderstanding or design, someone at the FFF chapter office gave the story to reporter Frank Smothers of the *Daily News*. The July 10 edition carried a public challenge by Scammon for a debate with Wood on the merits of the American occupation of Iceland.[17]

The following morning Dryer held a stormy conference with Benton. Not only did Benton condemn Scammon's stand on foreign policy, but the public challenge to Wood violated "Round Table" policy that its staff refrain from any public activity that might threaten the program's carefully cultivated image of impartiality. The two men discussed what to do about Scammon, with Benton directing considerable personal abuse at the young researcher. Benton later telephoned Dryer and told him to have Scammon resign immediately and cease all duties, but to continue paying him until the date Scammon had wished to quit, August 4. This was Benton's longstanding practice in dealing with departing employees.[18]

In the charged climate that existed during the summer of 1941, the attempt by Benton to bring the incident to a swift and silent conclusion died stillborn. Dryer was indiscreet when he talked with Scammon, disclosing details of Benton's comments concerning Scammon and the proposed debate with Wood. Shortly thereafter Scammon began talking with the press. He charged that Dryer had threatened to dismiss him, that Benton had demanded his ouster, and that due to his foreign policy views the university had reneged on a promise to grant him additional severance pay for joining the armed forces. Scammon believed himself to have been wronged, but he also saw an opportunity to publicize Fight For Freedom in Chicago. A plea from Benton prompted the *Daily*

News to kill the story, but it ran in the *Chicago Times*, the *New York Times*, *PM*, and the *St. Paul Pioneer Press*. Reporters from *Time* magazine questioned the participants but no article resulted. In the course of being interviewed, Benton—hardly an unbiased witness—gained the impression that the eastern press was seeking to use the affair to attack America First. Several reporters had suggested that the "Round Table" administration had acted out of fear that the university might lose financial support. Robert Wood and Lessing Rosenwald of America First were generous contributors to the school. The matter also attracted the attention of Secretary Ickes in Washington, who wrote Hutchins inquiring as to the facts of the Scammon case.[19]

Reaction on campus was also swift and hostile to the university administration. Most students had left for summer vacation, but a group of six faculty members pressured the administration on Scammon's behalf. At the head of the effort were two sociologists, Louis Wirth and Lloyd Warner, both of whom were in Fight For Freedom. They sent Hutchins a letter demanding a thorough investigation of the treatment given Scammon and raising the issue of bias with regard to foreign affairs programming on the "Round Table." The six professors suggested that a faculty advisory committee be set up to oversee the program. Although cool to this last idea, Hutchins did direct Benton to conduct a complete inquiry into the case and promised the Warner group that they would have access to the results. Meanwhile the faculty members interviewed both Scammon and Dryer in an attempt to ascertain for themselves whether or not the dismissal represented an abridgment of the right of free speech.[20]

Benton and his aides set about their investigation early in August. The university administration was still fearful of adverse publicity. At least one aide urged Hutchins to appoint a rival committee composed of friendly faculty members to offset anticipated criticism from Warner and the others. Cooler heads prevailed and the administration adhered to a policy of refusing to comment on the case in hopes that public attention would wither. Benton also continued his behind-the-scenes efforts with newspapermen. "Obviously the key here is to try to kill every possible story, to keep as much out of print as possible," he wrote to Dryer. This strategy was successful. After the initial wave of hostile coverage, the press lost interest. Repercussions among alumni and other academicians were modest.[21]

Meanwhile the official investigation continued. Hutchins forwarded statements from Benton, Dryer, and Scammon to three independent parties for judgment. Deans Spencer and Huth of the university administration and Chicago lawyer Laird Bell comprised the committee. If anything, these men were biased in Scammon's favor. Spencer had differed openly with Hutchins on the aid issue and Bell was a member of CDA and FFF. On balance, however, their reports favored Benton and Dryer. The harshest criticism of the university came from Bell. In light of the outspoken stances taken by Hutchins and Benton, he considered it "absurd" that the university required its administrative staff to refrain from open involvement in public controversies. Added Bell, "I submit that a neutral observer would find it hard to say that Scammon's interventionist activities had no part in his being relieved of his duties." Nevertheless, Bell admitted that no hard evidence existed to prove impropriety in the action. The lawyer confined his formal recommendations to an award of additional severance pay to Scammon. Huth believed that Scammon had no grounds for complaint whatsoever, and Spencer likewise denied that the university had acted improperly.[22]

The findings of the administration's own confidential report confirmed these conclusions. Central to the dispute was whether Dryer, in the meeting following the publication of Smothers's article, did in fact threaten to discharge Scammon unless he resigned immediately and, if such was the case, whether Benton had dictated such a policy out of political prejudice. The report concluded that Benton would have taken similar action had politics not been a factor. While accepting Scammon's assertion that Dryer indeed had threatened him with outright dismissal, the report rejected the notion that Dryer had acted from political prejudice. Scammon soon left for the army and the affair came to an end.[23]

There remained the allied issue of faculty supervision of "Round Table" programming, which by that time carried overtones of the larger foreign policy debate. John Howe, who prepared the confidential report for Benton, believed that the question of supervision had come to be the chief interest of the Warner group by the middle of August. In separate discussions with both

Warner and Wirth, Howe found each man dissatisfied with Dryer and Benton. An element of personal dislike was involved, but a more fundamental source of faculty discontent was the conviction among many that Benton and Dryer had emphasized showmanship over intellectual quality in choosing subjects and guests for the "Round Table." Wirth, Warner, and several other professors also believed that the program had been "unduly isolationist" in light of American national policy. To this faction, a faculty advisory committee appeared to be a useful corrective to shortcomings of the program's current staff. An advisory committee would also serve as a means to further promote their own foreign policy views.[24]

The Scammon episode thus had evolved into another effort by supporters of Roosevelt's foreign policy to undermine the presumed influence of their critics. In this case the drama played against a backdrop of campus politics and, perhaps, of personal jealousy. Alarmed, Hutchins and Benton had moved to defend the status quo at the "Round Table." Their motives had less to do with a desire to promote a political viewpoint, or even to uphold freedom of speech, than to prevent the creation of a committee whose members understood themselves to have a vested interest in the program and therefore a preferential claim to its guest spots. Neither Hutchins nor Benton believed that the program had shown any bias against Roosevelt supporters. Benton contended that the reverse held true. He noted that one leading America First spokesman, author John T. Flynn, had declined a recent invitation to appear on the "Round Table" due to its allegedly pro-Roosevelt orientation. In any case, the Warner group achieved even less than Scammon. Hutchins succeeded in routing their proposal for a supervisory committee to that traditional graveyard for unwanted ideas, the Faculty Senate, where it languished throughout the fall. By that time, too, the episode no longer agitated the campus. In itself the episode was of minor importance. That it attracted national attention illustrates how charged the atmosphere surrounding foreign policy questions had become in 1941.[25]

The university was far from quiet that autumn. In a new round of foreign policy debates, arguments remained similar to those of the previous spring. Supporters of Roosevelt revived their attacks on administration critics. Both Hutchins and Benton kept silent, leaving such figures as Maynard Kreuger to bear the burden of the antiwar cause. The Socialist party and the various pacifist groups on campus supplied most of the organizational backing for several peace rallies. They drew crowds equivalent to those attending proadministration meetings, but neither side was able to attract numbers close to those of the previous academic year. While a core of activists kept the discussions alive, most campus members seemed content to follow the government's lead and await events.[26]

This attitude of acquiescence was what America First and the other antiadministration groups were determined to combat. They admitted to having been badly, but not fairly, beaten on the lend-lease issue. If some of their leaders despaired, most of the key figures remained convinced that their cause of keeping America at peace retained public support. Many found encouragement in the belief that, as Roosevelt edged closer to open involvement, the public would grow more aware of the risks inherent in his policies and would demand an end to presidential meddling in events abroad. But the fundamental problem facing America First and like-minded organizations was to find some means by which their popular support could be channeled into decisive political influence.

Alone among the antiwar groups in Chicago, America First endured as a true mass organization throughout 1941. The Citizen's Keep America Out of War committee faded from view as it became a forum for right-wing fanatics to heap criticism on the administration. The most prominent of the independent women's groups in Chicago, We, the Mothers, Mobilize for America, could draw only 150 women to a meeting at the LaSalle Hotel in September. Pacifists retained a small following on campus and among certain church groups. Dr. Albert W. Palmer, president of the Chicago Theological Seminary and editor of *Christian Century*, headed a clergyman's antiwar group, the Minister's No-War Committee. They received generous publicity from the *Tribune*, but never became active with the public. Aside from these modest allies, and a score of more ephemeral groups, America First spoke for antiwar feeling in the Chicago area.[27]

Following the passage of lend-lease, the AFC soon shook off its disappointment. America First concentrated upon enlarging its membership and developing contacts with other types of organizations. The Chicago chapter sent letters to around 300 civic, church, and neighborhood groups in the metropolitan area, offering to furnish AFC speakers for local meetings. Committee spokespersons remained busy through March and April, but activity centered on a recruitment drive. The goal of the Chicago chapter, which supervised downstate operations as well, was to amass a state membership of one million. Each current member received ten application forms that they were to circulate among friends and associates. For weeks thereafter the *Tribune* trumpeted the gains as Illinoisans flocked by the thousands to join the struggle against war. Given the often fictitious nature of *Tribune* figures, the actual increase is impossible to tabulate. However, even the largest published figure, 135,000 for the state, fell far short of AFC's ostensible goal. Whatever the true amount, increases were dramatic. Committee leaders reported that the Illinois rolls had doubled since the beginning of 1941. Another sign of expansion was the founding of new chapters. By the middle of April, sixty AFC chapters existed throughout the state, with thirteen in Chicago alone. This figure is also misleading, for America First listed as chapters some local groups which were little more than kaffeeklatsches. Nationwide, for example, the Executive Committee considered only 148 of AFC's 648 units to be full-fledged chapters. Still, the numbers cannot be dismissed, and AFC leaders had ample reason to be proud of their strength in Illinois.[28]

Capping these efforts were a pair of mass meetings held in Chicago during the second half of April. Charles Lindbergh and Senator Burton Wheeler were the featured speakers. Such gatherings accomplished a variety of purposes. Of course the speakers spread AFC's latest message. Wheeler, for example, began to focus attention on the convoy issue. Aside from conveying messages, the mass meetings served to invigorate existing committee members and to recruit new ones. During slack periods, local AFC chapters often asked the national office to organize a major rally as a means of widening interest in the committee. While there are no figures for membership following the Chicago meetings, a Lindbergh rally in New York City during the same period brought 7,000 new recruits to the ranks of America First.[29]

The performance of individual chapters was affected by local conditions no less than by the mass meetings, the recommendations of AFC headquarters, or the ebb and flow of public affairs. The dedication and energy of local leaders, the cooperation of community media, and the availability of nearby resources all figured as keys to the success of a chapter. The same factors shaped the pattern of its operations. In areas such as Evanston, where a major university and a highly educated population provided a large reservoir of talent, chapters relied on local speakers and tended to meet as frequently as once a week. Where the ready fund of orators was thinner, chapters held fewer meetings and tried to attract prominent outsiders as centerpieces for their gatherings. The Rockford group, for example, favored political figures. Several antiwar congressmen addressed rallies there.

Wide variations existed in the quality, effectiveness, and the message of speakers at these local chapter meetings. Detailed records kept by the Evanston chapter during the autumn of 1941 suggest the diversity of arguments that could reach a single America First outpost. Five different speakers appeared in a period of seven weeks. Each was a Chicagoan of no special reputation. Two were lawyers and two were clergymen. The subjects of their addresses reflected the assorted viewpoints to be found among the forces arrayed against American involvement. The initial speaker described the conflict in Europe as a clash between rival economic systems. He denied that any single nation was responsible for the war and urged the United States to return to the principles of traditional neutrality. The following week Evanston AFCers heard a diatribe against American interventionists. The speaker alleged that they were prepared to subvert the Constitution if necessary to bring about a declaration of war. This man dismissed the risks of invasion or economic warfare against the United States as "bogeymen." The third speaker delivered a strong moral condemnation of war. His position flirted with outright pacifism, a stance at variance with national committee policy. Although the fourth speaker was a minister, his message substituted vehement anticommunism for the religious homilies of his predecessor. No one in Europe cared about America, declared the minister, so there was no reason for Americans to embroil themselves in European troubles. Americans instead should concentrate on ridding the nation of the 150,000 paid agents of the Communist party who, he said, were engaged in subversion. The first speaker returned on November 17 to urge America Firsters to back noninterventionists in Congress. He refused to believe that repeal of the Neutrality Act made war inevitable, and he pleaded with the chapter to redouble its lobbying efforts. He was again followed by the same attorney who had spoken during the second week. The lawyer employed arguments in many ways similar to those of the *Tribune*. He leveled extensive criticism at Great Britain, although he admired the British for pursuing their own self-interest. War would bring economic ruin and dictatorship to the United States and it was thus the duty of every citizen to oppose the administration's scheming. The final speaker echoed this latter theme. He contended that the greatest danger facing America came not from foreign ideology, but from the swelling power of the federal government in Washington. His address mixed bitter criticism of Roosevelt with warm praise for Colonel McCormick and the *Tribune*.[30]

Stray bits of evidence hinted at the response of Chicago audiences to the viewpoints they heard expressed by AFC spokespersons. Like the messages, the reactions varied. Patrick J. Quinn, an elderly Chicagoan, attended a meeting held by the Lincoln Park America First chapter in mid-April 1941. Janet Fairbank addressed the gathering and attempted to divide the nation into patriotic midwesterners and warmongering easterners. Then the featured speaker, Father John A. O'Brien of Notre Dame University, began a long antiadministration harangue. Quinn rose in the audience and denounced the speeches of Fairbank and O'Brien as traitorous. A mob scene ensued. Amidst shouts of "Kill him," "Put him out," and "Go down to Roosevelt," members of the crowd buffeted Quinn, cutting him in several places and breaking his eyeglasses. The police arrived in time to escort him home and no arrests were made as a result of the disturbances. While extreme, Quinn's experience was not wholly uncommon. Many observers noted that jeers often accompanied the mention of FDR's name at large AFC rallies. Yet other crowds rejected Roosevelt-baiting. An audience in Evanston booed AFCer Robert D. Ross for the "blind prejudice and little thinking" contained in his diatribe. In August Mrs. Fairbank warned Chicago chapters to avoid contact with a local movement to impeach Roosevelt, saying "we see no grounds for impeachment, and . . . we will have nothing whatever to do with such a plan." A similar warning went out to all AFC chapters in October, after one of them had passed a resolution favoring impeachment.[31]

Many observers detected a pervasive strain of anglophobia among the rank and file of America Firsters in Chicago and elsewhere. Following his speech to the crowd at the Coliseum on April 17, Charles Lindbergh confided in his diary that he "was also surprised by the amount of anti-British feeling in Chicago." Mention of the British Empire also drew boos at a mammoth AFC rally held in May at New York's Madison Square Garden. Northwestern University professor Howard G. Swann, who addressed dozens of AFC meetings around northern Illinois, observed the same phenomenon. Swann himself had no love for Albion, but he tried with indifferent success to avoid criticism of Britain out of a belief that it would best serve the cause of noninterventionism. Some other speakers showed less restraint. General Thomas Hammond, chairman of the Chicago America First Chapter, deemed Britain unworthy of American aid due to her failure to repay her World War I debts. The Rogers Park chapter heard Mrs. V. O. Joyce, a high school history teacher in Hyde Park, denounce British propaganda as subversive and declare the peoples of her empire "enslaved." British imperialism was also the target of Mrs. Lyrl Van Heineman's early July address to the Oak Park AFC. Yet at the mass meeting addressed by Senator Wheeler, which occurred less than two weeks after the Lindbergh rally, anti-British shouts came from only one small section of the 9,000 boisterous members in attendance. Still, anglophobia occurred often enough in AFC oratory to be a significant theme. But compared to the almost universal denunciation of "foreign wars" it was a secondary element.[32]

Controlling such a diverse assemblage as America First proved to be an impossible job. Although exercising formal command over all America First outposts in Illinois, as well as in Iowa and northern Indiana, the Chicago chapter was able to provide only limited supervision. By May 11 Mrs. Fairbank claimed a membership of over 200,000 for the AFC in Illinois, organized into twenty chapters in the Chicago area and fifty-nine more downstate. Inflated as these figures may be, the continued rapid growth of the committee far outstripped the facilities of the LaSalle Street office

to accommodate it. A lack of coordination between chapters resulted in a continuing undercurrent of friction.[33]

The heart of the problem was structural. America First never
became more than a loose coalition of volunteer citizens' groups.
Local chapters could flout policy guidelines and ignore directives
from regional or national headquarters. On June 26, for example,
a meeting of the chairpersons of the various chapters around Illinois voted to eliminate the normal question-and-answer period after speeches at AFC meetings. Mrs. Fairbank explained that the
committee undertook this action because extremists in the audience were undermining AFC's antiwar message by giving vent to
their personal prejudices. Yet the practice of question-and-answer
periods continued among many Illinois chapters throughout the
autumn. Partially to promote discipline among local chapters,
America First issued a *Chapter Manual* in the summer that emphasized the need to understand and adhere to committee policy and
procedures.[34]

The Chicago office itself constituted as serious a source of disruption as the activities of individual chapters around the state. As
vice-president of the Chicago chapter, Mrs. Fairbank had assumed
control in January over all operations within Illinois. In practice
her authority overlapped with that of Stuart's national headquarters. Local chapters were slow to grasp the new arrangement and
continued to request literature from Stuart, who would comply
and bill the costs to Fairbank. The result was that the Chicago
chapter repeatedly encountered unexpected debts. The two offices also issued duplicate and sometimes conflicting sets of instructions to local outposts. Personal relations between Stuart and
Fairbank had never been cordial. They soured further as the
muddle involving their respective offices persisted throughout the
spring. In an effort to resolve matters, the national headquarters
acceded to a series of demands by Mrs. Fairbank for complete
autonomy in running Illinois. Yet the nationals continued to respond to direct appeals from local groups.[35]

Divided authority confused the subordinate chapters and inefficiency within the Chicago office angered them. In April the Evanston chapter complained to Stuart's headquarters that the friction
between the national and the Chicago offices "made it very difficult for local people to know what to do." Furthermore, the situa-

tion had hindered local initiative. Discontent became so rife that seven Chicago-area chapter leaders appealed for a private meeting with General Wood to air their grievances. Wood agreed to meet with them on June 14. The chapter leaders voiced five major complaints. Because the Chicago office represented a bottleneck for mailings, the chapter heads wished to have the national headquarters mail all bulletins to the local chapters. They also urged that Mrs. Fairbank delegate authority to act on important decisions whenever she was absent from the Chicago office. The chairpersons asked to serve as an advisory body to Mrs. Fairbank's headquarters, and in particular they stressed the need for clear and specific short-term goals. Finally, they desired greater efficiency in the Chicago office's Speakers Bureau. The chairpersons charged that the previous scheduling of speakers had often been inept and unreliable. Furthermore, the local leaders wished "that the censorships which have obviously been imposed" upon the content of speeches be removed.[36]

How much actual change resulted from this meeting is unclear. Staff members at Stuart's office recommended against direct mailings of AFC literature to the chapters and suggested instead that they press the Chicago chapter to handle the task with more dispatch. Committee leaders recognized the need for specific goals, but they were seldom able to provide useful solutions. They refrained from comment on the other points.[37]

Whatever changes did come as a result of the June meeting were insufficient to quiet complaints about how the Chicagoans handled operations in Illinois. One example concerned a situation on the south side of the Windy City. Throughout the spring, the AFC outpost there had been little more than a letterhead on some stationery. Beginning in July, Mrs. Joan Scott had attempted to invigorate things by securing a new chairperson. Three months later Mrs. Scott was still trying to enlist the aid of the Chicago office in her effort. Headquarters staffers finally formulated a plan whereby the south-side supporters would merge with the more energetic Hyde Park chapter. Meanwhile Mrs. Scott wrote to Fairbank in hopes of eliciting her personal intervention in the affair. Mrs. Scott did not attempt to hide dismay when this letter found its way to the Chicago AFC office. "It is now back in the initial department of inertia," she wrote in a last appeal, this time to Stuart's headquarters. After months of delay on the problem, she told them, the Chicago staff had developed an unworkable plan. The national office refused to intercede because they had agreed in midsummer to refrain from any further interference in Mrs. Fairbank's fiefdom. So all the determination and energy exhibited by Mrs. Scott resulted in nothing.[38]

The top leadership of America First had troubles aplenty of its own. Chief among these was an issue raised by the seven Chicago chairpersons in their meeting with General Wood, the need to develop a positive program. If America First was to be successful, wrote the head of the Evanston chapter to Wood and Stuart, it was vital for the committee to come out for "a positive, constructive long range program. As we see it, we cannot forever take a negative program." Her letter went on to emphasize the psychological disadvantages of a consistently negative position and urged committee leaders to push for a negotiated peace in Europe.[39]

Wood and Stuart concurred with this evaluation, and under their guidance America First adopted a series of goals in the remaining months before Pearl Harbor. The first of these came in March, immediately following the passage of lend-lease. Most observers believed that the next step by the administration would be a call for American convoys to Britain, a move which the Committee to Defend America had endorsed already. On April 1 Senator Charles W. Tobey, a New Hampshire Republican, introduced a resolution to prohibit American naval or merchant vessels from being used to transport material to belligerent nations. Within days, America First put its support behind the measure. Although this was a logical decision, in fact the Tobey Resolution was a weak reed upon which to lean. Robert McCormick refused a request from Stuart to lobby for the resolution in the *Tribune* because sources in Washington assured the colonel that Tobey's measure had no chance for adoption. This information proved to be correct. After weeks passed without any move from the White House to endorse convoys, the issue faded.[40]

As committee leaders continued their search for a positive program, they began to return to the idea of advocating a negotiated peace for Europe. This too was a logical course for AFC to pursue, but again one with a remote chance of success. The concept of a negotiated peace at least cut to the heart of what America First sought to achieve, an end to the danger that America would be drawn into war. For Stuart, it offered a potential means to enhance AFC's standing among church groups and reformist circles, something he had all along been trying to promote. His perception of the continuing appeal of a negotiated peace was probably accurate. At a mass meeting of the Ministers' No-War Committee in Detroit, for example, the principal theme was that American policy should be to mediate an end to the war. General Wood agreed with Stuart's intentions, and Senator Wheeler often urged Roosevelt to appeal for negotiations. In June, Stuart discussed the issue with Robert Hutchins and William Benton. Hutchins feared that if America First tried to push Roosevelt into backing a negotiated peace, the wily president might turn the tables on the committee. Suppose Roosevelt championed a bid for peace negotiations, which then proved unsuccessful. He might be able to lead the country into war on the grounds that peace in Europe had proved to be unattainable by any other means. This argument impressed the America Firsters, but by late October Stuart again had taken up the idea with Hutchins. Stuart now contended that conditions in Europe were ripe for a settlement. He believed that Russia would soon be beaten, leaving Germany in control of all Europe from the Pyrenees to the Caucasus. "A clear cut [sic] geographical basis for peace has been established," Stuart wrote to Hutchins. The latest German triumph would surely convince the British that their chances of besting the Nazis were remote. Thus London would be more receptive to a suggestion of negotiations. Stuart admitted that this idea had little popular following in America. But he was convinced it would gain acceptance if publicized. The young national director wanted Hutchins to lead the campaign. Hutchins consented to lend his name to a new ad hoc group to be created for that purpose, but he refused to lead it. There the matter rested at the time of the Pearl Harbor attack.[41]

The continued pursuit by America First of the chimera of a negotiated peace reveals more than just frustration over Roosevelt's tactical successes and their own failure to develop compelling positive alternatives to the policy of aid to the Allies. In particular, the willingness to advocate a negotiated peace indicates how AFC-ers viewed the nature of the war. The differences between their views and the outlook of their opponents were vast. To find the idea of a negotiated peace acceptable in 1941, someone must not have placed much value on a moral distinction between the combating sides. Or the person must have believed either that America lacked the power to change the situation in Europe, or that war itself was a worse evil than fascism. Millions of people on both sides of the Atlantic had come to agree with Winston Churchill that the war was a crusade to defend civilization against a new onslaught of barbarism. *Fortune* surveyed public attitudes regarding the consequences of a Nazi victory. Only five percent of the respondents rated the results of a German victory "not serious." These findings held roughly constant for both upper- and lower-income groups. To those who viewed Nazism with alarm as well as repugnance, a negotiated peace seemed not only a foolishly unworkable dream, dead since Hitler had violated his Munich pledge, but a morally bankrupt concept as well. The idea was so unacceptable as to cast doubt on the motives of its advocates. These suspicions were made worse by AFC's timing. Committee officials reckoned that London was the real obstacle to concluding a treaty due to the stubborn unwillingness of Britons to recognize the hopelessness of their position. So America First tended to push the idea of negotiations just when British fortunes were at their ebb. This reflected a hope that the latest reverse would bring London to face reality at last. But the effect of such timing was to encourage doubts among committee opponents as to its true loyalty. The result was to further poison the atmosphere in which the debate was conducted.[42]

Of course committee leaders were also engaged in efforts to undermine their opponents while they were conducting the ineffectual search for a positive program. Among their major targets were public opinion polls, especially the Gallup Poll. America Firsters accepted and emphasized the pollsters' findings when they supported the antiwar position, especially the figures indicating that a solid 80 percent of the American public opposed an immediate declaration of war. What the committee found perplexing and worrisome was the recurring public support for each new Roosevelt proposal. In their own way, committeemen sought to explain away the central dilemma of the American reaction to the international crisis. Convinced as they were that the public's primary dedication was to peace, America Firsters contended that the proadministration figures came as a result of a deliberate manipulation by the pollsters. In other words, rather than blame the public for its confusion, or the leadership on both sides of the debate for failing to clarify issues, America First indicted the pollsters. They blamed the messenger for the message.

The committee considered two lines of attack in its efforts to discredit the damaging poll results. The first was to challenge the integrity and methodology of the pollsters. Gallup became the chief target. Throughout April and May, Stuart attempted to amass a compelling case against the pollster. Meanwhile, he solicited advice on whether or not to attack Gallup openly. The person whose opinion Stuart most valued was Chester Bowles, a former advertising partner of William Benton who assumed control of the firm when Benton retired. Bowles agreed that the Gallup polls were biased, but cautioned America First to have hard statistics to support any charges it might make. Otherwise, Bowles warned, the public would belittle AFC's criticism as an effort to disguise weaknesses in its position. Stuart sought data and opinions among academic circles to bolster his case. AFC inquiries elicited a meager response, and committee leaders decided to concentrate upon an alternative approach.[43]

Chester Bowles had suggested that the most telling indictment of Gallup might be for another poll to yield different results. Other administration opponents had reached a similar conclusion, and by late spring these alternative tabulations were appearing at various points around the country. The *New York Daily News*, run by McCormick's cousin and former *Tribune* cohort Joseph Patterson, distributed questionnaires to its readers and encouraged them to mail the completed forms back to the paper. New York Congressman Hamilton Fish conducted a similar poll in his home district, which included Franklin Roosevelt's home at Hyde Park. The *Tribune* sponsored a replica of the *New York Daily News* survey. None of these polls was remotely scientific, but the results in Chicago matched those elsewhere. Americans opposed immediate entry into the war by margins of around four to one, or almost exactly what Gallup reported.[44]

America First attempted a more elaborate and scientific procedure. They sought an independent and unimpeachable figure to head this effort, and induced Robert Maynard Hutchins to accept the job. The initial announcement promised an unbiased survey using the most precise methods available. America First would provide financing, but would exercise no influence over the conduct of the polling or its tabulation. Then the whole project came to a sudden halt when the original cost estimates proved to be low and the AFC was unable to secure adequate additional funding.[45]

Still another line of attack that the committee considered seriously was whether to organize a boycott of companies that sponsored certain interventionist-minded radio commentators. In early autumn AFC leaders discussed the possibility of calling for a boycott of the Pure Oil Company, which sponsored H. V. Kaltenborn, and the Jurgens Company, which sponsored Walter Winchell. General Wood even went so far as to write the head of Pure Oil to complain about Kaltenborn's alleged biases. Some committeemen likened the proposed boycott to colonial embargoes of British products during the pre-Revolutionary period. Other America Firsters, such as Sterling Morton, opposed the idea as an infringement of free speech and as unworthy of the standards AFC was trying to maintain in the debate. Morton believed that his salt company had lost some business due to his association with the committee, so there was perhaps an element of self-interest underlying his stance. In any case, committee leaders decided not to adopt the boycott proposal.[46]

The most celebrated—or notorious—incident among America First's diverse efforts to criticize its opponents came in September. Speaking at an AFC rally in Des Moines, Charles Lindbergh charged that the chief impetus for the drift toward war came from three groups within American society. He named the Roosevelt administration, anglophiles, and the Jews. The last reference aroused enormous controversy and brought charges from around the country that Lindbergh and the America First Committee were anti-Semitic. The furor came as a complete surprise to AFC leaders. Lindbergh wrote his own speeches and did not circulate advance copies of his texts. The Des Moines speech was not part of any organized AFC campaign to put its critics, and Jews in particular, on the defensive. But the nature of Lindbergh's address agreed with the broader spirit of the diverse efforts within America First to identify, confront, and discredit its opponents.

The speech also fit with the climate of bitterness that all sides in the debate had helped to foster.[47]

The Des Moines speech brought the issue of anti-Semitism within America First into the open. Lessing Rosenwald had resigned from AFC's national committee in December 1940, charging that he could not agree with the views of some members. He specified neither the persons nor the views in question, but he probably was referring to Henry Ford. In any case, Rosenwald's resignation had attracted little public comment in Chicago. The New York City newspaper *PM* had once accused certain AFC members of anti-Jewish feeling, but those charges too had failed to stick. The matter had continued to lurk under the surface throughout the debate. The *Tribune* published an editorial on the Des Moines speech, critical of Lindbergh, which contained the observation that "what follows here is printed in the belief that it is better to handle the subject in public discussion than to leave it to the savagery of irresponsible private conversations. We doubt if many of our readers are unaware of the prevalence of those conversations in the past year." The editorial went on to note that Jews, like many other groups in America, had special reasons for despising Hitler. These feelings were understandable and proper, said the *Tribune*, and no one need object to them. All one could ask of Jews or any other citizens was that they "think and act as Americans" on public issues, especially foreign policy. The *Tribune* gave no hint that Jews had failed this test.[48]

How widespread was anti-Semitism among America Firsters in Chicago? The available evidence suggests that, in its virulent variety at least, anti-Semitism in the upper echelons was minimal. Attitudes among the rank and file are impossible to determine with accuracy, but no evidence of widespread anti-Semitism at that level exists either. General Wood had told *PM* back in December that no one on the executive committee of America First bore any prejudice against the Jews. Wood admitted hearing rumored accusations against Chicago businessman William Regnery, but the general declared that he had never encountered any evidence to support them in his many contacts with Regnery. Among the other key AFC insiders, Stuart, Judson, and Mrs. Fairbank were above suspicion. Less than a month before the Des Moines rally, Mrs.

Fairbank issued an emphatic warning to all Illinois chapters to refuse all contact with a local anti-Semite, adding that "it is obvious that he knows nothing about the ideals upon which the America First Committee is founded . . . [We] are not anti-Semitic." So concerned was the committee to avoid infiltration by subversive or undesirable elements that it even sought, unsuccessfully, to obtain FBI evaluations of various groups and individuals with whom it had dealings.[49]

Many America Firsters, however, did agree with the views expressed in Lindbergh's address. These committeemen believed that Jews represented a separate, cohesive, and definable interest group on some foreign policy issues, one dedicated to promoting a policy of intervention and possessed of the influence to help bring it about. For this reason, some committee members regarded Jews as political enemies. But the stray references to Jews in the AFC records contain considerably less malice than those to communists, anglophiles, or Franklin D. Roosevelt. General Wood was a man given to forthright statements himself, and he believed that Lindbergh had been honest, accurate, and unprejudiced in his presentation of the issues. Sterling Morton was another blunt talker. In a letter to Stuart he defended the rights of Jews to use their influence as citizens however they saw fit, and he sympathized with the feelings of Jews in the current European war. But in the current heated political climate, declared Morton, "They must, however, be prepared to defend themselves against criticism and opposition by fact and logical argument, not merely by raising the cry of anti-Semitism." Morton was nonetheless critical of Lindbergh for raising the issue without first consulting the leaders of America First. He feared that the Des Moines address had tainted the entire committee. Other AFCers disagreed. The chairwoman of the Rockford chapter listened approvingly to Lindbergh over the radio and declared "no one could accuse him of anything but the best intentions toward any group of people." Leaders in other AFC chapters, such as Boston, agreed with this assessment.[50]

The avalanche of criticism that soon fell on America First more than confirmed that Morton had not misread the situation. Anxiously, AFC leaders gathered in Chicago to draft a formal statement about the opinions Lindbergh had expressed in Des Moines. However, due in large part to their internal divisions on what the proper response should be, the leadership mishandled this matter. They let twelve days elapse before holding the strategy session, thus appearing indifferent to public criticism. The press interpreted the internal disagreements as further evidence of anti-Semitism. At the meeting itself, Stuart and John T. Flynn of New York pressed for a strong denunciation of anti-Semitism. Wood at one point suggested that the committee disband and at another urged that it back Lindbergh without reservation. These diverse views produced a diffuse statement that satisfied no one in or out of the committee. It supported Lindbergh in general terms and denied the charge of anti-Semitism. The statement also deplored the injection of the Jewish issue into the debate and accused AFC's opponents of having done so. Even Mrs. Fairbank judged it a "deplorably weak" performance. Given the lack of consensus among AFC leaders, this vague and contradictory document was the best they could produce. It earned little praise and, like the entire affair, did incalculable damage to the committee's public standing.[51]

Perhaps the strongest evidence as to the views of rank-and-file members can be found in their actions following the Des Moines address. If there was no rush within America First to denounce Lindbergh, neither was there an upsurge of anti-Semitic activity by committeemen or anyone else. Such incidents as did occur continued to be few and isolated. Nor did the question of Jewish influence become a feature of AFC rhetoric at any level. Committee opponents continued to mention the Des Moines address in their campaign to discredit AFC and its allies, but this was essentially the only overt way the issue remained alive in the remaining weeks of peace.

On the same day that America First issued its formal statement on the Lindbergh address, the *Tribune* reported that President Roosevelt intended to ask for an almost total repeal of the Neutrality Act. This latest round in the long foreign policy debate found the AFC a more experienced and developed organization than during the lend-lease period. Yet committee leaders still operated under the same basic tactical premises that had guided them since AFC's inception.

The main method of lobbying used by America First continued to be the mass letter-writing campaign. Committee leaders persisted in emphasizing this weapon to the chapters despite abun-

dant signals that the membership had grown weary of the tactic
and doubted its effectiveness. When Mrs. Fairbank lauded the results of letter writing at a September meeting of the south side
AFC chapter, a man in the audience exclaimed, "Letters haven't
helped. I've written 1500 of them. We need a plan." His comments
drew applause from the crowd. A member of the Park Ridge chapter wrote to General Wood that the rank and file had long since
lost faith in letter campaigns. These and similar entreaties were
wasted. "I still believe it is possible to stop our going into war by
sending an immense amount of mail to the President and Congress," wrote Mrs. Fairbank to one of her chapter chairmen. Her
general instructions to all Illinois outposts declared that letters had
been effective in the past and would be useful again. They would
remain the centerpiece of the AFC's campaign against convoys.[52]

However familiar was their basic tactic, committee leaders had
become more discerning in its use. During the height of the convoy debate in late October, America First issued "Emergency Bulletin No. 1." The bulletin directed chapter chairpersons to place
dependable workers in charge of supervising the letter-writing activities of their peers, who were to be organized along an almost
military pattern for the purpose. Little evidence suggests that
many chapters fell into step with this elaborate scheme, but the
rest of the bulletin was of greater substance. "National headquarters will decide when, to whom, and, in general, what to write," it
stated. "Remember, this is not a problem of writing every day, it is
a problem of getting a specific number of letters to a specific person on a specific subject." Committee leaders had profited from
their mistakes during the lend-lease debate, when many AFCers
had written to congressmen already pledged to vote against the
bill. Now America First concentrated its efforts on undecided congressmen and on opposition members whom it believed were politically vulnerable.[53]

In Chicago, for example, Mrs. Fairbank directed AFC pressure
against Representative Raymond S. McKeough. She reported to
General Wood that both steelworkers and members of the University of Chicago community mounted major letter campaigns aimed
at the congressman. The outpouring of mail seemed to impress
the Chicago Democrat, who began to waver in his support for the
administration. The Roosevelt forces detected the potential defec-

tion, however, and a telephone appeal from Paul Douglas convinced McKeough to vote for the convoy bill. Chicago's other congressional representatives gave little comfort to America First either. Seven of the remaining nine members voted in favor of the' convoy measure. In disgust, Mrs. Fairbank labeled them "preachers of the Kelly-Nash machine."[54]

Much more encouraging were the relatively slender margins by which the revisions of the Neutrality Act passed each house of Congress. The narrowness of the loss buffered the depression America Firsters felt over another major defeat. A change of seven votes in the Senate or nine in the House would have doomed the bill. Thus General Wood had some reason for claiming that the vote represented a certain moral victory for America First. Observers on all sides of the foreign policy debate agreed that the administration had pushed close to the limits of public and congressional tolerance in its program to aid the Allies. America First had been convinced all along that the public would side with them once the issues came into focus. Now the closeness of the vote seemed to prove this contention, but it also heightened the frustration that pervaded the committee. Again they failed to translate this popular support into influence within the government, allowing Roosevelt to steal another victory.[55]

America First announced its latest, and what was to be its last, attempted solution to this problem on November 19. Fairbank declared that the committee would enter politics on a nonpartisan basis beginning with the 1942 primaries. Principle rather than party label would be its criterion for extending political support. As the *Daily News* observed sourly, AFC would "stump for appeasers in both existing parties." The national committee's decision evoked an enthusiastic response from local chapters around Chicago. A few area leaders wished to go even farther and convert America First into the basis for a new political party. The *Tribune* had issued a similar call as far back as the previous July. None of the key AFC leaders possessed personal political ambitions however, and there is no evidence the committee ever seriously contemplated becoming a third party.[56]

The decision to enter electoral politics emerged from yet another round of AFC strategic planning that came as a result of the defeat over neutrality revision. America First leaders weighed and rejected several alternative courses before settling on their choice. They discussed whether to attempt to have a sympathetic congressperson introduce a motion to declare war. Late in October, Wood had sent a open letter to Roosevelt asking the president to put the matter before Congress. Such a move would get the real issue out in the open at last, the general had declared, where it could be settled in a fair decision by which all must abide. The White House had ignored the original request and committee leaders saw no reason to believe that the strategy would be more successful a second time. Then, in mid-November, Wood traveled to Washington for a secret meeting with about a dozen legislators. Among several topics the group discussed was a possible effort to impeach the president. Most agreed that the idea was impractical for the moment, but some of those present held out hope that a movement to remove Roosevelt might form in the upcoming months. Finally, back in Chicago, America First encouraged Robert Hutchins to develop a comprehensive peace program around which all antiwar groups could rally. Hutchins accepted this task and began work on the plan in the latter half of November.[57]

The problems, resentments, frustrations, and hopes of the antiwar forces were well indicated by the nature and number of the strategies they chose to consider. In the face of repeated setbacks, antiadministration forces persisted in seeking the key to ultimate victory for their cause. Some members quit the movement, convinced that the times required a united nation. But most of the original leadership remained committed to the struggle against full military involvement. They were sustained by the convictions that their cause was righteous and that they enjoyed the support of the mass of citizens. Throughout their campaign, America First Committee leaders drew strength from the devotion of the rank and file to the cause of peace. "These meetings always amaze me," young Douglas Stuart wrote in June. "Everybody's against us but the people." This abiding faith that America First represented the popular will fueled its flagging spirits throughout the disheartening months of 1941. To the finish, members remained convinced that the committee's failures were those of means and not of ends.[58]

EIGHT

WAR ADJOURNS THE DEBATE

n retrospect, the normality with which December 7 began was what stood out in memory. Chicagoans awoke to sunshine and seasonably mild temperatures, good weather for football. The Bears needed a victory against their crosstown rivals, the Cardinals, to force a playoff with the Green Bay Packers for the western division championship of the National Football League. Those uninterested in the gridiron could tune in a variety of musical offerings over the radio. *I Pagliacci* was the featured afternoon offering over WGN. Listeners with different tastes could look forward to an appearance by Judy Garland on the Edgar Bergen and Charlie McCarthy show. Moviegoers were flocking to see *Sergeant York* and the new Abbott and Costello comedy, *Keep 'Em Flying*. Only fifteen shopping days remained before Christmas. To aid the holiday buyer, the *Tribune* recommended William L. Shirer's *Berlin Diary* as the best bet in nonfiction and Louis Bromfield's *Wild Is the River* as the top pick among novels. With unemployment falling and paychecks swollen by overtime, Christmas business was better than it had been for many seasons.[1]

The news that Sunday was the usual solemn fare. Much of it dealt with the war. Britain had just declared war on Finland, and the Roosevelt administration now placed all Finnish ships in American ports under "protective custody" to prevent their leaving. The president had also dispatched a personal note, contents unknown, to Emperor Hirohito of Japan. Word had reached Washington that a pair of Japanese convoys had been sighted sail-

ing toward the Gulf of Siam. Most newspaper accounts contended
that Japanese-American relations had reached a point of acute
crisis, and Southeast Asia appeared as if it would become the
flashpoint. A few reports continued to express hope that the Japanese would back down if Western resolve to oppose aggression
remained firm. Optimistic forecasts were as exceptional as the occasional warnings that war with Japan might be long and difficult.
Most accounts radiated confidence in American might and the
prospects for military success in the Pacific. Secretary of the Navy
Frank Knox reported that the U.S. Navy was beyond question the
"finest in the world." Even more luckless was a quote by Harold E.
Fey, an editor of *Christian Century* magazine, who had recently returned from a trip to Japan. He indicated that economic chaos
there had become so severe that it threatened to bring on a popular revolution. "The Japanese people are in no position to continue the war they have already started," Fey declared, "to say
nothing of taking on an opponent like America."[2]

The first radio bulletins announced the attack on Pearl Harbor
around midafternoon. Soon a stream of bulletins, reports, and
commentaries filled the airwaves. By evening, crowds had gathered in downtown Chicago. Observers noted that most people
seemed too distracted to pay much notice to the elaborate Christmas window displays. Chicagoans wandered aimlessly and asked
strangers for the latest news. Aside from some window breaking
at the Oriental Trading Company, a Japanese-owned firm on
Madison Street, there were no unusual instances of violence or
vandalism.[3]

Leading figures in the foreign policy debate reacted swiftly to
the news of the Japanese attack. In Chicago the *Tribune*, the *Defender*, and the *Daily News* pledged their complete support for the
war effort. Newspapers across the country were doing the same.
The *Daily News* called upon all the crisis committees to disband.
"Whatever threatens the security of this country," declared the *Defender*, "whatever endangers its sovereignty, imperils the safety of
us all regardless of creed, color, or race." In a short, front-page
editorial, McCormick declared that war had come to the United
States "through no volition of any American." The *Tribune* held
that the current emergency was no time to indulge in recrimina-
tions on the course of American foreign policy and vowed to re-

frain from such action itself. Robert Wood told newsmen that America First would back the government completely. The respective heads of Chicago's AFC and CDA chapters, Thomas Hammond and Harland Allen, released a joint call for all Americans to rally to the support of the nation. Leaders of the Republican party in Illinois issued a similar message.[4]

Not even the powerful shock generated by Pearl Harbor was sufficient to wipe away the passions and suspicions engendered during months of debate. Upon hearing news of the attack, Charles Lindbergh telephoned General Wood to discuss what America First's initial reaction should be. Wood greeted the aviator by saying, "Well, he got us in through the back door." A few America Firsters were convinced that the committee ought to continue its work. On December 8 Stuart dispatched a hastily composed message to all chapter chairpersons. He noted that Wood had pledged the group to full support for the war against Japan, but said nothing about the European situation. Stuart outlined several alternative courses: to dissolve outright, to adjourn activities but continue organizational existence, to persist with opposition to American intervention in Europe, or to transform the committee into a civilian service group. He asked the chairpersons to consider whether the AFC would want to become involved in such issues as Allied relations, partisan politics, peace terms, or the preservation of civil liberties in wartime. He urged them to telegraph their views in time for a December 11 meeting of the AFC national committee.[5]

America First's two main opponents were not inclined to dissolve automatically either. The Chicago chapter of the Committee to Defend America, which had been moribund for months, met on December 10 to decide its future. A heated argument developed between those who wanted to merge with Fight For Freedom and those who preferred to disband. Finally the chapter voted for outright dissolution. The fate of Fight For Freedom was less speedily resolved. Committee leaders disagreed about the country's needs. Many wished to promote national unity and contended that their mission had been accomplished; others desired to be of further use to the government and to work for postwar aims. Chairman Denison B. Hull had received word from New York that Clark Eichelberger of the CDA was trying to contact the Roosevelt administration to determine its wishes. Hull was inclined to disband the chapter, but FFF continued its formal existence into the spring of 1942. As late as March, Courtenay Barber was prepared to renew activity upon word that Washington had found a use for the committee. The signal never came and Fight For Freedom was finished.[6]

The national committee of America First gathered in Chicago on December 11 to decide the future of their group. AFC leadership too was divided. A faction centered in the New York chapter wished for America First to continue its announced strategy of entering electoral politics. Sterling Morton also saw an enduring need to watch over America's national interest. He believed that the committee should cease operations temporarily in order to reorient itself for a role as loyal wartime opposition. None of these views prevailed. The locus of power within the leadership of America First had always been in Chicago. This group again asserted itself. Wood, Stuart, Judson, and Fairbank rejected any idea of further opposition. Pressed by the Chicagoans, the national committee voted to disband America First. Wood issued the announcement the following day. The *New York Times*, among others, commended the action as a demonstration of patriotism.[7]

The decision to disband was a concession of defeat rather than an act of repentance. Wood's announcement contained no apologies. Personally, the general regretted that America First had been unsuccessful in keeping the nation at peace. Wood never abandoned his conviction that the AFC had been fundamentally correct in its stance. Stuart also remained a staunch defender of the committee. As expressed by Clay Judson, what had changed for these America Firsters was their sense of the immediate needs of the United States. They did not alter their basic views about American foreign policy and international affairs. Judson pointed out that the committee had pledged all along to abandon its efforts if the United States became engaged in hostilities. "The period of debate was over for me the day war was declared," Judson wrote. But he retained his fears of the effects a protracted war would have on American society and its system of government. Judson was also suspicious of the administration's postwar international aspirations. An expanded American role abroad threatened to breed resentment in Russia, Europe, and around the globe. He doubted that American national interests required this country to "police the world" politically. Judson warned against this "Roman Empire psychology" and deplored the type of hubris which he believed it represented. His letter revealed what America First had rarely managed to convey in its public pronouncements, that its primary concern was to preserve American values.[8]

The debate that convulsed the United States between 1939 and 1941 hinged on a disagreement over the nature of the contemporary threat to American institutions and principles. Did the dangers of Fascist expansion outweigh the debilitating effects of waging a modern war?

On one side were those who stressed the menace posed by Nazi Germany and its Axis allies. In their view, strengthening the American military was a necessary but dangerously inadequate response to aggression. They advocated an active policy of furnishing aid to those resisting Axis expansionism, above all Great Britain. The aid policy developed in a series of stages that took the United States from neutrality to limited belligerency. At no time did more than a minority of the proponents of aid view the policy as a springboard to full American entry into the war. Until Pearl Harbor, most Americans desired peace. But they wanted even more to see Hitler beaten. They hoped it would be possible to reconcile these goals. Most Americans therefore supported the aid policy precisely because, with all its risks, aid offered the best chance to achieve peace and victory. But the hope that the twin goals could be reconciled was not matched by an expectation that they would be. The public anticipated being drawn in, grasped that American military power would probably be needed to defeat the Axis, and balked at the prospect.

The proponents of aid were resisted at every step by a sizable segment of the public that judged war itself to be the paramount danger to national well-being. They believed that the United States would be severely harmed by participation in a major war, regardless of its outcome. Pacifists, of course, were numbered in this second group, but most of its members supported military preparedness as a sufficient safeguard against a successful foreign invasion. By these lights, the aid policy was needless. Worse still, it was dangerous. The obvious unneutrality of Roosevelt's program would probably lead to war, the outcome most Americans hoped to avoid.

Compromise between such antithetical positions was a virtual impossibility. Other factors made impasse even more certain. The existence of extremists on both sides encouraged mutual misperceptions. Fight For Freedom never represented more than a minority position, but it lent credence to the fears of America Firsters and others that a conspiracy existed to get the United States into war. Similarly, the presence of American Nazis at antiwar rallies tainted the entire cause. Media coverage, with its inherent tendency to spotlight the unusual and sensational, helped direct public attention to extremists on both sides and thus helped to foster misperceptions.

Media coverage contributed to the polarization of opinion in other ways as well. Until the fall of France, coverage in almost all quarters reflected the deep and pervasive commitment to peace that most Americans shared. As the French collapsed, an image of imposing German power came to dominate press accounts of the debacle. Though the specific content of most radio broadcasts is beyond recovery, the immediacy of radio coverage and the ability of the medium to render distant events intimate must have fueled the sense of threat arising so rapidly in so many Americans. But after the summer of 1940 the press did not contribute to consensus. The issue now was how far from neutrality the United States ought to go in opposing Axis expansionism. The Chicago experience suggests that readers of different newspapers received contrasting portraits of the world situation and of Washington's response to it. This fact assumes added importance because Roosevelt relied on events to educate public opinion on foreign policy. In effect, however, the public received different educational messages depending on what outlet they listened to or read. To the degree that views were shaped by the media, separate and conflicting "realities" were formed. Moreover, even when the press substantially agreed on an issue in 1941, such as that the Allies were capable of winning the war without American military intervention, the somewhat paradoxical effect was to contribute indirectly to continued polarization of opinion. Because the American public did not realize the full urgency of the military situation, it could afford to postpone decisive action still longer.

By the latter half of 1940, public involvement in foreign policy issues was extraordinarily high. The resulting debate became intense, especially as the focus moved beyond the issue of supplying material aid and on to questions of convoying and outright belligerency. Activity was by no means limited to elite forums, like the councils on foreign relations that existed in most major cities. Foreign policy debates were heard in most of the leading interest groups in American society, from veterans' organizations and labor unions to women's groups and business associations. The frequency with which divisions arose within organizations of all types attests to the ability of foreign policy issues to cut across factions formed by domestic affairs. No group escaped internal wrangling, though the seriousness of such disputes varied considerably. The pervasiveness of controversy indicates that when a foreign policy debate involved war or peace, as it did beginning in mid-1940, public disinterest evaporated. Especially noteworthy were the disputes within organizations like the League of Women Voters or the American Legion, which had not previously experienced divisions of this sort. The extensive publicity given these divisions contributed to the realization that the American public was deeply split in 1940–41. The internal ferment found in so many interest groups may have undercut the formal expressions of support for administration policy so many of them issued. Still, formal resolutions did represent "signals" to policymakers. It is therefore significant that so many mainstream interest groups seldom prodded the administration to more extreme action. Most resolutions either endorsed existing proposals or contained such vague wording as to prescribe no specific course of action. With the exception of ideologically committed groups such as the socialists or pacifists, whose political weight was marginal, the administration did not receive specific promptings from organized interests. This lack of popular pressure helps explain why Roosevelt proceeded with such caution in 1941.

To a greater degree than has been previously explored, the crisis committees reflected the internal divisions over foreign policy that characterized so many organizations prior to Pearl Harbor.

Much of the action took place below the level of national leadership. Both America First and the Committee to Defend America were composed of hundreds of local chapters. Understaffing at national headquarters guaranteed that supervision of local chapters would be ineffective, therefore allowing the locals considerable operational latitude. In practice, major metropolitan chapters functioned as middle-level management. They helped furnish speakers to local meetings, routed literature to small chapters, tried to coordinate activities, and conveyed local opinion to national leadership. But metropolitan chapters were themselves overburdened and unable to provide more than lax supervision. The haste with which the committees were formed and the urgency with which they viewed their missions added to the likelihood of internal turmoil. Each committee had to deal with extremists, though America First suffered more on this score than CDA or Fight For Freedom. But each of the three also experienced disagreement among those supporters it regarded as legitimate. The Committee to Defend America in effect split from top to bottom over the need to go to war. Even within Fight For Freedom, a smaller organization sharing a distinctly minority viewpoint, local chapters differed in the thrust of their activities. The Chicago chapter worked harder at discrediting the *Tribune* than at building support for war. America First was less burdened than the CDA by disagreements over policy. Indeed, R. Douglas Stuart and others sought with scant success to attract a greater diversity of opinion to the committee's top leadership. Disagreement within America First centered on tactics. Committee leaders believed that Roosevelt was taking the country into war despite public preferences to the contrary. How could the president be stopped? None of the logical possibilities was acceptable to all committee members. Focusing public attention on the trend toward war had failed to stop lend-lease. America First could call for a negotiated peace, but public support for such an agreement was low, and international prospects were dim. The committee was forced back on its mainstay, organized letter-writing campaigns, despite growing frustration within the ranks over the inability of such efforts to control government policy. America First eventually resolved to enter electoral politics by supporting antiwar candidates, but Pearl Harbor intervened before this strategy could be tested. Though

America First disbanded soon thereafter, many committeepersons and others among the antiwar forces remained convinced of the essential soundness of their position and bitter at what they regarded as Roosevelt's duplicity.

Bitterness was rife in America during 1941. Of course rancor was hardly an unusual element in American political life. The New Deal years had been filled with it, to cite only a proximate example. But the ugliness of 1941 had especially serious consequences, since it precluded the development of national unity in a period of crisis. During the lend-lease debate, both sides gradually abandoned their efforts to convert their opponents and sought instead to subvert them in the public mind. The resulting polarization became evident almost at once and deepened in subsequent months. Public support for lend-lease eroded in February and March, even though congressional approval remained certain. Public attitudes split along partisan political lines. Republican approval of lend-lease declined from 62 percent to 38 percent, while Democratic ranks held firm. Poll data for the rest of 1941 indicates that public attitudes on all major foreign policy issues remained stable. This hardening of opinion reflected in part the inability of either side to develop new arguments to justify its position. The open campaign for war was the only new position to emerge in 1941. Its impact was not decisive. The more general trend was for each side to seek to discredit the integrity of the opposition. Interventionists labeled America First a "Nazi Transmission Belt"; Roosevelt called Lindbergh a "copperhead"; America First looked for ways to disprove Gallup poll findings and have Walter Winchell removed from the airwaves—a complete listing of such attacks would be vast. Charles Lindbergh's speech at Des Moines, when he identified the Jews as one group working to get the United States into war, was part of a much larger trend. Attacks such as Lindbergh's damaged the noninterventionist cause, as has long been understood, but they hurt the other side as well. Proadministration forces had hoped to achieve national unity following the enactment of lend-lease, but that hope died in a chorus of invective emanating from all quarters.

The debate had its merits as well as its shortcomings. Countless Americans, tens of thousands of them in Chicago alone, took a direct part in the political process. Americans enjoyed the opportunity to air their views on issues of war and peace before hostilities began. Despite two major conflicts in subsequent decades, they have not enjoyed a similar opportunity. Participants in the 1939–41 debate educated themselves and their fellow citizens and expressed opinions on matters crucial to their government and their society. The debate was an exercise in democracy. All sides voiced their satisfaction with the roles they played, surely a sign of health in any political system.

But few Americans, regardless of viewpoint, were satisfied with their foreign policy by the summer of 1941. Even the majority supporting the aid program did so with the expectation that it would fail to keep the country out of war. To the last, the public and the government remained torn between their continuing desire for peace and their yearning to see Hitler beaten. While the United States agonized over its foreign policy, Europe underwent a far greater agony at the hands of the Nazis. By November the Germans seemed on the verge of adding the Soviet Union to their list of conquests, the British were losing the battle of the Atlantic, and Japan was poised to strike. That the United States could conduct such a debate in the turmoil of 1939–41 is impressive. That the debate produced such a flawed result is deeply disturbing.

APPENDIX

I n a sense the 1940 election has become a casualty of critical election theory, which has usually tended to focus on periods of realignment. While earlier scholars, notably Lazarsfeld and Lubell, published highly influential work on mass political behavior based in whole or in part on the 1940 election, most recent scholars have concentrated on the period from 1928 to 1936. There has been vigorous debate on virtually every aspect of when, why, and how the Democrats emerged as the new majority party, but only Allan J. Lichtman has put much emphasis on the importance of 1940 in that regard. Everyone else has argued, at least implicitly, that the electorate was essentially established in its loyalties not later than the end of the 1930s.[1]

The older work of Lazarsfeld and Lubell also addresses more directly the concerns of this study—the impact of foreign policy on voters—as well as its temporal focus. Of later scholars, Lichtman is again one of the exceptions, although the role of issues is only a secondary concern of his. Lichtman contends that the war not only induced Roosevelt to seek a third term, but was the element which made FDR acceptable to the voters. The main evidence in support of this contention is a Gallup poll taken just after Germany invaded Poland, over a year prior to the election. Lazarsfeld's study of Erie County, Ohio, furnished some evidence to buttress further the notion that the war had a significant impact on at least some voters. He found distinct differences over foreign policy between the two groups of voters. Republicans were much more likely than

Democrats to oppose both the draft and increased aid for Britain. In addition to scattered testimony from voters on the value of Roosevelt's experience in foreign affairs, the Erie County study revealed that voters who changed preferences for candidates often referred to foreign policy as a factor in their decisions. The number of such changes was relatively small, however, and economic arguments were more often cited than foreign policy issues as a reason for deciding to switch. While Lazarsfeld found foreign affairs to be a secondary factor at best, Lubell emphasized that it was the critical factor behind changes in voting patterns in 1940. The substantial losses Roosevelt suffered among rural voters were due largely, Lubell said, to the defection of German-Americans upset by FDR's outspoken antifascism. Lubell did not ignore the influence of economic issues, but contended that foreign affairs outweighed the other influences among German- and Italian-Americans in both country and city. Correspondingly, Roosevelt gained votes among Hitler's victims, notably the Poles. These ethnics contributed large numbers of new voters to the electorate in 1940 and, by going overwhelmingly Democratic, enabled FDR to amass even larger margins in many major cities than he had in 1936. To prove his claim of ethnic influence, Lubell noted that Roosevelt's steepest losses from 1936 came overwhelmingly in counties or wards with heavy German-American populations, while his most lopsided majorities were provided by Eastern European wards.[2]

Recent research by Andersen amplified greatly Lubell's observation about the role of new voters. She established that increased participation by new immigrants was a trend extending back into the late 1920s. Her research leaves open the question of how much of the surge between 1936 and 1940 was due to foreign affairs, and how much was a continuation of an existing movement. Voting data cannot answer this question, but Andersen at least revealed that new immigrants had found compelling reasons to mobilize themselves in large numbers on behalf of the New Deal long before events abroad had become critical. She also examined ethnic voting in a small number of Chicago wards in 1940. The Democratic vote in a highly German-American ward fell sharply, as Lubell had indicated, but Andersen figured increases in the voting-age populations into her calculations and showed that, in fact, German-Americans did not switch to Willkie when they abandoned the Democrats. Instead they refrained from voting at all. Andersen did not examine a heavily Italian ward, but she did analyze one containing a mixture of Italians, Poles, and Russians (many of them, presumably, Jews), with the Poles predominating. Here too there was only a slight increase in the Republican vote over 1936, while the Democratic vote remained almost constant and the percentage of nonvoters fell slightly. Given the diverse composition of this ward, all analysis of ethnic influence is necessarily conjectural. But the results could conceivably support Lubell's interpretation. If the Polish vote adhered to the national trend of increasing both in size and in the percentage of its support for Roosevelt, then a noticeable drop in Italian support for the president would explain the overall steadiness of the Democratic vote in this ward. However, a third ward examined by Andersen, overwhelmingly Czech in composition, does not fit Lubell's account. There the Democratic percentage remained almost fixed, while the Republican totals actually increased. Since the Czechs had quite as much reason as the Poles to loathe Hitler, it would seem that other factors were at work in this ward, and perhaps in others as well.[3]

My own research in Illinois confirms Lubell's findings regarding German-Americans, but not for Italian-Americans or for Irish-Americans—another group often cited as isolationist but curiously ignored by Lubell for 1940. Using census figures and county-level election data, counties were ranked by their ethnic composition (German-, Irish-, and Italian-Americans) and by the degree to which the Democratic vote fell in percentage. There was a strong tendency for the Democratic vote to drop less heavily in counties with a low population of these ethnic groups than it dropped on average throughout the state. Counties with large German-American populations showed a very strong tendency for the Democratic vote to fall off more sharply than the statewide average, but this held true for neither of the other two groups, each of which tended to lose less than the statewide averages. From a different perspective the results are similar. Counties where the Democrats suffered their worse percentage losses were twice as likely to have higher-than-average German-American populations than lower-than-average populations. However, few counties with above-average Italian- or Irish-American populations were found in the group where the Democrats suffered their worst percentage losses. But many counties with below-average Italian- and Irish-American populations were found in that group. In the counties where Democratic percentage losses were smallest, below-average German-American populations were three times more likely to appear than in counties with above-average populations, but twice as many *high* Italian-American populations appeared as in counties with below-average Italian-American populations. Counties where the Democrats' losses were relatively modest did however tend to have below-average Irish-American populations. Thus there was a fairly clear and consistent correlation only between one potential group of defectors, the German-Americans, and actual Democratic losses. There is no similar relationship with either of the other groups. Moreover, Democratic losses were not limited to German-American counties by any means, as nine of the twenty-five counties where Democratic defections were most severe contained either average or below-average components of German-Americans. As no observer would deny, factors other than foreign policy were also clearly at work among the electorate, but foreign affairs did count among German-Americans.

NOTES

ABBREVIATIONS

AES Papers
: The Adlai E. Stevenson Papers, the Seely G. Mudd Library, Princeton, New Jersey

AFC Papers
: The America First Committee Papers, the Hoover Institution on War, Revolution and Peace, Palo Alto, California

CCFR Papers
: The Chicago Council on Foreign Relations Papers, the University of Illinois at Chicago Circle Library, Chicago, Ilinois

CDA Papers
: The Committee to Defend America by Aiding the Allies Papers, the Seely G. Mudd Library, Princeton, New Jersey

FFF Papers
: The Papers of the Chicago Chapter of the Fight For Freedom Committee, the University of Chicago Library, Chicago, Illinois

NLWV Papers
: The National League of Women Voters Papers, the Library of Congress, Washington, D.C.

Stevenson Papers
: Walter Johnson and Carol Evans, eds., *The Papers of Adlai E. Stevenson. Vol. 1.* Boston: Little, Brown, 1972.

Note: Shortened titles will be used in the notes for all Chicago newspapers—for example, *Tribune* for the *Chicago Tribune*.

PREFACE

1. Divine, *Reluctant Belligerent*, ably surveys foreign policy in the prewar period. On public opinion, Levering, *Public and American Foreign Policy*, is a valuable introduction, while many of the polls themselves have been collected in Cantril and Strunk, *Public Opinion*, and Gallup, *Gallup Poll*.

2. Beard, *American Foreign Policy* and *President Roosevelt*; Barnes, *Perpetual War*; Tansill, *Back Door to War*; Rauch, *Roosevelt*; Sherwood, *Roosevelt and Hopkins*; Feis, *Road to Pearl Harbor*; Langer and Gleason, *Challenge to Isolation* and *Undeclared War*; Dallek, *Roosevelt*; Steele, "The Great Debate"; Reynolds, *Anglo-American Alliance*; Prange, *At Dawn We Slept*; Cole, *Roosevelt*; Ickes, *Secret Diary*, 2:659. Quote from Dallek, *Roosevelt*, p. vii.

3. The best overall account of Roosevelt's presidency is still Burns, *Lion and the Fox* and *Soldier of Freedom*.

4. Hull, *Memoirs*; Welles, *Time for Decision* and *Seven Decisions*; Blum, *Morganthau Diaries*; Ickes, *Secret Diary*; Sherwood, *Roosevelt and Hopkins*; Stimson and Bundy, *On Active Service*.

Among the noteworthy lower-level officials, the following are especially important: Berle, *Navigating the Rapids*; Grew, *Ten Years in Japan*; Hooker, *Moffat Papers*; Long, *War Diary*; Pogue, *Marshall: Ordeal*; Leahy, *I Was There*.

On the impact of bureaucracy, see Utley, *War with Japan*.

5. Divine, *Illusion of Neutrality*, pp. 333–35; Cole, *Roosevelt*, pp. 3–9; Kimball, *Most Unsordid Act*; Guinsburg, *Pursuit of Isolationism*; Porter, *Seventy-Sixth Congress*. Among the memoirs of legislative leaders are Vandenberg, *Private Papers*; Wheeler, *Yankee from the West*; Connally and Steinberg, *Tom Connally*; Bloom, *Autobiography*; Martin and Donovan, *Fifty Years*; Barkley, *That Reminds Me—*.

6. Lubell, *American Politics*, pp. 137–67; Adler, *Isolationist Impulse*; Osgood, *Ideals and Self-Interest*; DeConde, *Isolation and Security*; Jonas, *Isolationism in America*; Rieselbach, *Roots of Isolationism* all deal with isolationism. On pacifism see Detzer, *Appointment on the Hill*; Libby, *To End War*; Curti, *Peace or War*; Wittner, *Rebels Against War*; Chatfield, *For Peace and Justice*; DeBenedetti, *Peace Reform*.

7. Johnson, *Battle against Isolation*; Cole, *America First*; Chadwin, *Warhawks*; Cole, *Lindbergh*; Lindbergh, *Wartime Journals*; Johnpoll, *Pacifist's Progress*; Stenehjem, *American First*; Kennedy, *Beard*; Hofstadter, *Progressive Historians*; Johnson, *White's America*.

8. Williams, *Tragedy*, pp. 9–16; Levering, *American Opinion*; Lauderbaugh, *American Steelmakers*; Martin, *Liberalism and World Politics*.

9. Steele, "The Great Debate," pp. 69–92; Culbert, *News for Everyman*; Manvell, *Films*; Fielding, *March of Time*.

10. Lippmann, *Public Opinion*; Cohen, *Public's Impact*; Graber, *Foreign Policy*; Friedrich, *Man and His Government*; Luttbeg, *Opinion and Public Policy*; Walther, *Orientations*; Rosenau, *Public Opinion and Foreign Policy*, *National Leadership*, and *Domestic Sources*.

11. Lowenheim, Langley, and Jonas, *Roosevelt and Churchill*, pp. 117, 159–60; Sherwood, *Roosevelt and Hopkins*, p. 227; Brinkley, *Voices of Protest*, pp. 134–37; Leigh, *Mobilizing Consent*, p. 30; Steele, "The Great Debate," pp. 69–71.

12. Steele, "American Popular Opinion," pp. 704–23; Lubell, *American Politics*, pp. 140–42, 236–39.

13. A good, brief discussion of the technical aspects of polling and how these affect survey results can be found in Mueller, *War, Presidents and Public Opinion*, pp. 1–18.

14. Wohlstetter, *Pearl Harbor*.

15. May, *"Lessons" of the Past*, pp. ix–xiv, 52, 81–83, 112–13.

CHAPTER ONE

1. *Tribune*, September 1, 1939, p. 1; *Daily News*, September 1, 1939, p. 1. Gallup, *Gallup Poll*, pp. 154, 80, 131, 197; *New York Times*, December 3, 1939, p. 42.

2. Bailey, *Diplomatic History*, p. 711.

3. *U.S. Census: 1940*, pp. 34, 58; Kleppner, *Chicago Divided*, pp. 17–19. Most of the voluminous literature on Chicago avoids the 1939–41 period. Mayer and Wade, *Chicago*, pp. 283–373, contains an overview of the city between the wars; Terkel, *Division Street: America*, contains the impressions and memories of many Chicagoans and best captures the flavor of the city.

4. Holli and Jones, *Ethnic Frontier*, pp. 180–208, 264–89. A pair of works shed light on Chicago's ethnics in earlier times, Zorbaugh, *Gold Coast*, and Nelli, *Italians of Chicago*, esp. pp. 201–44.

5. Newell, *Labor Movement*, pp. 230–31.

6. Holli and Jones, *Ethnic Frontier*, pp. 180–208, 264–89.

7. Jensen, *Illinois*, p. 133; Biles, *Big City Boss*, pp. 15–17, 44–46, 76–84; Kleppner, *Chicago Divided*, pp. 15–27; Kantowicz, *Polish-American Politics*, pp. 202–14; Rakove, *Don't Make No Waves*, pp. 21–42.

8. Jensen, *Illinois*, p. 133; Biles, *Big City Boss*, p. 22; Mayer and Wade, *Chicago*, p. 360.

9. Biles, *Big City Boss*, pp. 46, 61, 79–80.

10. Biles, *Big City Boss*, pp. 61–63; Jensen, *Illinois*, p. 136; Newell, *Labor Movement*, pp. 204–5, 223–29, 252.

11. Culbert, *News for Everyman*, pp. 5, 20–24; Kendrick, *Prime Time*, pp. 139–41, 164, 169.

12. *Current Biography, 1942*, p. 546.

13. Ibid., pp. 545–48; *New York Times*, April 1, 1955, p. 17. See also Waldrop, *McCormick of Chicago*, and Wendt, *Chicago Tribune*.

14. *Current Biography, 1942*, pp. 545–48; *New York Times*, April 1, 1955, p. 17; Giles, *Colonel of Chicago*, pp. 4–5.

15. *Current Biography, 1942*, pp. 545–48; Giles, *Colonel of Chicago*, pp. 4–5; *New York Times*, April 1, 1955, p. 17; April 3, 1955, sec. 4, p. 2; Friendly, *Minnesota Rag*.

16. *Current Biography, 1940*, pp. 461–64.

17. Ibid.; *New York Times*, April 29, 1944, pp. 1, 8; *New York Herald-Tribune*, April 29, 1944, p. 8.

18. *Tribune*, April 29, 1944, p. 5; *Current Biography, 1940*, p. 463.

19. Gallup, *Gallup Poll*, p. 193.

20. *Tribune*, September 2, 1939, p. 10; September 6, 1939, p. 1; *Daily News*, September 7, 1939; October 12, 1939, p. 10.

21. *Tribune*, September 2, 1939, p. 10; September 21, 1939, p. 12; *Daily News*, September 7, 1939, p. 1; *Los Angeles Times*, September 2, 1939, sec. 2, p. 4; *Boston Globe*, September 4, 1939, p. 4; *Denver Post*, September 2, 1939, p. 2; *San Francisco Chronicle*, September 14, 1939, p. 14; *Atlanta Constitution*, September 4, 1939, p. 4. The *Constitution* had waffled initially, however; see September 1, 1939, p. 4. In the *Louisville Courier Journal*, September 3, 1939, sec. 3, p. 21, Herbert Agar was prescient on the dilemmas facing America.

22. *Tribune*, September 6, 1939, p. 1; September 4, 1939, p. 18; September 7, 1939, p. 14; *Daily News*, September 9, 1939, p. 1; *Louisville Courier-Journal*, September 2, 1939, sec. 1, p. 4; September 4, 1939, sec. 1, p. 4; September 7, 1939, sec. 2, p. 12; *St. Louis Post-Dispatch*, September 2, 1939, p. 4A; *Los Angeles Times*, September 3, 1939, pt. 2, p. 4. The *Cleveland Plain Dealer* ran a series by propaganda expert H. C. Peterson on how to avoid being influenced by propaganda, see September 14, 1939, p. 5; September 15, 1939, p. 6; September 18, 1939, p. 3.

23. *Tribune*, October 17, 1939, p. 12; December 1, 1939, p. 11; *Daily News*, December 1, 1939, pp. 2, 22; October 10, 1939, p. 4; *Louisville Courier-Journal*, November 1, 1939, sec. 1, p. 1; *San Francisco Chronicle*, September 2, 1939, p. 12; *Boston Globe*, September 1, 1939, p. 16; *New York Times*, September 1, 1939, p. 16.

24. *Tribune*, September 30, 1939, p. 1; October 1, 1939, pt. 1, p. 16; *Daily News*, September 2, 1939, pp. 1, 15.

25. *Daily News*, September 12, 1939, p. 1; William Allen White to Frank Knox, September 23, 1939; and reply, September 25, 1939; Knox to White, October 18, 1939, White Papers; *Journal of Commerce*, September 6, 1939, p. 16.

26. Bailey, *Diplomatic History*, pp. 713–15. The other major debate concerned aid to Finland during the Russo-Finnish War.

27. *Tribune*, September 6, 1939, p. 1.

28. *Daily News*, September 16, 1939, p. 6.

29. *Daily News*. September 16, 1939, p. 1; *Tribune*, September 16, 1939, p. 8.

30. *Tribune*, September 16, 1939, p. 8; Frank Knox to Joseph W. Martin, Jr., October 23, 1939, White Papers. Knox lobbied for repeal of the Embargo as lessening the risk of war. On those grounds he stressed the political dangers of opposing repeal.

31. *Journal of Commerce*, September 7, 1939, p. 16.

32. Drake and Clayton, *Black Metropolis*, pp. 399–404; *Defender*, September 9, 1939, p. 1; January 6, 1940, p. 7.

33. *Defender*, August 19, 1939, p. 14; September 9, 1939, p. 1; September 16, 1939, p. 1; January 20, 1940, p. 6; January 27, 1940, p. 15.

34. *Defender*, September 9, 1939, p. 14; September 30, 1939, p. 14; October 7, 1939, p. 14.

35. *New York Times*, October 22, 1939, sec. 4, p. 6; November 4, 1939, p. 14; *Cleveland Plain Dealer*, September 19, 1939, p. 6; September 16, 1939, sec. 1, p. 7; September 27, 1939, p. 24; *Louisville Courier-Journal*, November 4, 1939, sec. 1, p. 6; *St. Louis Post-Dispatch*, September 6, 1939, p. 2C; *Atlanta Constitution*, September 20, 1939, p. 8.

36. *Tribune*, November 3, 1939, p. 1; November 4, 1939, p. 14; *Daily News*, November 3, 1939, p. 1; November 28, 1939, p. 1; *Defender*, December 23, 1939, p. 16; January 6, 1940, p. 14; March 2, 1940, p. 14; March 16, 1940, p. 14; March 23, 1940, p. 16; April 13, 1940, p. 14.

37. *Daily News*, December 5, 1939, p. 1; *Tribune*, November 19, 1939, pt. 1, p. 11; November 25, 1939, p. 8; December 18, 1939, p. 1; *Daily News*, January 10, 1940, p. 10; *Tribune*, December 15, 1939, p. 20.

38. Tebel, *American Dynasty*, p. 208; Waldrop, *McCormick of Chicago*, pp. 50, 54; *Tribune*, November 1, 1939, p. 14; November 8, 1939, p. 16; December 16, 1939, pt. 1, pp. 1, 16; January 2, 1940, p. 8; January 4, 1940, p. 18; January 10, 1940, p. 3; January 20, 1940, p. 11; February 21, 1940, p. 12; January 12, 1940, p. 1; March 17, 1940, pt. 1, p. 14.

39. *Daily News*, January 23, 1940, p. 3; March 13, 1940, p. 1; March 18,

1940, p. 6; October 9, 1939, p. 2.

40. *Tribune*, September 23, 1939, p. 10; October 1, 1939, pp. 1, 16; November 8, 1939, p. 16; November 27, 1939, p. 10; January 20, 1940, p. 1; January 22, 1940, p. 1; January 23, 1940, p. 5; April 19, 1940, p. 4; April 20, 1940, p. 10.

41. *Daily News*, January 26, 1940, p. 1; April 18, 1940, p. 12; April 24, 1940, p. 10.

42. Cantril and Strunk, *Public Opinion*, p. 775.

43. *Daily News*, September 1, 1939, p. 14.

44. *Tribune*, September 17, 1939, pt. 8, p. 1; September 24, 1939, pt. 8, pp. 1–2; September 5, 1939, p. 19; November 12, 1939, pt. 6, p. 3; *Daily News*, September 20, 1939, p. 10; February 14, 1940, p. 14; October 12, 1939, p. 10; September 22, 1939, p. 9; *Defender*, September 19, 1939, pp. 1, 6, 11; October 26, 1939, p. 6.

45. *Tribune*, September 2, 1939, p. 6; October 11, 1939, p. 18; November 22, 1939, p. 18; *Daily News*, October 5, 1939, p. 18; *Defender*, September 16, 1939, p. 5; *Atlanta Constitution*, September 28, 1939, p. 2; November 1, 1940, p. 1; *Louisville Courier-Journal*, September 4, 1939, sec. 1, p. 5.

46. *Daily News*, September 4, 1939, p. 3; September 7, 1939, p. 4; September 21, 1939, p. 10; September 25, 1939, p. 1; September 27, 1939, p. 1; September 28, 1939, p. 1; *Tribune*, September 22, 1939, p. 5; September 25, 1939, p. 1; September 26, 1939, p. 3; September 27, 1939, p. 1; September 28, 1939, p. 15; *New York Times*, September 2, 1939, p. 32; September 14, 1939, p. 5; *St. Louis Post-Dispatch*, September 6, 1939, p. 3C.

47. "Know Your League," August 1938, and Louise Leonard Wright to Chairman of Government and Foreign Policy, September 20, 1939, NLWV Papers.

48. Program for the National League of Women Voters, 1938–1940; Memorandum on Changes in Foreign Policy Program, April 1939; Marguerite Wells to State Presidents, September 19, 1939; Louise Wright to Wells, November 3, 1939, NLWV Papers.

49. "Request for Action," September 14, 1939 and September 27, 1939; Freida Kirlin to Marguerite Wells, September 15, 1939; Wells to State Presidents, October 25, 1939; Lolita E. Bogert to Wells, October 26, 1939; Summary: Activity Regarding Neutrality Legislation, November 30, 1939; Bogert to Colleagues, and attachment, October 12, 1939, NLWV Papers.

50. Frayn Utley to Anne Johnson, October 24, 1939; Lolita E. Bogert to Marguerite Wells, October 26, 1939, NLWV Papers.

51. *Daily News*, September 20, 1939, p. 6.

52. *Daily News*, September 15, 1939, p. 39; October 24, 1939, p. 3; *Tribune*, October 21, 1939, p. 23; November 16, 1939, p. 33.

53. *Defender*, September 16, 1939, p. 11; October 7, 1939, p. 24; October 21, 1939, p. 11; *Tribune*, September 26, 1939, p. 3; October 12, 1939, p. 1; *Daily News*, October 14, 1939, p. 3.

54. *Daily News*, October 3, 1939, p. 1; *Tribune*, October 3, 1939, pp. 1, 10; Ickes, *Secret Diary*, 3:110.

55. *Daily News*, September 6, 1939, p. 5; September 7, 1939, p. 7; September 30, 1939, p. 6.

56. *Daily News*, September 2, 1939, p. 5; October 27, 1939, p. 10; January 22, 1940, p. 1; January 27, 1940, p. 4; *Tribune*, October 20, 1939, p. 1; January 28, 1940, pt. 1, p. 16; February 4, 1940, pt. 8, p. 2; February 10, 1940, p. 4; February 11, 1940, pt. 1, p. 4. Clarke Papers, Box 137. Weinstein Papers, Sermons, 1927–1941, Box 1.

57. *Defender*, September 16, 1939, pp. 17, 22; September 30, 1939, p. 14; October 14, 1939, p. 23; November 4, 1939, p. 16; November 25, 1939, p. 14.

58. *Defender*, September 16, 1939, p. 6; September 23, 1939, p. 14; December 16, 1939, p. 16; December 30, 1939, p. 4; May 20, 1940, p. 16.

59. Quincy Wright to Scott Lucas, September 18, 1939; Clay Judson to Quincy Wright, September 27, 1939, Wright Papers; *New York Times*, January 28, 1939, p. 5; *Daily Maroon*, October 3, 1939, p. 1; October 12, 1939, p. 2; October 13, 1939, p. 2.

60. *Daily Maroon*, October 10, 1939, p. 1; October 11, 1939, p. 1; October 12, 1939, pp. 1–2; October 13, 1939, p. 2; October 17, 1939, p. 2; October 25, 1939, p. 1.

61. *Daily Maroon*, October 31, 1939, p. 1; November 8, 1939, p. 2; November 9, 1939, p. 1; April 2, 1940, p. 1.

62. *Daily Maroon*, April 24, 1940, p. 2; April 25, 1940, p. 1.

63. *Tribune*, February 22, 1940, p. 14.

64. *Denver Post*, January 4, 1940, p. 2; *Atlanta Constitution*, November 13, 1939, p. 2; November 15, 1939, p. 1; November 26, 1939, p. 11; *Cleveland Plain Dealer*, September 10, 1939, p. 12; *Journal of Commerce*, January 1, 1940, p. 16; *New York Times*, January 1, 1940, p. 22; January 5, 1940, pt. 4, p. 1; April 20, 1940, p. 6.

CHAPTER TWO

1. Gallup, *Gallup Poll*, pp. 220, 225, 226, 229, 231, 234, 236, 238, 245; Cantril and Strunk, *Public Opinion*, pp. 494, 775, 981, 1189; *New York Times*, May 12, 1940, sec. 4, p. 7; May 19, 1940, sec. 4, p. 9; June 2, 1940, sec. 4, p. 3; June 16, 1940, sec. 4, p. 7; August 25, 1940, sec. 4, p. 1; *Atlanta*

Constitution, May 30, 1940, p. 8; *Los Angeles Times*, May 27, 1940, sec. 2, p. 4; *San Francisco Chronicle*, May 28, 1940, p. 18.

2. *Tribune*, May 11, 1940, p. 14; *Daily News*, May 6, 1940, p. 1; *Journal of Commerce*, May 22, 1940, p. 16; *Defender*, July 20, 1940, p. 16.

3. Ibid.

4. *Daily News*, May 11, 1940, p. 1; May 16, 1940, p. 31; August 28, 1940, p. 8.

5. *Tribune*, May 13, 1940, p. 1; May 16, 1940, p. 9; June 20, 1940, p. 14; *Journal of Commerce*, May 28, 1940, pp. 1, 16; *Los Angeles Times*, May 16, 1940, p. 4.

6. *Tribune*, June 20, 1940, pp. 1, 12; July 10, 1940, p. 10; May 17, 1940, p. 14; *Boston Globe*, May 24, 1940, p. 16.

7. *Defender*, June 1, 1940, p. 15; July 6, 1940, p. 24; July 20, 1940, p. 16; August 3, 1940, p. 14; August 10, 1940, p. 14; September 14, 1940, p. 16; September 28, 1940, p. 16.

8. *Daily News*, June 6, 1940, p. 10; June 22, 1940, p. 2; December 9, 1940, p. 10; July 20, 1940, p. 4.

9. *Tribune*, May 19, 1940, pt. 1, p. 18; June 6, 1940, p. 12; Steel, *Walter Lippmann*, p. 28; *New York Times*, May 12, 1940, sec. 4, p. 8; May 24, 1940, p. 8; May 26, 1940, sec. 6, pp. 1, 20; *Journal of Commerce*, May 20, 1940, p. 16; *Los Angeles Times*, May 17, 1940, sec. 2, p. 4.

10. *Tribune*, May 19, 1940, pt. 1, p. 18; June 6, 1940, p. 12.

11. *Defender*, April 27, 1940, p. 1; May 18, 1940, p. 16; May 25, 1940, pp. 1, 16, 17; June 1, 1940, p. 1; June 15, 1940, p. 1; August 31, 1940, p. 7; September 21, 1940, p. 16.

12. *Tribune*, July 19, 1940, p. 10; June 8, 1940, p. 12; June 10, 1940, p. 12; *Boston Globe*, May 24, 1940, p. 18.

13. *Daily News*, June 17, 1940, p. 1; June 24, 1940, p. 8; June 6, 1940, p. 10; October 11, 1940, p. 16. For the change in cartoon imagery, compare the *Cleveland Plain Dealer*, September 12, 1939, p. 8, with the *Los Angeles Times*, May 29, 1940, sec. 2, p. 4. On the tendency to focus on Hitler, see the *Atlanta Constitution*, May 26, 1940, p. 3C.

14. *Defender*, September 14, 1940, p. 16; September 28, 1940, p. 15.

15. *Daily News*, June 8, 1940, p. 12; July 15, 1940, p. 2; August 23, 1940, p. 1; July 23, 1940, p. 1; January 20, 1941, pp. 1, 16. Kendrick, *Prime Time*, pp. 169, 181, 193; Culbert, *News for Everyman*, p. 27; Fielding, *March of Time*, pp. 35–36; Manvell, *Films*, pp. 86–92.

16. *Tribune*, May 17, 1940, p. 1; June 3, 1940, p. 1; June 10, 1940, p. 3; *New York Times*, May 20, 1940, p. 1; Cole, *Lindbergh*, pp. 88–94.

17. *Tribune*, August 2, 1940, p. 8; September 14, 1940, p. 12.

18. *Tribune*, August 2, 1940, p. 8; June 17, 1940, p. 1; August 1, 1940,

p. 6; September 25, 1940, p. 1; *New York Times*, May 18, 1940, p. 9; May 23, 1940, p. 14; *Louisville Courier-Journal*, May 24, 1940, sec. 1, p. 4.

19. *Daily News*, May 31, 1940, p. 2; June 20, 1940, p. 4; August 19, 1940, p. 5; Dallek, *Roosevelt*, pp. 205, 233–34.

20. *Daily News*, May 21, 1940, p. 1; *Tribune*, May 23, 1940, p. 1; July 18, 1940, p. 12; August 22, 1940, p. 12; August 28, 1940, p. 10; September 29, 1940, p. 1; *Defender*, April 12, 1940, p. 1; May 25, 1940, p. 10; June 1, 1940, p. 15; December 21, 1940, p. 18; January 18, 1941, p. 16; *Journal of Commerce*, May 28, 1940, p. 16; *New York Times*, June 2, 1940, sec. 7, p. 16.

21. *Daily News*, August 22, 1940, p. 6; September 3, 1940, p. 1.

22. *Tribune*, August 6, 1940, pp. 3, 10; August 15, 1940, p. 12; August 17, 1940, p. 4; September 1940, pp. 1, 3, 14. McCormick was not unique. Interventionists claimed more for actions in retrospect than they tended to admit at the time of action.

23. *Louisville Courier-Journal*, November 4, 1940, sec. 1, p. 14; *Atlanta Constitution*, November 4, 1940, p. 4; *Cleveland Plain Dealer*, November 6, 1940, p. 14; *San Francisco Chronicle*, November 6, 1940, p. 1.

24. *Tribune*, May 16, 1940, p. 16; June 17, 1940, p. 1; June 13, 1940, p. 1; *Journal of Commerce*, May 18, 1940, p. 1; May 24, 1940, p. 3; May 25, 1940, p. 16; *Denver Post*, May 30, 1940, p. 2; *San Francisco Chronicle*, November 1, 1940, p. 18.

25. *Tribune*, June 22, 1940, p. 1; June 25, 1940, p. 1; *Daily News*, June 25, 1940, p. 1; *New York Times*, June 26, 1940, p. 1.

26. *Daily News*, June 25, 1940, p. 8; June 28, 1940, p. 10.

27. *Daily News*, July 19, 1940, p. 12; September 7, 1940, p. 10; September 23, 1940, p. 10; October 28, 1940, p. 8; November 1, 1940, p. 1. Ultimately the *Daily News* endorsed Willkie. The *Louisville Courier-Journal*, November 1, 1940, sec. 1, p. 8.

28. *Tribune*, September 16, 1940, p. 12; October 23, 1940, pp. 1, 14; October 17, 1940, p. 1; October 25, 1940, p. 12.

29. *Cleveland Plain Dealer*, November 1, 1940, p. 10; *Denver Post*, November 1, 1940, p. 2; *San Francisco Chronicle*, November 4, 1940, p. 16; *Journal of Commerce*, November 5, 1940, p. 16.

30. *Defender*, June 29, 1940, p. 17; July 6, 1940, pp. 6, 14; September 21, 1940, p. 17; September 28, 1940, p. 10; October 12, 1940, pp. 5, 16; October 19, 1940, pp. 6, 7, 11.

31. *Tribune*, November 6, 1940, p. 18.

32. *Daily News*, November 6, 1940, p. 1.

33. Dallek, *Roosevelt*, pp. 244–45, 253; Reynolds, *Anglo-American Alliance*, pp. 132, 143–44.

34. *Daily News*, November 8, 1940, p. 1; November 18, 1940, p. 6; December 7, 1940, p. 4.

35. *Tribune*, November 19, 1940, pt. 1, p. 18; November 27, 1940, p. 12; December 1, 1940, pt. 1, p. 20; December 9, 1940, pt. 1, p. 14; November 29, 1940, p. 12.

36. *Tribune*, January 11, 1941, p. 1; January 12, 1941, pt. 1, p. 1; *Journal of Commerce*, March 11, 1941, p. 16; *New York Times*, February 8, 1941, p. 6. The *Times* was also capable of editorializing in its headlines; see "For Our Defense," December 22, 1940, sec. 4, p. 1.

37. *Tribune*, January 3, 1941, p. 8. For example, the National Maritime Union, which otherwise seldom agreed with the *Tribune*, voiced similar concerns about lend-lease in the *New York Times*, February 14, 1941, p. 9.

38. *Tribune*, January 4, 1941, p. 10.

39. *Daily News*, January 14, 1940, p. 1.

40. *Cleveland Plain Dealer*, December 27, 1940, p. 6; December 27, 1940, p. 6; *Louisville Courier-Journal*, March 10, 1941, sec. 1, p. 4; *Atlanta Constitution*, December 25, 1940, p. 8; March 8, 1941, p. 4; *Los Angeles Times*, March 9, 1941, sec. 5, p. 4; *San Francisco Chronicle*, December 30, 1940, p. 12.

41. *Daily News*, February 5, 1941, p. 1.

42. *Defender*, January 4, 1941, p. 14; January 18, 1941, p. 17; January 25, 1941, p. 15; February 8, 1941, p. 15; February 15, 1941, p. 18; February, 22, 1941, pp. 8, 15; March 8, 1941, p. 15.

43. Kimball, *Most Unsordid Act*, pp. 156–60, 165, 171–87. Polls suggest the outlines of national opinion. At the end of the lend-lease debate only 17 percent of those surveyed were willing to declare war immediately, Gallup, *Gallup Poll*, p. 270. The public favored aid at the risk of war over preserving peace by 2 to 1, ibid., p. 273; up from a 50–50 split on this question seven months earlier, ibid., p. 243. But fewer than 40 percent favored any concrete extension of American involvement, ibid., p. 275. The polls do not reveal the bitterness of the opposing sides, but for evidence outside Chicago see the *Louisville Courier-Journal*, March 9, 1941, sec. 3, p. 6; *New York Times*, February 9, 1941, sec. 4, p. 3; *Atlanta Constitution*, March 8, 1941, p. 4.

CHAPTER THREE

1. Cantril and Strunk, *Public Opinion*, p. 973. Average attendance in the 1939–40 series of programs exceeded 1,100, CCFR Papers. Insights into the temper of Chicago elites were drawn from the following: Oates interview; Almond correspondence; William B. Benton to Robert M.

Hutchins, December 6, 1939, Hutchins Papers. *News Letter,* June 10, 1940, NLWV Papers.

2. Johnson, *Battle against Isolation,* chap. 1. Johnson was an instructor at the University of Chicago at that time and was himself active with the Chicago CDAAA chapter. Johnson interview.

3. Jackson, *Chicago Council on Foreign Relations,* pp. 18–23; Minutes: Executive Committee Meeting, August 20, 1940; Speakers' Committee Minutes, April 1, 1940, August 7, 1940, October 2, 1940, CCFR Papers.

4. Jackson, *Chicago Council on Foreign Relations,* p. 19.

5. *Stevenson Papers,* pp. 453–54; Martin, *Stevenson of Illinois,* pp. 164–65; *Daily News,* May 18, 1940, p. 1.

6. C. M. Eichelberger to Lucy McCoy, May 25, 1940, CDA Papers. McCoy was the secretary for the Chicago Office of the League of Nations Association and the local CDAAA chapter.

7. Johnson interview; Lucy McCoy to Mrs. Harrison Thomas, June 25, 1940, CDA Papers.

8. *Current Biography Yearbook, 1961,* pp. 440–42; Martin, *Stevenson of Illinois,* chapters 1–4, esp. p. 165; Johnson interview. In addition to Edgar Mowrer, who was a foreign correspondent for the *News,* his brother, Paul Scott Mowrer, was its editor.

9. Stevenson to Charles G. Dawes, January 18, 1939; Congressman John C. Martin to Stevenson, March 6, 1939; Stevenson to Loring C. Merwin, May 31, 1940; Stevenson to E. L. Ryerson, July 8, 1940, AES Papers.

10. Martin, *Stevenson of Illinois,* p. 165; *Stevenson Papers,* p. 456; Stevenson to David McDouglas, June 24, 1940; Stevenson to Lucy McCoy, July 6, 1940; Stevenson to Gilbert Schribner, July 8, 1940, AES Papers; Eichelberger to Lucy McCoy, June 3, 1940; Lucy McCoy to Mrs. Harrison Thomas, June 25, 1940, CDA Papers.

11. *Stevenson Papers,* pp. 456–57, 460–61, 508–10; *Daily Maroon,* June 6, 1940, p. 1; Lucy McCoy to Mrs. Harrison Thomas, June 25, 1940, CDA Papers.

12. Minutes of the Executive Committee—CDAAA, I, August 2, 1940, Theodore Smith, Summary Report, August 14, 1940, CDA Papers; *Stevenson Papers,* pp. 463–68; Johnson interview. The chapter eventually was made the center of midwest operations, Memorandum, October 2, 1940, CDA Papers.

13. Fenn letter; *Stevenson Papers,* pp. 464–65, 508–10; Lucy McCoy to Stevenson, August 26, 1940, AES Papers; *Daily News,* August 8, 1940, p. 3.

14. Hart Perry to William Allen White, May 23, 1940; Walter Johnson to Eichelberger, September 9, 1940, CDA Papers; *Daily News,* August 13,

1940, p. 3; August 14, 1940, p. 4; Johnson interview. Johnson served as faculty advisor to the student group and attended the rally.

15. Lucy McCoy to Stevenson, August 26, 1940; Stevenson to English Speaking Union, September 6, 1940; Stevenson to James B. Forgan, Jr., September 12, 1940; Stevenson to John Guteknecht, September 16, 1940; Stevenson to Eichelberger, September 10, 1940, AES Papers; *Stevenson Papers*, p. 475; *Daily News*, September 9, 1940, p. 3; September 16, 1940, p. 5; *Defender*, September 14, 1940, p. 7.

16. Stevenson to William McCormick Blair, Jr., September 23, 1940; *Stevenson Papers*, pp. 490, 458–87. John A. Morrison to Eichelberger, September 19, 1940, CDA Papers; *Daily News*, September 19, 1940, p. 1.

17. Plan of the Chicago CDAAA Meeting, September 18, 1940, AES Papers; *Tribune*, September 19, 1940, p. 3; *Daily News*, September 19, 1940, p. 1; *Defender*, July 6, 1940, p. 14; September 21, 1940, p. 5.

18. Josef Martinek to CDAAA Headquarters, July 9, 1940; Mrs. Harrison Thomas to Lucy McCoy, July 31, 1940, CDA Papers.

19. Stevenson to Morrison, September 20, 1940; Stevenson to M. J. Spiegel, November 15, 1940; Leo S. Samuels to Stevenson, February 12, 1941, AES Papers. Martin discusses Stevenson and the Jewish issue in *Stevenson of Illinois*, pp. 70–71, 175–77, 182, and notes that Stevenson also worried that the White Committee would be linked to Britain. It is indicative of attitudes among the largely Anglo-Saxon elite that keeping ethnics out of leadership positions in CDAAA would be taken as proof of the committee's Americanism and devotion to the national interest.

20. Neither Stevenson's nor the Committee's records refer at all to this matter. No significant records on the internal workings of the Kelly-Nash machine are known to exist. My source for this is the Johnson interview. Kelly's biographer claims that the mayor was outspoken on behalf of Roosevelt's foreign policy. If so, the Chicago press, including the *Daily News*, ignored him almost completely. He is scarcely mentioned at all throughout this period. Biles, *Big City Boss*, pp. 115–16.

21. *Tribune*, November 4, 1940, p. 12; *Daily News*, November 4, 1940, p. 15.

22. *Stevenson Papers*, pp. 494–95, 518–20. Stevenson himself admitted that the opposition had demolished the military threat argument, ibid., p. 502.

23. *New York Times*, February 2, 1941, p. 15; *Atlanta Constitution*, December 31, 1940, p. 4; *Denver Post*, December 27, 1940, p. 2.

24. *San Francisco Chronicle*, December 30, 1940, p. 1; *Cleveland Plain Dealer*, December 30, 1940, pp. 1, 3; Dallek, *Roosevelt*, pp. 256–57.

25. Proceedings of the Midwest Regional Conference, November 11, 1940, CDA Papers; *Daily News*, November 11, 1940, p. 5; November 12,

1940, p. 12; November 26, 1940, p. 8. Johnson contends that Stevenson advocated use of American convoys to deliver supplies to Britain at that November 11 meeting. If so, it was not recorded in the proceedings of the meeting, *Stevenson Papers*, p. 527. *San Francisco Chronicle*, December 27, 1940, pp. 1, 2.

26. Johnson, *Battle against Isolation*, pp. 171–96; Tuttle, "Aid-to-the-Allies," pp. 840–58; White's letter to Howard appears in Eichelberger, *Organizing for Peace*, pp. 145–46.

27. Stevenson to Howard Mayer, December 5, 1940, *Stevenson Papers*, p. 520; Stevenson to Webster D. Todd, January 1, 1941; Stevenson to Herbert Agar, December 13, 1940, AES Papers; Johnson interview; Johnson, *Battle against Isolation*, pp. 196–97.

28. William Emerson to John A. Morrison, January 4, 1941; Stevenson to Lewis Douglas, January 1, 1941; Eichelberger to Morrison, January 18, 1941, AES Papers; Johnson, *Battle against Isolation*, pp. 201–3; Martin, *Stevenson of Illinois*, p. 183.

29. Utley's speech is in the CDA File, AFC Papers; *Tribune*, January 10, 1941, p. 5; February 4, 1941, p. 3; *Daily News*, January 22, 1941, p. 7; *Daily Maroon*, January 29, 1941, p. 1.

30. *Daily Maroon*, January 29, 1941, p. 1; "The Atlantic Is Not 3000 Miles Wide Because –"; Mrs. Harrison Thomas to Morrison, January 13, 1941, CDA Papers.

31. *Daily News*, February 11, 1941, p. 8; Stevenson to Frank Knox, January 31, 1941; Stevenson to Mrs. Paul Magnusen, February 3, 1941, *Stevenson Papers*, pp. 533–35.

32. *Louisville Courier-Journal*, March 8, 1941, sec. 3, p. 6; *Cleveland Plain Dealer*, March 9, 1941, p. 14; *New York Times*, October 30, 1940, p. 22; Stevenson to Arthur Krock, October 31, 1940, *Stevenson Papers*, p. 506; *Tribune*, September 7, 1940, p. 10; "The Atlantic Is Not 3000 Miles Wide Because –," CDA Papers; *Daily News*, November 12, 1940, p. 12.

33. *Tribune*, September 14, 1940, p. 5; Stevenson to Morrison, September 23, 1940, AES Papers; Stevenson to the Editor, *Daily News*, December 23, 1940, p. 10.

34. *Daily News*, March 16, 1941, p. 1; Morrison to Roger Greene, February 25, 1941, CDA Papers; Stevenson to Ernest Gibson, March 3, 1941; Stevenson to Thomas K. Finletter, February 3, 1941; Morrison to Stevenson, March 22, 1941, AES Papers.

35. Morrison to Stevenson, March 22, 1941, AES Papers; Martin, *Stevenson of Illinois*, pp. 174, 183–85; Stevenson to Mrs. Stanley McCormick, December 17, 1940, *Stevenson Papers*, pp. 524–25; Oates interview. The case for pressure on Stevenson's law firm rests on the Stevenson-McCormick letter alone. Oates was in a position to know, and his denial

was emphatic, although he was interviewed many years afterward. John Bartlow Martin states that Stevenson's displeasure with the Century Group caused him to decide to quit CDAAA, but an earlier biographer, Kenneth S. Davis, cites a personal interview with Stevenson to contend that his decision did not come until April 1941 and was based on a conviction that America must fully enter the war. Davis, *Politics of Honor*, p. 61. As my account indicates, I believe both authors underestimate the complexity of factors involved.

36. The *St. Louis Post-Dispatch*, March 10, 1941, p. 28; McCoy to Stevenson, February 19, 1941; Stevenson to Ernest Gibson, March 8, 1941, AES Papers; *Daily News*, March 15, 1941, p. 3.

37. *Daily News*, June 15, 1940, p. 16; October 22, 1940, p. 9; February 11, 1940, pp. 1, 4; June 12, 1940, p. 2; June 12, 1940, p. 15. *Louisville Courier-Journal*, May 26, 1940, sec. 1, p. 1; May 27, 1940, sec. 1, p. 4.

38. *Defender*, August 31, 1940, p. 1; September 14, 1940, p. 11; September 21, 1940, p. 1; May 3, 1941, p. 6.

39. *Tribune*, May 24, 1940, p. 3; June 4, 1940, p. 5; *Defender*, May 25, 1940, p. 1; *Daily News*, July 30, 1940, p. 14; August 6, 1940, p. 6; August 26, 1940, p. 8; *Boston Globe*, May 28, 1940, p. 23.

40. Dallek, *Roosevelt*, pp. 224–27; *Los Angeles Times*, May 27, 1940, sec. 1, p. 1; *Denver Post*, May 24, 1940, p. 2; *New York Times*, June 22, 1940, p. 6; May 21, 1940, p. 14; May 26, 1940, p. 6; May 29, 1940, p. 16; *Atlanta Constitution*, May 26, 1940, pp. 1, 10; May 29, 1940, p. 1.

41. *Denver Post*, May 26, 1940, p. 1.

42. *Defender*, June 22, 1940, p. 14; June 29, 1940, p. 16; August 10, 1940, pp. 1, 2; August 24, 1940, pp. 1, 14.

43. *Daily News*, June 21, 1940, p. 9; July 6, 1940, p. 7; August 31, 1940, p. 6; October 19, 1940, p. 4; *New York Times*, June 9, 1940, p. 30; June 12, 1940, p. 17; June 24, 1940, p. 4; August 20, 1940, p. 6.

44. *Daily News*, September 4, 1940, p. 10.

45. *Daily News*, June 19, 1940, p. 6; June 21, 1940, p. 7; *Tribune*, June 22, 1940, p. 11.

46. *Tribune*, October 27, 1940, pt. 3 (West), p. 1; *Daily News*, June 22, 1940, p. 11.

47. *Daily News*, November 2, 1940, p. 3; Lubell, *American Politics*, pp. 55, 140–41, 155.

48. *Tribune*, September 10, 1940, p. 7; *Daily News*, September 12, 1940, p. 12. The others were, *Dr. Mambock, I Was a Captive in Nazi Germany, Inside Nazi Germany* (a *March of Time* feature), *Concentration Camp, The Opperman Family, Hitler, the Beast of Berlin*, and *The Living Dead*. Manvell, *Films*, p. 64, summarizes of the plot of *Pastor Hall*.

49. *Daily News*, September 12, 1940, p. 12; September 13, 1940, p. 7;

Tribune, September 13, 1940, p. 12; *Defender*, September 21, 1940, p. 13.

50. *Daily News*, September 12, 1940, p. 3; September 14, 1940, p. 3.

51. *Tribune*, September 27, 1940, p. 12; *Daily News*, September 25, 1940, p. 1; September 30, 1940, p. 12; January 16, 1941, p. 10; February 20, 1941, p. 1; February 21, 1941, p. 5; *New York Times*, December 30, 1940, p. 71.

52. *Louisville Courier-Journal*, March 11, 1941, sec. 1, p. 8; *New York Times*, December 31, 1940, p. 16; January 24, 1941, p. 8; February 10, 1941, p. 10.

53. *News Letter*, December 19, 1940; draft of letter to state League presidents, December 31, 1940 and attachment; Referenda, January 10, 1941; Marguerite Wells to the Members of the National Board of Directors, January 10, 1941; Press Release, January 10, 1941; *News Letter*, January 24, 1941, NLWV Papers.

54. Lolita Bogert to Marguerite Wells, January 18, 1941, and attachments; Mrs. George Bogert to Colleagues, February 12, 1941, and attachments; excerpt from Mrs. Quincy Wright to unknown, February 10, 1941, NLWV Papers.

55. Lolita Bogert to Marguerite Wells, February 5, 1941, and attachments; Request for Action, February 25, 1941, NLWV Papers.

56. Lolita Bogert to Marguerite Wells, February 5, 1941, and attachments; Request for Action, February 25, 1941; Bogert to Wells, February 7, 1941; Bogert to Wells, February 21, 1941; Bogert to Wells, March 1, 1941; petition by members of the Flossmoor LWV, n.d., NLWV Papers.

57. Lolita Bogert to Marguerite Wells, February 21, 1941; Bogert to Wells, February 21, 1941, NLWV Papers.

58. *Daily Maroon*, April 20, 1940, p. 1; May 7, 1940, pp. 1, 3; May 16, 1940, p. 1; *Journal of Commerce*, May 23, 1940, p. 14.

59. *Tribune*, May 20, 1940, p. 8; *Daily Maroon*, June 6, 1940, p. 1; *Daily News*, August 13, 1940, p. 3; August 14, 1940, p. 4; *New York Times*, May 26, 1940, p. 2; *Los Angeles Times*, May 17, 1940, sec. 1, p. 12; May 26, 1940, sec. 1, p. 12.

60. *Tribune*, October 6, 1940, pt. 3 (South), p. 7; *Daily Maroon*, September 11, 1940, p. 2; September 23, 1940, p. 2; October 11, 1940, p. 2.

61. *Daily Maroon*, October 15, 1940, p. 1; October 25, 1940, p. 1; January 31, 1941, p. 1.

62. *Daily Maroon*, October 29, 1940, pp. 1, 2; November 12, 1940, p. 1; November 13, 1940, p. 1; November 20, 1940, p. 1; December 5, 1940, p. 4; December 10, 1940, p. 1. The colonels, of course, are Charles Lindbergh and Robert R. McCormick, respectively.

63. *Daily Maroon*, January 14, 1941, p. 2.

64. *Daily Maroon*, January 24, 1941, pp. 1–4; January 27, 1941, pp. 1–4;

January 28, 1941, p. 2; January 20, 1941, p. 1; January 30, 1941, p. 1.
65. *Daily Maroon*, February 27, 1941, p. 2.

CHAPTER FOUR

1. *Tribune*, May 15, 1940, p. 5; May 24, 1940, p. 23; *New York Times*, May 23, 1940, p. 19; May 26, 1940, sec. 4, p. 7.

2. *Tribune*, June 15, 1940, p. 3; June 30, 1940, pt. 3 (Southwest), p. 1; July 21, 1940, pt. 3 (South), p. 2; *Cleveland Plain Dealer*, March 8, 1941, p. 7; *New York Times*, February 14, 1941, p. 5; *San Francisco Chronicle*, May 26, 1940, p. 57; February 20, 1941, p. 6.

3. *Tribune*, June 23, 1940, pt. 1, p. 3; June 20, 1940, pt. 1, p. 6 and pt. 3 (North), p. 2; July 14, 1940, pt. 1, p. 5; July 15, 1940, p. 3; *Los Angeles Times*, May 28, 1940, sec. 1, p. 5; May 31, 1940, sec. 1, p. 1; *New York Times*, July 1, 1940, p. 5.

4. *Tribune*, June 27, 1940, p. 2; July 24, 1940, p. 4; July 26, 1940, p. 4; July 27, 1940, p. 4; July 30, 1940, p. 5; *Daily News*, July 26, 1940, p. 10; August 3, 1940, p. 3; Stevenson to Claude Pepper, August 12, 1940, *Stevenson Papers*, pp. 466–67; *New York Times*, October 5, 1946, p. 9; August 4, 1940, p. 6.

5. Adlai Stevenson to Claude Pepper, August 12, 1940, *Stevenson Papers*, pp. 466–67; *Daily News*, August 5, 1940, p. 7; *Tribune*, August 5, 1940, pp. 1, 4, 28. The text of Lindbergh's address is in *New York Times*, August 5, 1940, p. 4.

6. *Defender*, May 18, 1940, p. 22; June 22, 1940, p. 14; June 29, 1940, p. 14; August 3, 1940, p. 7; August 24, 1940, p. 17; September 7, 1940, p. 14; October 26, 1940, pp. 3, 7; November 30, 1940, p. 6.

7. *Daily News*, July 1,1940, p. 32; July 5, 1940, p. 10.

8. *Daily News*, July 18, 1940, p. 1; July 28, 1940, pt. 3 (North), p. 2.

9. *Daily News*, August 2, 1940, p. 1; August 5, 1940, p. 7; August 8, 1940, p. 1; *Tribune*, August 14, 1940, p. 14.

10. *Tribune*, September 22, 1940, pt. 1, p. 16; *Daily News*, October 5, 1940, p. 1; February 12, 1941, p. 1; *New York Times*, June 12, 1940, p. 20.

11. *Tribune*, June 11, 1940, p. 3; February 8, 1941, p. 2; *Daily News*, August 27, 1940, p. 1; November 23, 1940, p. 4; *Los Angeles Times*, May 27, 1940, sec. 2, p. 1; *San Francisco Chronicle*, May 30, 1940, p. 11.

12. *New York Times*, May 24, 1940, p. 13; June 22, 1940, p. 12; July 1, 1940, p. 19; January 1, 1941, p. 7; February 16, 1941, p. 12.

13. Cantril and Strunk, *Public Opinion*, p. 1119; Lauderbaugh, *American*

Steelmakers, pp. 18–19, 41, 71, 117; *New York Times*, May 25, 1940, sec. 2, p. 3; May 19, 1940, p. 10; December 14, 1940, p. 11.

14. Cole, *America First*, pp. 71–4, emphasizes the conservatism of the businessmen. His is much the standard view. Since Cole wrote, however, historians have become much more sensitive to the ambiguities of terms like "conservative" and "liberal." There is probably little profit in debating which labels best fit particular individuals. My point is only that America First was not created by refugees from the Liberty League. Rather its key leadership had shown itself considerably more open to innovation and divergent viewpoints during the New Deal years than that. Doenecke, "Robert E. Wood," pp. 162–75, emphasizes the bitter opposition to the Fair Deal and similar proposals by Wood and others in the late 1940s. The intense conservatism of their postwar years stems in part, I suspect, from their being radicalized during the foreign policy debate of 1939–41.

15. Undated copies of the original letter and petition can be found in the Hutchins Papers. For an account of the Yale Group see Sarles, "A Story of America First," chap. 1, pp. 2, 3–5, AFC Papers; Stuart interview.

16. Stuart interview; Confidential Folder on America First, CDA Papers.

17. Stuart interview; Confidential Folder on America First, CDA Papers.

18. Stuart interview; Confidential Folder on America First, CDA Papers; Sarles, "Story of America First," chap. 1, pp. 2, 9–12, AFC Papers; Robert E. Wood to Frank Knox, June 21, 1940; Wood to Edgar B. Stern, August 14, 1940, Wood Papers.

19. *Current Biography, 1941*, pp. 933–35; Doenecke, "Robert E. Wood," pp. 162–75; Oates interview; William Benton to Robert Wood, November 18, 1940; John Howe to Robert Hutchins, October 4, 1940, Benton Papers.

20. "Proposed Committee" undated mailing list, Hutchins Papers; Robert Wood to Herbert Hoover, July 22, 1940, Wood Papers; "Emergency Committee to Defend America First," Morton Papers.

21. *Tribune*, September 5, 1940, p. 3; Stuart interview; Sarles, "Story of America First," chap. 1, p. 1, chap. 2, p. 19, AFC Papers.

22. Stuart interview; Judson's views are ably summarized in a series of letters to Quincy Wright, September 27–October 3, 1939, Wright Papers.

23. *Tribune*, September 5, 1940, p. 3; Stuart interview; Hanford MacNider to Robert Wood, December 20, 1940; Sarles "Story of America First," chap. 2, p. 21, AFC Papers; Stenehjem, *American First*, pp. 121–23.

24. Hanford MacNider to Robert Wood, July 11, 1941, AFC Papers; *Daily News*, September 5, 1940, p. 1.

25. *Tribune*, September 5, 1940, p. 3; October 23, 1940, p. 13; *Daily News*, November 1, 1940, p. 18; Sarles, "Story of America First," chap. 2, p. 26, AFC Papers.

26. "Our Foreign Policy," AFC Pamphlet, AES Papers; *Daily News*, October 4, 1940, p. 11; *Tribune*, October 5, 1940, pp. 1, 6. Wood's speech won a very respectful hearing in the *Daily News*, October 10, 1940, p. 12; *New York Times*, May 12, 1940, sec. 4, p. 3.

27. *Tribune*, December 13, 1940, p. 1; *New York Times*, November 13, 1940, p. 10.

28. *Tribune*, December 13, 1940, p. 1; *New York Times*, November 13, 1940, p. 10.

29. Sarles, "Story of America First," chap. 2, p. 33, AFC Papers.

30. Stuart interview; *Tribune*, September 5, 1940, p. 12.

31. The rhetoric emerges most clearly in the "America First Club Plan," n.d. but probably January 1941; see also *Guide for State Organization*, January 1941, AFC Papers.

32. Stuart interview; *Guide for District Organization*; *Chapter Manual*, AFC Papers.

33. *New York Times*, December 18, 1940, p. 12; *Denver Post*, December 30, 1940, p. 13; Lindbergh, *Wartime Journals*, pp. 421–22, 426–32, 436, 438–40.

34. "Outline of Projects," February 25, 1941, AFC Papers.

35. R. Douglas Stuart to Robert Wood, December 6, 1940; Chicago AFC Weekly Payroll, February 18, 1941; Speakers Bureau Reports; Janet Fairbank to Robert Wood, February 20, 1941, AFC Papers; *Tribune*, January 4, 1941, p. 5; January 5, 1941, pt. 1, p. 11; January 30, 1941, p. 1.

36. Cole, *America First*, pp. 30–31; Cole, "America First and the South," pp. 36–47; Irish, "Foreign Policy and the South," pp. 306–26; Gallup, *Gallup Poll*, pp. 231, 239, 245, 254, 256, 259–61, 263, 275, 280.

37. *Daily News*, January 21, 1941, p. 8.

38. *Tribune*, January 22, 1941, p. 3; January 29, 1941, p. 1; February 22, 1941, p. 4; *Daily News*, January 31, 1941, p. 11; March 3, 1941, p. 5; *New York Times*, September 2, 1940, p. 8; February 14, 1941, p. 9.

39. *Defender*, February 8, 1941, pp. 2, 4; February 15, 1941, p. 26; May 10, 1941, p. 4.

40. "Address to Advertising Men's Post Number 38," February 3, 1941, AFC Papers; *Daily News*, February 3, 1941, p. 1; Clay Judson to James Bryant Conant, February 3, 1941, Hutchins Papers.

41. *Tribune*, January 24, 1941, pp. 1, 2; *Daily Maroon*, January 24, 1941, pp. 4, 6.

42. William Benton to Robert Hutchins, July 12, 1940; Benton to

Hutchins, October 3, 1940; Benton to Hutchins, November 1, 1940; Hutchins to Benton, January 29, 1941; Benton to Ralph Ingersoll, April 10, 1941, Benton Papers; "Statement by Members of the Faculty of the University of Chicago," January 23, 1941, Hutchins Papers; *Daily Maroon*, January 24, 1941, pp. 1–6; January 28, 1941, p. 2. The situation at Harvard, for example, was almost the mirror image of Chicago. Harvard's president, James Bryant Conant, was an outspoken proponent of aid while the *Harvard Crimson* opposed it. *Boston Globe,* May 31, 1940, p. 16.

43. R. Douglas Stuart to William Benton, February 15, 1941; Stuart to Benton, February 19, 1941, AFC Papers; "Confidential Profile—AFC," CDA Papers.

44. Sterling Morton to Hanford MacNider, April 1, 1941; Sterling Morton to Robert Wood, April 3, 1941, Morton Papers.

45. Robert Wood to Sterling Morton, April 7, 1941, Morton Papers; William Benton to Robert Hutchins, December 17, 1940, Benton Papers.

CHAPTER FIVE

1. Robert Wood to Sterling Morton, April 7, 1941, Morton Papers; *New York Times*, May 10, 1941, sec. 4, p. 3. All percentages are based on those respondents who expressed an opinion. Cantril and Strunk, *Public Opinion*, p. 267.

2. Morison, *The Two Ocean War*, pp. 35–36; Liddell Hart, *Second World War*, 1:377–82; Stokesbury, *History of World War II*, pp. 123–49.

3. Reynolds, *Anglo-American Alliance*, pp. 141–42, 149, 168, 199, 214–19; *New York Times*, July 5, 1941, p. 1; July 8, 1941, p. 8.

4. Burns, *Soldier of Freedom*, pp. 84–92, 101–6; Dallek, *Roosevelt*, pp. 263–67; Reynolds, *Anglo-American Alliance*, pp. 20–24; Lindbergh, *Wartime Journals*, pp. 478, 481, 488; *New York Times*, April 25, 1941, p. 1; May 13, 1941, p. 13; May 18, 1941, sec. 4, p. 3; May 26, 1941, p. 1; May 29, 1941, pp. 2, 4.

5. Utley, *War with Japan*, pp. 102–18, 153–56; Thorne, *Allies*, pp. 51–83; Schroeder, *Japanese-American Relations*, pp. 168–216; Reynolds, *Anglo-American Alliance*, pp. 226–36; *Louisville Courier-Journal*, September 8, 1941, sec. 1, p. 4.

6. *Tribune*, May 5, 1941, p. 13; November 11, 1941, p. 36; September 14, 1941, pt. 6, p. 4; *Daily News*, September 17, 1941, p. 14.

7. *Tribune*, July 19, 1941, p. 6; *Daily News*, October 11, 1941, p. 17; November 18, 1941, p. 18; May 10, 1941, Comics Section; May 17, 1941, Comics Section.

8. *New York Times*, April 22, 1941, p. 26.

9. *Tribune*, May 3, 1941, p. 10; April 12, 1941, p. 1; July 9, 1941, p. 6; October 28, 1941, p. 12.

10. *Tribune*, May 25, 1941, pt. 1, p. 14; May 28, 1941, p. 14; May 29, 1941, p. 12.

11. *Tribune*, March 17, 1941, p. 12; May 24, 1941, p. 8; May 8, 1941, p. 1; June 23, 1941, p. 1; June 24, 1941, p. 12; June 28, 1941, pp. 1, 8; Edwards, *McCormick's Tribune*, pp. 148, 153, 172. The *Tribune* continued its infrequent exposure and denunciation of Nazi atrocities long after the Russian invasion. See *Tribune*, October 3, 1941, p. 1; October 19, 1941, pt. 1, p. 16; October 23, 1941, p. 18; October 27, 1941, p. 12.

12. *Daily News*, April 19, 1941, p. 10; April 9, 1941, p. 12; July 7, 1941, p. 1; July 24, 1941, p. 8; September 12, 1941, p. 1.

13. *Daily News*, April 12, 1941, p. 2; April 23, 1941, p. 1; May 5, 1941, p. 1; April 19, 1941, p. 10; June 20, 1941, p. 8; November 8, 1941, p. 10.

14. *New York Times*, August 1, 1941, p. 4; *San Francisco Chronicle*, September 28, 1941, p. 1; *Louisville Courier-Journal*, September 11, 1941, sec. 1, p. 4; *Atlanta Constitution*, November 12, 1941, p. 6; *Cleveland Plain Dealer*, November 8, 1941, p. 8; *Denver Post*, November 8, 1941, p. 2.

15. *New York Times*, August 1, 1941, p. 4; September 3, 1941, p. 22; November 2, 1941, sec. 4, p. 6; *Los Angeles Times*, September 12, 1941, sec. 2, p. 4.

16. *Defender*, March 15, 1941, p. 14; March 21, 1941, p. 14; May 10, 1941, pp. 1, 15; July 5, 1941, pp. 1, 2; July 12, 1941, p. 1; August 23, 1941, p. 16.

17. *Defender*, January 18, 1941, p. 16; March 15, 1941, p. 14; April 5, 1941, p. 16; April 12, 1941, p. 14; April 19, 1941, p. 16; November 16, 1941, p. 16; November 23, 1941, p. 14.

18. *Daily News*, June 4, 1941, p. 1; August 2, 1941, p. 1; August 4, 1941, p. 8; October 30, 1941, p. 12; November 2, 1941, p. 10.

19. *Tribune*, August 8, 1941, p. 8; April 20, 1941, pt. 1, p. 3; October 4, 1941, p. 3; March 21, 1941, p. 1; June 1, 1941, p. 1; June 30, 1941, p. 9; April 25, 1941, p. 10; April 27, 1941, pt. 1, p. 1; June 8, 1941, pt. 1, pp. 1, 8; November 4, 1941, p. 5.

20. *Daily News*, April 8, 1941, p. 10; July 23, 1941, p. 10; July 26, 1941, p. 10; November 12, 1941, p. 1.

21. *Tribune*, March 22, 1941, p. 10.

22. *New York Times*, March 17, 1941, p. 16; March 24, 1941, p. 16; April 14, 1941, p. 19; April 15, 1941, p. 9; May 6, 1941, p. 5; March 21, 1941, p. 7; April 10, 1941, p. 2; April 24, 1941, pp. 1, 12; *San Francisco Chronicle*, September 23, 1941, p. 12; November 8, 1941, p. 12.

23. Langer and Gleason, *Undeclared War*, pp. 419–64, 568–92, 732–60; Bailey, *Diplomatic History*, pp. 729–32; Dallek, *Roosevelt*, pp. 260–62, 287–89.

24. *Los Angeles Times*, September 12, 1941, pt. 2, p. 4; *Atlanta Constitution*, September 13, 1941, p. 4; *St. Louis Post-Dispatch*, September 12, 1941, p. 2E; *Denver Post*, September 12, 1941, p. 2; *Cleveland Plain Dealer*, September 12, 1941, p. 10; *Journal of Commerce*, September 13, 1941, pp. 1, 12.

25. *Tribune*, April 1, 1941, p. 12; September 6, 1941, p. 8; October 9, 1941, p. 10; October 7, 1941, p. 12; October 16, 1941, pp. 1, 4.

26. *Daily News*, September 6, 1941, p. 1; October 15, 1941, p. 10; November 11, 1941, p. 1; November 26, 1941, p. 10.

27. *Los Angeles Times*, September 18, 1941, sec. 2, p. 4; November 1, 1941, sec. 2, p. 4; *San Francisco Chronicle*, September 23, 1941, p. 12; November 8, 1941, p. 1; *New York Times*, October 7, 1941, p. 22.

28. *Denver Post*, November 13, 1941, p. 2; November 14, 1941, p. 2; *Cleveland Plain Dealer*, November 13, 1941, p. 1; *Los Angeles Times*, November 13, 1941, sec. 1, pp. 1, 15; *San Francisco Chronicle*, November 14, 1941, p. 1; *New York Times*, November 14, 1941, pp. 1, 4; November 16, 1941, sec. 4, p. 3.

29. Gallup, *Gallup Poll*, pp. 304, 307; Burns, *Soldier of Freedom*, pp. 148–49; *Daily News*, May 29, 1941, p. 1; June 14, 1941, p. 12; August 12, 1941, p. 1; August 23, 1941, p. 2.

30. *Tribune*, June 16, 1941, p. 10; July 4, 1940, p. 4; *Daily News*, July 12, 1940, p. 2; December 12, 1940, p. 2; November 9, 1940, p. 2.

31. *San Francisco Chronicle*, December 24, 1940, p. 3; July 7, 1941, p. 2; *New York Times*, June 23, 1940, sec. 4, pp. 1, 5; February 16, 1941, sec. 4, p. 3; *Boston Globe*, January 5, 1940, p. 5 (Red Streak); *Denver Post*, November 3, 1940, sec. 3, p. 3; *Los Angeles Times*, September 12, 1941, pp. 1, 8; *Atlanta Constitution*, November 10, 1941, p. 3; November 12, 1941, p. 5; Culbert, *News for Everyman*, p. 5; Manvell, *Films*, p. 87.

32. *Daily News*, July 12, 1940, p. 2; September 26, 1940, p. 12; September 28, 1940, p. 14; October 1, 1940, p. 8; November 28, 1940, p. 12; December 18, 1940, p. 2; January 29, 1941, p. 1.

33. *San Francisco Chronicle*, December 3, 1941, p. 16; *New York Times*, June 23, 1940, sec. 4, pp. 1, 5; February 16, 1941, sec. 4, p. 3; February 23, 1941, sec. 4, p. 1; *Louisville Courier-Journal*, March 9, 1941, sec. 3, p. 1; November 11, 1941, sec. 1, p. 6; *Cleveland Plain Dealer*, November 11, 1941, p. 22.

34. *Tribune*, August 3, 1940, p. 8; September 28, 1940, pp. 1, 10; September 29, 1940, p. 10.

35. *Tribune*, August 21, 1941, p. 10.

36. *Tribune*, June 16, 1941, p. 10; July 26, 1941, p. 6; August 2, 1941, p. 10.

37. *Daily News*, October 18, 1941, p. 1; November 3, 1941, p. 5; December 5, 1941, p. 2; *Tribune*, October 17, 1941, p. 1; November 18, 1941, p. 14; November 28, 1941, p. 1; *Louisville Courier-Journal*, November 10, 1941, pt. 1, p. 2; *Cleveland Plain Dealer*, November 11, 1941, p. 2; *New York Times*, November 28, 1941, p. 1; November 30, 1941, sec. 4, p. 1; *San Francisco Chronicle*, December 3, 1941, p. 3; *Denver Post*, December 1, 1941, p. 1; *Journal of Commerce*, December 4, 1941, p. 16; December 5, 1941, p. 20.

CHAPTER SIX

1. By far the most complete account of the Fight For Freedom Committee is Chadwin, *Warhawks*.

2. *Tribune*, March 18, 1941, p. 3; *Daily News*, April 17, 1941, p. 1; April 23, 1941, p. 9.

3. "Meeting of Chicago Council of Committee to Defend America," February 18, 1941, FFF Papers; Minutes of the Executive Committee Meeting, March 20, 1941, AES Papers.

4. Johnson interview; *Daily News*, April 25, 1941, p. 4; Morrison to Harland H. Allen, June 11, 1941, AES Papers.

5. Chicago CDA *News Bulletin*, June 23, 1941, CDA Papers.

6. Ibid.; *Daily News*, April 25, 1941.

7. *St. Louis Post-Dispatch*, March 14, 1941, p. 30; *New York Times*, May 11, 1941, sec. 4, p. 10; Gallup, *Gallup Poll*, pp. 259, 273, 275–76, 297, 300, 304.

8. See Eichelberger, *Organizing For Peace*; Chicago CDA *News Bulletin*, July 16, 1941, CDA Papers.

9. Chicago CDA *News Bulletin*, July 16, 1941, CDA Papers.

10. *Daily News*, May 21, 1941, p. 1.

11. Minutes, CDA Regional Conference, February 1, 1941; Stevenson to Paul W. Steer, April 10, 1941, AES Papers; Adlai Stevenson to Albert A. Sprague, May 6, 1941; Stevenson to Wendell Willkie, May 20, 1941; *Stevenson Papers*, pp. 547–48, 552.

12. Adlai Stevenson to Albert A. Sprague, May 6, 1941; Stevenson to Edward J. Kelly, May 28, 1941, *Stevenson Papers*, pp. 547–48, 553–54; Morrison to Roger S. Greene, June 9, 1941, CDA Papers.

13. *New York Times*, June 7, 1941, pp. 1, 6; *Tribune*, June 7, 1941, p. 3; *Daily News*, June 7, 1941, pp. 13, 42; June 13, 1941, p. 4; John Morrison

to Roger S. Greene, June 9, 1941, CDA Papers; Paul Douglas to Harold L. Ickes, June 10, 1941, Ickes Papers.

14. Harland Allen to Clark Eichelberger, July 12, 1941, CDA Papers.

15. Mrs. Bertha K. Fenn to Adlai Stevenson, July 17, 1941; Charles P. Megan to Stevenson, August 22, 1941, AES Papers; Paul Lyness to Clark Eichelberger, July 26, 1941; Lyness to Mrs. Thomas, August 26, 1941; Doris Hargis to Mrs. Thomas, September 9, 1941, CDA Papers.

16. *Cleveland Plain Dealer*, September 19, 1941, p. 3.

17. Chadwin, *Warhawks*, pp. 159–90; *Daily News*, April 21, 1941, p. 5; memo, Courtenay Barber, Jr., and Albert Parry to the Executive Committee of the Chicago Chapter of the Fight For Freedom, December 1941, FFF Papers; *New York Times*, April 20, 1941, p. 21.

18. Carlson, "Fight For Freedom Committee," pp. 11–13; memo, Courtenay Barber, Jr., and Albert Parry to FFF Executive Committee, December 1941, FFF Papers.

19. *Cleveland Plain Dealer*, December 3, 1941, p. 7; *New York Times*, October 6, 1941, pp. 1, 7.

20. FFF Press Release, July 29, 1941, FFF Papers.

21. *New York Times*, March 12, 1941, p. 15; April 7, 1941, p. 14; May 22, 1941, p. 11; May 25, 1941, p. 3; May 26, 1941, p. 12; July 15, 1941, p. 13; September 16, 1941, p. 18; September 20, 1941, p. 5; *Louisville Courier-Journal*, December 4, 1941, sec. 1, p. 6; *Denver Post*, November 8, 1941, p. 1; *Boston Globe*, September 12, 1941, p. 22.

22. *New York Times*, March 3, 1941, p. 8; June 16, 1941, p. 6; *Los Angeles Times*, March 8, 1941, sec. 3, p. 1.

23. Francis P. Miller to Carroll Binder, November 29, 1940; Paul Scott Mowrer to Ickes, June 10, 1941; Ickes to Mowrer, June 23, 1941, Ickes Papers.

24. Harold Ickes to Robert R. McCormick, June 30, 1941, Ickes Papers; *Tribune*, April 15, 1941, p. 14.

25. Becker, *Marshall Field III*, pp. 273–88; Tebbel, *The Marshall Fields*, pp. 224–37.

26. Courtenay Barber, Jr., to Harold Ickes, July 27, 1941; Ickes to Barber, July 28, 1941, Ickes Papers.

27. Courtenay Barber, Jr., to Ulric Bell, July 30, 1941; Barber to Mrs. Emmons Blaine, July 31, 1941; Felix Mendelsohn, Jr., to the Chicago FFF, August 1, 1941, FFF Papers; Paul V. Perry to Harold Ickes, July 30, 1941, Ickes Papers; *Tribune*, July 30, 1941, p. 5.

28. Courtenay Barber, Jr., to Ulric Bell, July 30, 1941; Albert Parry to Jean Dawson, August 4, 1941, FFF Papers; Carlson, "Fight For Freedom," p. 23.

29. *Daily News*, August 26, 1941, p. 4; Courtenay Barber, Jr., to Mrs.

Helena Clayton, August 27, 1941; Albert Parry to Richard E. Gutstadt, August 9, 1941, FFF Papers.

30. *New York Times*, August 23, 1941, p. 2; Paul Scott Mowrer to Albert Parry, August 21, 1941; FFF Press Release, September 15, 1941; Parry to George F. Havell, September 15, 1941, FFF Papers; *Tribune*, August 15, 1941, p. 2; *Daily News*, August 22, 1941, p. 14; October 4, 1941, p. 5.

31. *Tribune*, September 10, 1941, p. 3; Albert Parry to *Chicago Tribune*, September 10, 1941; FFF Press Release, August 9, 1941, FFF Papers.

32. A. Lidden Gresham to Albert Parry, September 3, 1941; Lois E. Barnes to Parry, September 19, 1941; Resolution No. 2, FFF Rally, October 3, 1941, FFF Papers; Tebbel, *The Marshall Fields*, p. 225; Becker, *Marshall Field III*, p. 283.

33. Courtenay Barber, Jr., to Peter Cusick, June 21, 1941; Barber to Howard M. Landau, July 10, 1941; Minutes of the Chicago FFF Executive Committee meeting, November 14, 1941; Minutes of the Chicago FFF Executive Committee meeting, November 28, 1941; Barber to Paul Douglas, November 14, 1941; Barber to Dorian Cairns, September 20, 1941; Barber to Robert Eiger, October 14, 1941, FFF Papers.

34. *Daily News*, August 26, 1941, p. 4; November 17, 1941, p. 11; *Tribune*, November 20, 1941, p. 1; Edna C. Hall to FFF, October 10, 1941; Albert Parry to Denison Hull, August 21, 1941; Parry to Arthur J. Goldberg, September 6, 1941; Ethnic Files; Courtenay Barber, Jr., to Peter Cusick, June 21, 1941; FFF Press Release, December 4, 1941, FFF Papers.

35. *Tribune*, April 16, 1941, p. 1; April 17, 1941, p. 11; *Daily News*, April 16, 1941, p. 1; *New York Times*, April 17, 1941, p. 19.

36. *Daily News*, April 16, 1941, p. 3; *St. Louis Post-Dispatch*, September 13, 1941, p. 4A.

37. *New York Times*, April 18, 1941, p. 5; October 13, 1940, p. 5

38. *Daily News*, June 24, 1941, p. 1; July 14, 1941, p. 4; July 16, 1941, p. 1; *New York Times*, July 28, 1941, p. 6.

39. *Tribune*, September 21, 1941, pt. 1, p. 1; *New York Times*, June 1, 1941, p. 21; September 21, 1941, p. 12; *Cleveland Plain Dealer*, November 8, 1941, p. 6.

40. *Defender*, March 15, 1941, p. 14; June 14, 1941, p. 16; July 5, 1941, p. 15; August 2, 1941, p. 14; August 30, 1941, p. 14; September 6, 1941, p. 7; October 4, 1941, p. 3; October 18, 1941, p. 10; November 15, 1941, p. 10; December 6, 1941, p. 1.

41. *Daily News*, June 16, 1941, p. 7; John Fitzpatrick to FFF, July 28, 1941; Albert Parry to Arthur Goldberg, September 4, 1941; Parry to Goldberg, September 6, 1941; Samuel Levin to Parry, July 22, 1941; Abe Rosenfield to Courtenay Barber, Jr., October 21, 1941, FFF Papers.

42. *CIO Newsletter*, September 24, 1941, p. 3, and November 3, 1941,

p. 4; John T. Bobbitt to Albert Parry, September 30, 1941, FFF Papers; *New York Times*, May 27, 1941, p. 14; August 24, 1941, sec. 1, p. 19.

43. *Tribune*, April 4, 1941, p. 5; June 5, 1941, p. 1; *Daily News*, May 24, 1941, p. 4; June 5, 1941, pp. 1, 4.

44. *Tribune*, August 17, 1941, pt. 1, p. 1; August 18, 1941, p. 4; August 20, 1941, p. 5; August 30, 1941, p. 7; *Daily News*, August 18, 1941, p. 4; August 21, 1941, p. 6; August 28, 1941, p. 1; *New York Times*, August 29, 1941, p. 36.

45. *Daily News*, August 20, 1941, p. 8; August 25, 1941, p. 1; *Tribune*, August 21, 1941, p. 11; August 23, 1941, p. 6; August 24, 1941, pt. 1, p. 3; August 25, 1941, p. 2.

46. *Daily News*, September 9, 1941, p. 3; September 16, 1941, p. 1; October 25, 1941, p. 3; *Tribune*, September 16, 1941, p. 1; September 18, 1941, p. 2; September 19, 1941, p. 14; *Los Angeles Times*, September 12, 1941, sec. 1, p. 10; *New York Times*, September 18, 1941, p. 1; October 9, 1941, p. 15.

47. *News Letter*, March 28, 1941; May 23, 1941; October 24, 1941; November 21, 1941; Press Release, May 9, 1941; "Rejected Items," November 14, 1941; Government and Foreign Policy: State Chairman's Recommendations for 1942, November 12, 1941, NLWV Papers.

48. *Daily Maroon*, March 26, 1941, p. 2; April 2, 1941, p. 2; April 3, 1941, p. 1; April 18, 1941, p. 2.

49. *Daily Maroon*, April 11, 1941, p. 2; April 24, 1941, pp. 1, 2; April 29, 1941, p. 2.

50. *Daily Maroon*, October 7, 1941, p. 1; *New York Times*, April 25, 1941, p. 16.

51. *Daily Maroon*, October 10, 1941, pp. 1, 2; October 22, 1941, pp. 1, 2; October 24, 1941, pp. 1, 2; October 31, 1941, p. 1; November 11, 1941, p. 4; November 12, 1941, pp. 1, 3.

52. *Daily Maroon*, October 8, 1941, p. 2.

53. *Daily Maroon*, October 28, 1941, p. 2.

54. Paul Douglas to Harold Ickes, October 6, 1941; Douglas to Scott W. Lucas, November 3, 1941, Ickes Papers; *Daily News*, October 20, 1941, p. 5.

55. Albert Parry to Richard M. Scammon, November 10, 1941; Clarence Randall to Denison Hull, November 15, 1941; Courtenay Barber, Jr., to F. H. P. Cusick, November 11, 1941; Barber to Laird Bell, December 4, 1941, FFF Papers; *New York Times*, October 21, 1941, p. 4.

56. *New York Times*, February 10, 1941, p. 10; April 5, 1941, p. 7; April 25, 1941, pp. 1, 12; April 29, 1941, p. 9; May 1, 1941, p. 3; May 14, 1941, pp. 1, 12; June 27, 1941, p. 7; June 28, 1941, p. 13; September 24, 1941, p. 17; November 12, 1941, p. 9.

57. *Los Angeles Times*, September 18, 1941, sec. 2, p. 1; *Cleveland Plain Dealer*, November 18, 1941, p. 4; *San Francisco Chronicle*, November 12, 1941, p. 12; December 1, 1941, pp. 1, 5; *Boston Globe*, November 12, 1941, p. 19; *New York Times*, November 8, 1941, p. 6.

58. *New York Times*, May 22, 1941, p. 10; October 11, 1941, p. 22; October 17, 1941, p. 15.

CHAPTER SEVEN

1. Gallup, for example, showed only a modest increase during 1941 in the percentage of respondents who favored an immediate declaration of war. At no time did the figure rise above 26 percent; Gallup, *Gallup Poll*, pp. 263, 270, 276, 281, 286, 290, 307. Stuart interview.

2. *Tribune*, April 9, 1941, p. 1; *Los Angeles Times*, September 16, 1941, sec. 1, p. 4; *Cleveland Plain Dealer*, September 12, 1941, p. 3; *Boston Globe*, September 13, 1941, p. 4.

3. *Tribune*, October 1, 1941, p. 1.

4. *Tribune*, April 22, 1941, p. 5; *Daily News*, April 10, 1941, p. 1.

5. *Daily News*, April 10, 1941, p. 1; *Tribune*, June 23, 1941, pp. 4, 5; August 16, 1941, p. 4; September 20, 1941, p. 1; William Grace to Courtenay Barber, Jr., July 10, 1941, FFF Papers.

6. "America First—Nazi Transmission Belt," AFC Papers.

7. L. M. Birkhead to Anton J. Carlson, March 18, 1941; Carlson to Birkhead, March 20, 1941; *New York Herald-Tribune*, March 17, 1941 (clipping, no page number), AFC Papers. See also the telegrams between AFC and various members of the Friends in the same folder.

8. Benton to Hutchins, April 7, 1941, Benton Papers.

9. *Tribune*, March 31, 1941, pp. 1, 4; for the complete text see the *Daily Maroon*, April 8, 1941, pp. 1, 2, 4. Hutchins formulated his ideas in discussions with William Benton, John Nif, Philip LaFollette, and Harold Laswell; Benton to Hutchins, March 18, 1941, and March 25, 1941, Benton Papers.

10. *Daily News*, April 12, 1941, p. 12; *Daily Maroon*, April 1, 1941, pp. 1, 2.

11. *Daily Maroon*, April 8, 1941, p. 1; *Tribune*, April 7, 1941, p. 12.

12. *Daily Maroon*, April 11, 1941, p. 2; William Benton to Ralph Ingersoll, April 10, 1941, AFC Papers.

13. *Daily Maroon*, April 3, 1941, p. 1; April 8, 1941, pp. 1, 4; April 18, 1941, p. 2.

14. William Benton to Robert Hutchins, April 7, 1941, Hutchins Papers.

15. Quincy Wright to William Benton, April 3, 1941; Benton to Hutchins, April 26, 1941, Benton Papers.

16. *Daily News*, July 10, 1941, p. 4; John Howe to Robert Hutchins, July 28, 1941; Sherman Dryer to William Benton; statement to the *New York Times*, July 31, 1941, Benton Papers. Scammon letter.

17. *Daily News*, July 10, 1941, p. 4; John Howe to William Benton, August 11, 1941, Benton Papers.

18. John Howe to Robert Hutchins, and addenda, July 28, 1941; Howe to Dean Laing, August 5, 1941, Benton Papers.

19. John Howe to Robert Hutchins, and addenda, July 28, 1941; Howe to William Benton, July 28, 1941; Sherman Dryer to Benton, July 15, 1941; Howe to Hutchins, July 25, 1941; Harold Ickes to Hutchins, July [?], 1941; Hutchins to Ickes, July 28, 1941, Benton Papers; *New York Times*, July 23, 1941, p. 9; *PM*, July 23, 1941, p. 3.

20. Louis Wirth et al. to Robert Hutchins and Hutchins's addenda, July 25, 1941, Benton Papers.

21. John Howe to William Benton, August 11, 1941; Benton to Howe, July 28, 1941; Benton to Sherman Dryer, July 29, 1941; Howe to Robert Hutchins, July 26, 1941; Dryer to Benton, July 21, 1941, Benton Papers.

22. John Howe to William Benton, August 11, 1941; Laird Bell to Robert Hutchins, August 6, 1941; Sherman Dryer to Hutchins and Benton, July 31, 1941, Benton Papers.

23. John Howe to Robert Hutchins, August 8, 1941, Benton Papers.

24. Louis Gottschalk et al. to Robert Hutchins, August 19, 1941; John Howe to William Benton, August 11, 1941, Benton Papers.

25. Louis Gottschalk et al. to Robert Hutchins, August 19, 1941; John Howe to William Benton, August 11, 1941; Hutchins to Gottschalk, August 22, 1941, Benton Papers.

26. *Daily Maroon*, November 7, 1941, p. 4; November 12, 1941, p. 3.

27. *Tribune*, May 11, 1941, pt. 1, p. 23; September 28, 1941, pt. 1, p. 14; May 25, 1941, p. 1; October 14, 1941, p. 7.

28. *Tribune*, March 16, 1941, pt. 1, p. 8; March 23, 1941, pt. 1, p. 9; March 27, 1941, pt. 1, p. 10; April 6, 1941, pt. 1, p. 1; April 10, 1941, p. 10; April 11, 1941, p. 12; Executive Committee Minutes, February 24, 1941, AFC Papers.

29. Edith W. Kimbark to Mrs. E. A. Prugh, May 5, 1941; Helen Lamont to Cornelia Howe, September 17, 1941; Lamont to Mrs. Janet A. Fairbank, September 27, 1941; Lamont to Martha Murphy, June 16, 1941, AFC Papers.

30. Report on Speakers, AFC Papers.

31. *Daily News*, April 15, 1941, p. 10; August 8, 1941, p. 9 (letter from Patrick J. Quinn); August 14, 1941, p. 15; Mrs. Frank McKibben to Edith

W. Kimbark, June 2, 1941; Janet Ayer Fairbank to all Chapter Chairmen, August 19, 1941; Page Hufty to all Chapter Chairmen, October 25, 1941, AFC Papers.

32. Lindbergh, *Wartime Journals*, pp. 474–75; Howard G. Swann to Barbara MacDonald, March 10, 1941, AFC Papers; *Daily News*, May 23, 1941, p. 1; July 8, 1941, p. 5; *Tribune*, June 29, 1941, pt. 3 (North), p. 1; *New York Times*, April 28, 1941, p. 10; May 24, 1941, pp. 1, 6.

33. *Tribune*, May 11, 1941, pt. 1, p. 15.

34. Janet Ayer Fairbank to Chapter Chairmen, July 5, 1941; *Chapter Manual*, AFC Papers.

35. Janet Ayer Fairbank to Bertha Tallman, April 2, 1941; Robert Bliss to Fairbank, April 7, 1941; Fairbank to Bliss, May 3, 1941; Bliss to Fairbank, May 7, 1941, AFC Papers.

36. S. E. Aiken to Robert Bliss, April 5, 1941; memo from Harry Schnibbe to Robert Wood, June 14, 1941, AFC Papers.

37. Ibid.

38. Mrs. Joan Scott to Janet Ayer Fairbank, undated (probably October 1941); Cornelia Howe to Mrs. Scott, October 9, 1941; Mrs. Scott to Bertha Tallman, October 19, 1941; R. Douglas Stuart to Robert R. McCormick, n.d., AFC Papers.

39. Mrs. Edith W. Kimbark to Robert Wood, R. Douglas Stuart, and Janet Ayer Fairbank, May 18, 1941, AFC Papers.

40. *New York Times*, March 19, 1941, p. 3; April 1, 1941, p. 13; *Tribune*, April 13, 1941, pt. 1, p. 4; Robert McCormick to R. Douglas Stuart, April 26, 1941; Robert Wood to Chapter Chairmen, April 28, 1941; Bulletin No. 192, "Stop Convoys," April 10, 1941, AFC Papers.

41. R. Douglas Stuart to Robert Wood, July 7, 1941; Stuart to Robert Hutchins, October 29, 1941, and Hutchins to Stuart, November 2, 1941, AFC Papers; Stuart interview. Hard-line anti–New Dealers such as Hanford MacNider strongly opposed the idea of a negotiated peace, labeling it "misguided meddling, just like FDR," MacNider to Wood, July 11, 1941, AFC Papers; *New York Times*, May 24, 1941, pp. 1, 7; May 25, 1941, p. 3.

42. Cantril and Strunk, *Public Opinion*, p. 1119.

43. Chester Bowles to Stuart, May 1, 1941, Hutchins Papers; "Gallup Poll File," AFC Papers, especially an untitled paper by Ross Stagner of Dartmouth. Stagner made some perceptive criticisms of the ways in which Gallup designed his questions. Gallup tended to pair "yes" answers with proadministration positions and to mention authority figures in the questions. But Stagner's own suggested substitutions were wildly biased in the opposite direction.

44. Chester Bowles to R. Douglas Stuart, May 1, 1941, Hutchins Papers;

Tribune, July 3, 1941, pp. 1, 7; July 1, 1941, p. 1; July 6, 1941, pt. 1, p. 4; July 15, 1941, p. 1.

45. Sterling Morton to Robert Hutchins, July 18, 1941, Hutchins Papers; Sarles, "America First," chap. 11, pp. 7–9, AFC Papers.

46. J. O. Richardson to Page Hufty, September 14, 1941; Sterling Morton to Hufty, September 29, 1941; Morton to Hufty, October 20, 1941; Harry Schnibbe to Morton, October 4, 1941; Morton to R. Douglas Stuart, October 10, 1941, AFC Papers.

47. Lindbergh's address appeared in full in both the *Des Moines Register* and the *Tribune* on September 13, 1941. The pertinent paragraphs appear in Cole, *Lindbergh*, pp. 171–72, which contains a good brief account of the affair. For examples of the critical reaction, see the *Louisville Courier-Journal*, September 13, 1941, sec. 1, p. 6; *Boston Globe*, September 13, 1941, pp. 6, 9; *New York Times*, September 13, 1941, p. 1; September 15, 1941, p. 2; *St. Louis Post-Dispatch*, September 14, 1941, p. 2C; *Denver Post*, September 14, 1941, p. 2; *Los Angeles Times*, September 16, 1941, sec. 1, p. 4; September 17, 1941, sec. 1, p. 5; *San Francisco Chronicle*, September 25, 1941, pp. 1, 4, 14.

48. Cole, *Lindbergh*, pp. 171–85; *Tribune*, September 13, 1941, p. 10; Stuart interview; *PM*, December 2, 1940, copy in AFC Papers; Robert Wood to Kenneth Crawford, December 6, 1940, and reply, December 12, 1940, AFC Papers.

49. Robert Wood to Kenneth Crawford, December 21, 1940; Janet Ayer Fairbank to Chapter Chairmen, August 19, 1941; Robert Bliss to the Chicago office of the Federal Bureau of Investigation, March 13, 1941, and reply March 27, 1941, AFC Papers. The stray references to Jews that remain in the committee's papers suggest that the collection had not been combed to remove incriminating evidence

50. Stuart interview; Speaker's Report, Dr. Howard Swann to Washington Boulevard Temple, January 21, 1941; O. H. Goetz to Robert Wood, November 23, 1941; Cornelia Howe to Helen Lamont, September 12, 1941, and reply, September 13, 1941, AFC Papers; Sterling Morton to R. Douglas Stuart, September 22, 1941, Morton Papers; *Boston Globe*, September 16, 1941, p. 4. The left wing of the antiwar movement, as represented by the Keep America Out of War Congress, disagreed with those AFCers who believed that Jews represented an identifiable interest group on foreign policy issues. KAOWC deplored the Des Moines speech. *New York Times*, September 21, 1941, p. 27.

51. *Daily News*, September 19, 1941, p. 3; September 22, 1941, p. 1; *Tribune*, September 25, 1941, p. 2; Robert Wood to Hanford MacNider, September 22, 1941, MacNider Papers; Sarles, "America First," chap. 9,

pp. 29–39; Fairbank to Page Hufty, September 24, 1941, AFC Papers.

52. *Daily News*, September 26, 1941, p. 9; O. H. Goetz to Robert Wood, November 23, 1941; Janet Ayer Fairbank to Helen Lamont, September 13, 1941; Fairbank to Chapter Chairmen, September 27, 1941, AFC Papers.

53. Emergency Bulletin Number 1, October 26, 1941, AFC Papers; Stenehjem, *American First*, pp. 105–6.

54. Robert Wood to Janet Ayer Fairbank, November 17, 1941, and reply, November 18, 1941, AFC Papers.

55. Burns, *Soldier of Freedom*, pp. 148–49; the vote total was 50 to 37 in the Senate, 212 to 196 in the House; *Daily News*, November 14, 1941, p. 4.

56. *Daily News*, November 19, 1941, p. 4; for the overwhelming approval of local chapters, see AFC Papers; Mrs. Edith Kimbark to Robert Wood, November 24, 1941, AFC Papers; *Tribune*, July 20, 1941, p. 10.

57. Robert Wood to President Franklin Roosevelt, October 22, 1941, AFC Papers; William Benton to Robert Hutchins, November 21, 1941, and November 13, 1941, Hutchins Papers.

58. R. Douglas Stuart to Cmdr. E. F. MacDonald, Jr., June 23, 1941, AFC Papers.

CHAPTER EIGHT

1. *Tribune*, December 7, 1941, pt. 1, p. 1; pt. 2, p. 1; pt. 3, p. 6; pt. 5, p. 3; pt. 6, p. 7.

2. Ibid., pt. 1, pp. 1, 11, 15; *New York Times*, December 7, 1941, pp. 1, 2; *Denver Post*, December 7, 1941, p. 1; *St. Louis Post-Dispatch*, December 4, 1941, p. 2C; December 7, 1941, p. 6C.

3. *Tribune*, December 8, 1941, pp. 1, 11; Rose, "How the U.S. Heard," pp. 285–98.

4. *Tribune*, December 8, 1941, p. 1; *Defender*, December 13, 1941, p. 1; *Daily News*, December 8, 1941, pp. 1, 5, 9, 12; *Atlanta Constitution*, December 9, 1941, p. 12; *San Francisco Chronicle*, December 8, 1941, p. 1.

5. Lindbergh, *Wartime Journals*, p. 561; R. Douglas Stuart to All Chapter Chairmen, December 8, 1941, Hutchins Papers.

6. Denison Hull to the Members of the Executive Committee, December 11, 1941; Courtenay Barber to Ulric Bell, December 8, 1941; Hull to Executive Committee, December 22, 1941; Barber to Claude A. Barnett, March 13, 1941, FFF Papers.

7. Sterling Morton to Robert Wood, December 8, 1941; and Morton to R. Douglas Stuart, December 12, 1941, Morton Papers; Stuart interview;

Tribune, December 12, 1941, p. 16; *Daily News*, December 12, 1941, p. 8; *New York Times*, December 13, 1941, p. 20.

8. *Daily News*, December 11, 1941, p. 1; December 12, 1941, p. 8; *Tribune*, December 12, 1941, p. 16; R. Douglas Stuart to Robert Hutchins, January 3, 1942; Clay Judson to James B. Conant, January 3, 1942, Hutchins Papers.

APPENDIX

1. Among the most important works in the now voluminous literature on realignment, those that concern the New Deal era include: Burnham, *Critical Elections*; Shivley, "New Deal Realignment"; Burner, *Politics of Provincialism*; Clubb and Allen, "The Cities and the Election of 1928"; Lichtman, "Critical Election Theory"; Nie, Verba, and Petrocik, *Changing American Voter*; Andersen, *Creation of the Democratic Majority*. The basic works on 1940 are Lazarsfeld, Berelson, and Gaudet, *People's Choice*, and Lubell, *American Politics*. For a now dated analysis of Illinois, see MacRae and Meldrun, "Critical Elections in Illinois, 1888–1958."

2. Lichtman, "Critical Election Theory," pp. 343–44; Gallup, *Gallup Poll*, 1:183. Lazarsfeld, Borelson, and Gaudet, *People's Choice*, pp. 29–36, 130–34; Lubell, *American Politics*, pp. 54–59, 140–42.

3. Andersen, *Creation of the Democratic Majority*, pp. 23–29, 74–76, 107–10.

BIBLIOGRAPHY

PRIMARY SOURCES

Manuscript Collections

Chicago, Illinois
   The Chicago Historical Society
      The Sterling Morton Papers
      The Jacob J. Weinstein Papers
   The Newberry Library
      The John T. McCutcheon Papers
   The University of Chicago Library
      The William B. Benton Papers
      The Files of the Department of History of the University of Chicago
      The Papers of the Chicago Chapter of the Fight For Freedom
         Committee
      The Papers of the President of the University of Chicago, 1925–
         1945
      The Robert M. Hutchins Papers
      The Thomas V. Smith Papers
      The Louis Wirth Papers
      The World Citizens Council Papers
      The Quincy Wright Papers
   The University of Illinois at Chicago Circle Library
      The Philip Ream Clarke Papers
      The Chicago Council on Foreign Relations Papers
Madison, Wisconsin
   The State Historical Society of Wisconsin
      The American Federation of Labor Papers
      The H. V. Kaltenborn Papers

The Philip LaFollette Papers
The Raymond Robbins Papers
New York, New York
  The New York Public Library
    The Clark M. Eichelberger Papers
Palo Alto, California
    The Hoover Institution on War, Revolution and Peace
    The America First Committee Papers
Princeton, New Jersey
  The Seely G. Mudd Library
    The Committee to Defend America by Aiding the Allies Papers
    The Adlai E. Stevenson Papers
Springfield, Illinois
  The Illinois State Historical Society
    The Henry Horner Papers
    The Scott W. Lucas Papers
Washington, D.C.
  The Library of Congress
    The Hanna-McCormick Family Papers
    The Harold L. Ickes Papers
    The Franklin Knox Papers
    The National League of Women Voters Papers
    The Edgar Ansell and Lillian Thomson Mowrer Papers
    The William Allen White Papers
West Branch, Iowa
  The Herbert Hoover Presidential Library
    The Hanford MacNider Papers
    The Robert E. Wood Papers

Newspapers

Chicago, Illinois
  Chicago Daily News
  Chicago Defender
  Chicago Journal of Commerce
  Chicago Sun
  Chicago Tribune
  Daily Maroon

Other Cities
  Atlanta Constitution
  Boston Globe
  Cleveland Plain Dealer

Denver Post
Los Angeles Times
Louisville Courier-Journal
New York Herald-Tribune
New York Times
PM
St. Louis Post-Dispatch
San Francisco Chronicle

Interviews

Clark M. Eichelberger, April 14, 1978.
T. Walter Johnson, December 29, 1978.
James F. Oates, Jr., October 18, 1977.
Robert Douglas Stuart, Jr., November 29, 1977.

Note: All interviews were conducted by the author.

Correspondence

Gabriel A. Almond, October 17, 1978.
Mrs. John F. Fenn, February 28, 1977.
William T. R. Fox, December 21, 1978.
Klaus Knorr, October 11, 1978.
Robert E. Merriam, January 12, 1978.
Richard M. Scammon, October 24, 1978.

Note: All correspondence was with the author.

SECONDARY WORKS

Books

Abbazia, Patrick. *Mr. Roosevelt's Navy: The Private War of the U.S. Atlantic Fleet, 1939–1942*. Annapolis, Md.: Naval Institute Press, 1975.
Adler, Selig. *The Isolationist Impulse: Its Twentieth Century Reaction*. New York: Collier Books, 1957.
Allswang, John M. *A House for All Peoples: Ethnic Politics in Chicago, 1890–1936*. Lexington, Ky.: University Press of Kentucky, 1971.
Andersen, Kristi. *The Creation of the Democratic Majority, 1928–1936*. Chicago: University of Chicago Press, 1983.
Andrews, Wayne. *Battle for Chicago*. New York: Harcourt, Brace, 1948.
Bailey, Thomas A. *A Diplomatic History of the American People*. 8th ed. New York: Appleton-Century-Crofts, 1969.

————. *The Man in the Street: The Impact of American Public Opinion on Foreign Policy.* New York: Macmillan, 1948.

Baker, Roscoe. *The American Legion and Foreign Policy.* New York: Bookman Associates, 1954.

Barkley, Alben W. *That Reminds Me—.* Garden City, N.Y.: Doubleday, 1954.

Barnes, Harry Elmer, ed. *Perpetual War for Perpetual Peace.* Caldwell, Idaho: Caxton Printers, 1953.

Beard, Charles A. *American Foreign Policy in the Making, 1932–1940.* New York: Alfred A. Knopf, 1948.

————. *President Roosevelt and the Coming of the War, 1941.* New Haven, Conn.: Yale University Press, 1948.

Becker, Stephen D. *Marshall Field III: A Biography.* New York: Simon and Schuster, 1964.

Berle, Adolph A. *Navigating the Rapids, 1918–1971.* Edited by Beatrice Berle and Travis Beal Jacobs. New York: Harcourt, Brace, 1973.

Biles, Roger. *Big City Boss in Depression and War: Mayor Edward J. Kelly of Chicago.* De Kalb, Ill.: Northern Illinois University Press, 1984.

Bloom, Sol. *The Autobiography of Sol Bloom.* New York: G. P. Putnam's Sons, 1948.

Blum, John Morton, ed. *From the Morganthau Diaries.* 3 vols. Boston: Houghton Mifflin, 1959–68.

Brinkley, Alan. *Voices of Protest: Huey Long, Father Coughlin, and the Great Depression.* New York: Alfred A. Knopf, 1982.

Burner, David. *The Politics of Provincialism: The Democratic Party in Transition, 1918–1932.* New York: Alfred A. Knopf, 1968.

Burnham, Walter Dean. *Critical Elections and the Mainsprings of American Politics.* New York: W. W. Norton, 1970.

Burns, James MacGregor. *Roosevelt: The Lion and the Fox.* New York: Lippincott, 1956.

————. *Roosevelt: The Soldier of Freedom.* New York: Lippincott, 1970.

Cantril, Hadley, and Mildred Strunk, eds. *Public Opinion, 1935–1946.* Princeton, N.J.: Princeton University Press, 1951.

Carlson, John Roy [Arthur Derounian] *Under Cover.* New York: E. P. Dutton, 1943.

Chadwin, Mark Lincoln. *The Warhawks: American Interventionists before Pearl Harbor.* Chapel Hill, N.C.: University of North Carolina Press, 1968.

Chatfield, Charles, Jr. *For Peace and Justice: Pacifism in America, 1914–1941.* Knoxville, Tenn.: University of Tennessee Press, 1971.

Cohen, Bernard C. *The Press and Foreign Policy.* Princeton, N.J.: Princeton University Press, 1963.

_____. *The Public's Impact on Foreign Policy*. Boston: Little, Brown, 1972.

Cole, Wayne S. *America First: The Battle against Intervention*. Madison, Wis.: University of Wisconsin Press, 1953.

_____. *Charles A. Lindbergh and the Battle against American Intervention in World War II*. New York: Harcourt Brace Jovanovich, 1974.

_____. *Roosevelt and the Isolationists, 1932–1945*. Lincoln, Neb.: University of Nebraska Press, 1983.

_____. *Senator Gerald P. Nye and American Foreign Relations*. Minneapolis, Minn.: University of Minnesota Press, 1962.

Connally, Tom, and Alfred Steinberg. *My Name is Tom Connally*. New York: Thomas Y. Crowell, 1954.

Culbert, David Holbrook. *News for Everyman: Radio and Foreign Affairs in Thirties America*. Westport, Conn.: Greenwood Press, 1976.

Current Biography, 1940. New York: The H. W. Wilson Company, 1940.

Current Biography, 1941. New York: The H. W. Wilson Company, 1941.

Current Biography, 1942. New York: The H. W. Wilson Company, 1942.

Current Biography Yearbook, 1961. New York: The H. W. Wilson Company, 1961.

Curti, Merle. *Peace or War: The American Struggle, 1935–1936*. New York: W. W. Norton, 1936.

Dallek, Robert. *Franklin D. Roosevelt and American Foreign Policy, 1932–1945*. New York: Oxford University Press, 1979.

Darilek, Richard E. *A Loyal Opposition in Time of War: The Republican Party and the Politics of Foreign Policy from Pearl Harbor to Yalta*. Westport, Conn.: Greenwood Press, 1976.

Davis, Forrest, and Ernest K. Lindley. *How War Came: An American White Paper*. New York: Simon and Schuster, 1942.

Davis, Kenneth S. *The Politics of Honor: A Biography of Adlai E. Stevenson*. New York: G. P. Putnam's Sons, 1967.

_____. *A Prophet in His Own Country: The Triumphs and Defeats of Adlai E. Stevenson*. Garden City, N.Y.: Doubleday and Co., 1957.

DeBenedetti, Charles. *The Peace Reform in American History*. Bloomington, Ind.: Indiana University Press, 1980.

DeConde, Alexander, ed. *Isolation and Security: Ideas and Interests in the Twentieth Century American Foreign Policy*. Durham, N.C.: Duke University Press, 1957.

Detzer, Dorothy. *Appointment on the Hill*. New York: Holt, 1948.

Devine, Donald J. *The Attentive Public: Polyarchial Democracy*. Chicago: Rand McNally, 1970.

Diamond, Sander A. *The Nazi Movement in the United States, 1924–1941*. Ithaca, N.Y.: Cornell University Press, 1974.

Diggins, John P. *Mussolini and Fascism: The View from America*. Princeton,

N.J.: Princeton University Press, 1972.

Divine, Robert A. *The Illusion of Neutrality*. Chicago: University of Chicago Press, 1962.

————. *The Reluctant Belligerent*. New York: John Wiley and Sons, 1965.

————. *Roosevelt and World War II*. Baltimore: Johns Hopkins University Press, 1969.

Douglas, Paul H. *In the Fullness of Time*. New York: Harcourt Brace Jovanovich, 1971.

Drake, St. Clair, and Horace R. Clayton. *Black Metropolis: A Study of Negro Life in a Northern City*. New York: Harcourt Brace and World, 1945.

Drummond, Donald F. *The Passing of American Neutrality, 1937–1941*. Ann Arbor, Mich.: University of Michigan Press, 1955.

Edwards, Jerome. *The Foreign Policy of Colonel McCormick's Tribune, 1929–1941*. Reno, Nev.: University of Nevada Press, 1971.

Eichelberger, Clark M. *Organizing for Peace: A Personal History of the Founding of the United Nations*. New York: Harper and Row, 1977.

Feis, Herbert. *The Road to Pearl Harbor: The Coming of the War Between the United States and Japan*. Princeton, N.J.: Princeton University Press, 1950.

Fielding, Raymond. *The March of Time, 1935–1951*. New York: Oxford University Press, 1978.

Friedrich, Carl J. *Man and His Government*. New York: McGraw-Hill, 1963.

Friendly, Fred W. *Minnesota Rag: The Dramatic Story of the Landmark Supreme Court Case That Gave New Meaning to Freedom of the Press*. New York: Random House, 1981.

Gallup, George H. *The Gallup Poll: Public Opinion, 1935–1971*. 3 vols. Vol. 1, *1935–1948*. New York: Random House, 1972.

Gerson, Louis L. *The Hyphenate in Recent American Politics*. Lawrence, Kans.: University of Kansas Press, 1964.

Giles, Joseph. *The Colonel of Chicago*. New York: E. P. Dutton, 1979.

Gove, Samuel K. *Illinois Votes, 1900–1958: A Compilation of Illinois Election Statistics*. Urbana, Ill.: Institute of Government and Public Affairs, University of Illinois, 1959.

Graber, Doris. *Public Opinion, the President, and Foreign Policy*. New York: Holt, Rinehart and Winston, 1968.

Grant, Bruce. *Fight for a City: The Story of the Union League Club of Chicago*. Chicago: Rand McNally, 1955.

Grassmuck, George L. *Sectional Biases in Congress on Foreign Policy*. Baltimore, Md.: Johns Hopkins University Press, 1951.

Grew, Joseph C. *Ten Years in Japan*. New York: Simon and Schuster, 1944.

_____. *Turbulent Era: A Diplomatic Record of Forty Years*. Boston: Houghton Mifflin Co., 1952.

Guinsburg, Thomas N. *The Pursuit of Isolationism in the United States Senate From Versailles to Pearl Harbor*. New York: Garland, 1982.

Hofstadter, Richard. *The Progressive Historians: Turner, Beard, Parrington*. New York: Knopf, 1968.

Holli, Melvin G., and Peter d'A. Jones, eds. *The Ethnic Frontier: Essays in the History of Group Survival in Chicago and the Midwest*. Grand Rapids, Mich.: William B. Erdmans, 1977.

Hooker, Nancy H., ed. *The Moffat Papers*. Cambridge, Mass.: Harvard University Press, 1956.

Hughes, Edward J. *Blue Book of the State of Illinois, 1939–1940*. Springfield: State of Illinois, 1941.

_____. *Blue Book of the State of Illinois, 1941–1942*. Springfield: State of Illinois, 1943.

Hull, Cordell. *The Memoirs of Cordell Hull*. New York: Macmillan, 1948.

Ickes, Harold. *The Secret Diary of Harold Ickes. The Lowering Clouds, 1939–1941*. New York: Simon and Schuster, 1954.

Jackson, Kenneth T. *The Chicago Council on Foreign Relations*. Chicago: Chicago Council on Foreign Relations, 1964.

Jacobs, Travis Beal. *America and the Winter War, 1939–1940*. New York: Garland, 1981.

Jensen, Richard. *Illinois: A Bi-Centennial History*. New York: W. W. Norton, 1978.

Johnpoll, Bernard K. *Pacifist's Progress: Norman Thomas and the Decline of American Socialism*. Chicago: Quadrangle Books, 1970.

Johnson, Walter. *The Battle against Isolation*. Chicago: University of Chicago Press, 1944.

_____. *William Allen White's America*. New York: Henry Holt, 1947.

_____, ed. *Selected Letters of William Allen White, 1899–1943*. New York: Henry Holt, 1947.

Johnson, Walter, and Carol Evans, eds. *The Papers of Adlai E. Stevenson. Vol. I*. Boston: Little, Brown, 1972.

Jonas, Manfred. *Isolationism in America, 1935–1941*. Ithaca, N.Y.: Cornell University Press, 1966.

Kantowicz, Edward R. *Polish-American Politics in Chicago, 1888–1940*. Chicago: University of Chicago Press, 1975.

Kendrick, Alexander. *Prime Time: The Life of Edward R. Murrow*. Boston: Little, Brown, 1969.

Kennedy, Thomas C. *Charles A. Beard and American Foreign Policy*. Gainesville, Fla.: University of Florida Press, 1975.

Kimball, Warren F. *The Most Unsordid Act: Lend-Lease, 1939–1941*. Baltimore, Md.: Johns Hopkins University Press, 1969.

Kinsella, Richard E. *Leadership in Isolation: FDR and the Origins of the Second World War*. Boston: G. K. Hall, 1978.

Kleppner, Paul. *Chicago Divided: The Making of a Black Mayor*. De Kalb, Ill.: Northern Illinois University Press, 1985.

Langer, William L., and S. Everett Gleason. *The Challenge to Isolation, 1937–1940*. New York: Harper and Brothers, 1954.

————. *The Undeclared War, 1940–1941*. New York: Harper and Brothers, 1953.

Lash, Joseph P. *Roosevelt and Churchill, 1939–1941: The Partnership That Saved the West*. New York: W. W. Norton, 1976.

Laswell, Harold D. *Propaganda Technique in the World War*. New York: Alfred A. Knopf, 1927.

Lauderbaugh, Richard A. *American Steelmakers and the Coming of World War II*. Ann Arbor, Mich.: University of Michigan Institute Research Press, 1980.

Lazarsfeld, Paul F. *Radio and the Printed Page*. New York: Arno Press and The New York Times, 1971.

Lazarsfeld, Paul F., Bernard Berelson, and Hazel Gaudet. *The People's Choice: How the Voter Makes Up His Mind in a Presidential Campaign*. New York: Columbia University Press, 1963.

Leahy, William D. *I Was There*. New York: Whittlesey House, 1950.

Leigh, Michael. *Mobilizing Consent: Public Opinion and American Foreign Policy, 1937–1947*. Westport, Conn.: Greenwood, 1976.

Leutze, James R. *Bargaining for Supremacy: Anglo-American Naval Cooperation, 1937–1941*. Chapel Hill, N.C.: University of North Carolina Press, 1977.

Levering, Ralph B. *American Opinion and the Russian Alliance, 1939–1945*. Chapel Hill, N.C.: University of North Carolina Press, 1976.

————. *The Public and American Foreign Policy, 1918–1978*. New York: William Morrow, 1978.

Libby, Frederick J. *To End War*. Nyack, N.Y.: Fellowship Publications, 1948.

Liddell Hart, B. H. *History of the Second World War*. New York: Capricorn Books, 1972.

Liggio, Leonard P., and James J. Martin. *Watershed of Empire: Essays on New Deal Foreign Policy*. Colorado Springs, Colo.: Ralph Myles, 1976.

Lindbergh, Charles A. *Autobiography of Values*. New York: Harcourt Brace Jovanovich, 1977.

————. *The Wartime Journals of Charles A. Lindbergh*. New York: Harcourt Brace Jovanovich, 1970.

Lippmann, Walter. *Public Opinion*. 1922. Reprint. New York: Free Press, 1965.

Loewenheim, Francis L., Harold D. Langley, and Manfred Jonas, eds. *Roosevelt and Churchill: Their Secret Wartime Correspondence*. New York: Saturday Review, 1975.

Long, Breckenridge. *The War Diary of Breckenridge Long*. Edited by Fred L. Israel. Lincoln, Neb.: University of Nebraska Press, 1966.

Lubell, Samuel. *The Future of American Politics*. New York: Harper and Row, 1965.

Luttbeg, Norman R., ed. *Public Opinion and Public Policy: Models of Political Linkage*. Homewood, Ill.: Dorsey, 1968.

McCutcheon, John T. *Drawn From Memory*. Indianapolis, Ind.: Bobbs-Merrill, 1950.

Manvell, Roger. *Films and the Second World War*. South Brunswick, N.J.: A. S. Barnes, 1974.

Martin, James J. *American Liberalism and World Politics, 1931–1941*. 2 vols. New York: Devin Adair, 1964.

Martin, Joe, and Robert J. Donovan. *My First Fifty Years in Politics*. New York: McGraw Hill, 1960.

Martin, John Bartlow. *Adlai Stevenson of Illinois: The Life of Adlai E. Stevenson*. Garden City, N.Y.: Doubleday, 1976.

May, Ernest R. *"Lessons" of the Past: The Use and Misuse of History in American Foreign Policy*. New York: Oxford University Press, 1973.

Mayer, Harold M., and Richard C. Wade. *Chicago: Growth of a Metropolis*. Chicago: University of Chicago Press, 1969.

Morison, Samuel Eliot. *The Two Ocean War*. Boston: Little, Brown, 1963.

Mowrer, Edgar Ansel. *Triumph and Turmoil: A Personal History of Our Time*. New York: Weybright and Talley, 1968.

Mueller, John E. *War, Presidents and Public Opinion*. New York: John Wiley and Sons, 1973.

Nelli, Humbert S. *The Italians of Chicago, 1820–1930: A Study in Ethnic Mobility*. New York: Oxford University Press, 1970.

Newell, Barbara. *Chicago and the Labor Movement: Metropolitan Unionism in the 1930s*. Urbana, Ill.: University of Illinois Press, 1961.

Nie, Norman, Sidney Verba, and John H. Petrocik. *The Changing American Voter*. Cambridge, Mass.: Harvard University Press, 1976.

Osgood, Robert Endicott. *Ideals and Self-Interest in America's Foreign Relations: The Great Transformation of the Twentieth Century*. Chicago and London: University of Chicago Press, 1953.

Pastor, Robert A. *Congress and the Politics of Foreign Economic Policy, 1929–1976*. Los Angeles and Berkeley, Calif.: University of California Press, 1980.

Pierce, Bessie L. *A History of Chicago.* 3 vols. New York: Knopf, 1937–1950.

Pogue, Forrest C. *George C. Marshall: Ordeal and Hope, 1939–1942.* New York: Viking, 1966.

Porter, David L. *Congress and the Waning of the New Deal.* Port Washington, N.Y.: Kennikat Press, 1980.

———. *The Seventy-Sixth Congress and World War II, 1939–1940.* Columbia, Mo.: University of Missouri Press, 1979.

Prange, Gordon W. *At Dawn We Slept: The Untold Story of Pearl Harbor.* New York: McGraw Hill, 1981.

Radosh, Ronald. *Prophets on the Right: Profiles of Conservative Critics of American Globalism.* New York: Simon and Schuster, 1975.

Rakove, Milton L. *Don't Make No Waves—Don't Back No Losers: An Insider's Analysis of the Daley Machine.* Bloomington, Ind.: Indiana University Press, 1975.

Rauch, Basil. *Roosevelt: From Munich to Pearl Harbor.* New York: Creative Age, 1950.

Reynolds, David. *The Creation of the Anglo-American Alliance, 1937–1941: A Study in Competitive Cooperation.* Chapel Hill, N.C.: University of North Carolina Press, 1982.

Rieselbach, Leroy N. *The Roots of Isolationism: Congressional Voting and Presidential Leadership in Foreign Policy.* Indianapolis: Bobbs-Merrill, 1966.

Roper, Elmo. *You and Your Leaders: Their Actions and Your Reactions, 1935–1956.* New York: William Morrow, 1957.

Rosenau, James N., ed. *Domestic Sources of Foreign Policy.* New York: Free Press, 1967.

———. *National Leadership and Foreign Policy.* Princeton, N.J.: Princeton University Press, 1963.

———. *Public Opinion and Foreign Policy.* New York: Random House, 1961.

Russett, Bruce. *No Clear and Present Danger: A Skeptical View of United States Entry into World War II.* New York: Harper and Row, 1972.

Sayers, Michael, and Albert E. Kahn. *Sabotage! The Secret War against America.* New York: Harper and Brothers, 1942.

Schroeder, Paul W. *The Axis Alliance and Japanese-American Relations.* Ithaca, N.Y.: Cornell University Press, 1958.

Schwartz, Andrew I. *America and the Russo-Finnish War.* Washington: Public Affairs, 1960.

Sherwood, Robert. *Roosevelt and Hopkins: An Intimate History.* New York: Grosset and Dunlap, 1948.

Steel, Ronald. *Walter Lippmann and the American Century*. Boston: Little, Brown, 1980.

Stenehjem, Michelle Flynn. *An American First: John T. Flynn and the America First Committee*. New Rochelle, N.Y.: Arlington House, 1976.

Stimson, Henry, and McGeorge Bundy. *On Active Service in Peace and War*. New York: Harper and Brothers, 1947.

Stokesbury, James L. *A Short History of World War II*. New York: William Morrow, 1980.

Tansill, Charles Callan. *Back Door to War: The Roosevelt Foreign Policy, 1933–1941*. Chicago: Charles Regnery, 1952.

Tebel, John. *An American Dynasty*. Garden City, N.Y.: Doubleday, 1947.

_____. *The Marshall Fields: A Study in Wealth*. New York: E. P. Dutton, 1947.

Terkel, Studs. *Division Street: America*. New York: Pantheon Books, 1967.

Thorne, Christopher. *Allies of a Kind: The United States, Britain, and the War Against Japan, 1941–1945*. New York: Oxford University Press, 1978.

Trohan, Walter. *Political Animals*. Garden City, N.Y.: Doubleday, 1975.

United States. Bureau of the Census. *Sixteenth Census of the United States: 1940*. Washington, D.C.: United States Government Printing Office, 1942.

Utley, Jonathan W. *Going to War with Japan, 1937–1941*. Knoxville, Tenn.: University of Tennessee Press, 1985.

Vandenberg, Arthur H. *The Private Papers of Senator Vandenberg*. Edited by Joe Alex Morris. Boston: Houghton Mifflin, 1952.

Waldrop, Frank C. *McCormick of Chicago*. Englewood Cliffs, N.J.: Prentice-Hall, 1966.

Walther, Regis. *Orientations and Behavior Styles of Foreign Service Officers*. New York: Carnegie Endowment for International Peace, 1965.

Welles, Sumner. *Seven Decisions That Shaped History*. New York: Harper, 1950.

_____. *The Time for Decision*. New York: Harper and Brothers, 1944.

Wendt, Lloyd. *Chicago Tribune: The Rise of a Great American Newspaper*. Chicago: Rand, McNally, 1979.

Wheeler, Burton K., and Paul F. Healy. *Yankee from the West*. Garden City, N.Y.: Doubleday, 1962.

Whyte, William F. *Street Corner Society: The Social Structure of an Italian Slum*. Chicago: University of Chicago Press, 1943.

Williams, William Appleman. *The Tragedy of American Diplomacy*. New York: Dell, 1962.

Wittke, Carl F. *The German Language Press in America*. Lexington, Ky.:

University of Kentucky Press, 1957.

Wittner, Lawrence S. *Rebels against War: The American Peace Movement, 1941–1960.* New York: Columbia University Press, 1969.

Wohlstetter, Roberta. *Pearl Harbor: Warning and Decision.* Stanford, Calif.: Stanford University Press, 1962.

Young, Roland A. *Congressional Politics and the Second World War.* New York: DaCapo, 1972.

Zorbaugh, Harvey Warren. *The Gold Coast and the Slum: A Sociological Study of Chicago's Near North Side.* 1929. Reprint. Chicago: University of Chicago Press, 1976.

Articles

Alexander, Jack. "The Duke of Chicago." *Saturday Evening Post* 214, no. 3 (July 19, 1941): 10–11, 70–75.

————. "The World's Greatest Newspaper." *Saturday Evening Post* 214, no. 4 (July 26, 1941): 27, 80–89.

"All in the Family." *Time* 34, no. 8 (February 24, 1941): 46–48.

"America First." *Time* 36, no. 26 (December 23, 1940): 37–38.

"America First Roughhouse." *Life* 11, no. 16 (October 26, 1941): 40–41.

"Battle of Newspapers." *Time* 38, no. 23 (December 1, 1941): 60–64.

Billington, Ray Allen. "The Origins of Middle Western Isolationism." *Political Science Quarterly* 60, no. 1 (March 1945): 44–64.

Butterfield, Roger. "Lindbergh." *Life* 9, no. 6 (August 11, 1941): 64–75.

Cantril, Hadley, Donald Rigg, and Frederick Williams. "America Faces the War: Shifts in Public Opinion." *Public Opinion Quarterly* 4, no. 4 (December 1940): 651–56.

————. "America Faces the War: A Study in Public Opinion." *Public Opinion Quarterly* 4, no. 3 (September 1940): 387–407.

Carleton, William G. "Isolationism and the Middle West." *Mississippi Valley Historical Review* 33 (June 1946): 377–90.

Clubb, Jerome, and Howard Allen. "The Cities and the Election of 1928: Partisan Realignment?" *American Historical Review* 74, no. 5 (December 1969): 1205–20.

Cole, Wayne S. "America First and the South, 1940–1941." *Journal of Southern History* 44, no. 1 (February 1956): 36–47.

"Colonel McCormick Rides Again." *Time* 39, no. 8 (February 23, 1942): 42.

Costello, Helen Murchie. "Colonel McCormick's Tribune, 1910–41." *New Republic* 105, no. 22 (December 1, 1941): 724–26.

Doenecke, Justus D. "General Robert E. Wood: The Evolution of An

American Conservative." *Journal of the Illinois State Historical Society* 71 (August 1978): 162–75.

Donovon, John C. "Congressional Isolationists and the Roosevelt Foreign Policy." *World Politics* 3 (April 1951): 292–316.

Dubsky, Phyllis. "Carrie Nations of Fascism." *The Nation* 153, no. 8 (August 23, 1941): 160–61.

"Follow What Leader." *Time* 38, no. 14 (October 6, 1941): 18–20.

"General Robert E. Wood, President." *Fortune* 17, no. 5 (May 1938): 66–69, 104–10.

Gleck, L. E. "96 Congressmen Make Up Their Minds." *Public Opinion Quarterly* 4, no. 1 (March 1940): 3–24.

"How Isolationist is the Midwest?" *Life* 11, no. 22 (December 1, 1941): 16–20.

Hutchins, Robert M. "On Democracy and Defense." *Common Ground* 1, no. 1 (Autumn 1940): 57–61.

_____. "The Path to War." *Vital Speeches of the Day* 7, no. 9 (February 15, 1941): 258–61.

_____. "The Proposition is Peace." *Vital Speeches of the Day* 7, no. 13 (April 15, 1941): 389–92.

_____. "What Shall We Defend?" *Vital Speeches of the Day* 6, no. 18 (July 1, 1940): 546–49.

Irish, Marion D. "Foreign Policy in the South." *Journal of Politics* 10, no. 2 (May 1948): 306–26.

Jacob, Philip E. "Influences of World Events on U.S. 'Neutrality Opinion.'" *Public Opinion Quarterly* 4, no. 1 (March 1940): 48–65.

"Keep Out of War." *Newsweek* 16, no. 27 (December 30, 1941): 9–10.

Knox, Frank. "Our Southern Arteries." *Atlantic Monthly* 164, no. 1 (July 1939): 75–80.

Lasch, Robert. "Chicago Patriot: 'The World's Greatest Newspaper.'" *Atlantic Monthly* 169, no. 1 (June 1942): 691–95.

"The Legion Strikes a Blow." *Time* 38, no. 13 (September 29, 1941): 21.

"Legion Transition." *Newsweek* 18, no. 13 (September 29, 1941): 15.

Lichtman, Allan J. "Critical Election Theory and the Reality of American Presidential Politics, 1916–1940." *American Historical Review* 81, no. 2 (April 1976): 317–51.

Lubell, Samuel. "Who Votes Isolationist and Why." *Harper's Magazine* 202 (April 1951): 29–36.

McCormick, Robert R. "The Lessons of This War." *Vital Speeches of the Day* 7, no. 21 (August 15, 1941): 644–46.

_____. "Lessons of Military History." *Vital Speeches of the Day* 7, no. 24 (October 1, 1941): 753–55.

McCoy, Donald R. "Republican Opposition During Wartime, 1941–1945."
    Mid-America 49 (September 1967): 714–39.
McKelway, St. Clair. "A Reporter At Large." *New Yorker* 17, no. 42
    (November 10, 1941): 40–47.
McKenzie, Vernon. "Treatment of War Themes in Magazine Fiction."
    Public Opinion Quarterly 5, no. 2 (June 1941): 227–32.
MacRae, Duncan, and James A. Meldrun. "Critical Elections in Illinois,
    1888–1958." *American Political Science Review* 54, no. 3 (September
    1960): 669–83.
"Mad at McCormick." *Time* 38, no. 6 (August 11, 1941): 54–55.
Maseland, John W. "The 'Peace' Groups Join the Battle." *Public Opinion
    Quarterly* 4, no. 4 (December 1940): 664–73.
Mayer, Milton S. "Hutchins of Chicago." *Harper's Monthly Magazine* 178
    (March–April 1939): 344–55, 543–52.
———. "I Think I'll Sit This One Out." *Saturday Evening Post* 212, no. 15
    (October 7, 1939): 23, 96–100.
Nichols, Jeanette P. "The Middle West and the Coming of World War II."
    Ohio State Archaeological and Historical Quarterly 62 (April 1953): 122–
    45.
"No Alibi." *Time* 37, no. 17 (April 28, 1941): 15.
Rieselbach, Leroy N. "The Basis of Isolationist Behavior." *Public Opinion
    Quarterly* 24 (September 1960): 645–57.
"Rising Torrent." *Newsweek* 18, no. 13 (September 29, 1941): 14.
Rose, Ernest D. "How the U.S. Heard about Pearl Harbor." *Journal of
    Broadcasting* 5, no. 4 (Fall 1961): 285–98.
Roucek, Joseph S. "Foreign Language Press in World War II." *Sociology
    and Social Research* 27 (July–August 1943): 462–71.
Sadler, Charles. "Political Dynamite: The Chicago Polonia and President
    Roosevelt in 1944." *Journal of the Illinois State Historical Society* 71, no. 2
    (May 1978): 119–32.
"Scientist's Scientist." *Time* 37, no. 6 (February 10, 1941): 44–48.
Shively, W. Philip. "A Reinterpretation of the New Deal Realignment."
    Public Opinion Quarterly 35, no. 4 (Winter 1971–72): 621–24.
"Smoke Out 'America First.'" *New Republic* 105, no. 14 (October 6, 1941):
    422–23.
Smuckler, Ralph H. "The Region of Isolationism." *American Political
    Science Review* 47 (June 1953): 386–401.
Steele, Richard W. "American Popular Opinion and the War against
    Germany: The Issue of a Negotiated Peace." *Journal of American History*
    65, no. 3 (December 1978): 704–23.
———. "The Great Debate: Roosevelt, the Media, and the Coming of the

War, 1940–1941." *Journal of American History* 71, no. 1 (June 1984): 69–92.

_____. "The Pulse of the People." *Journal of Contemporary History* 9 (October 1974): 195–216.

Stromburg, Roland N. "American Business and the Approach of War, 1935–1941." *Journal of Economic History* 13 (Winter 1953): 58–78.

"The Sun Comes Out." *Time* 38, no. 24 (December 15, 1941): 55–56.

Tuttle, William H., Jr. "Aid-to-the-Allies Short-of-War versus American Intervention, 1940: A Reappraisal of William Allen White's Leadership." *Journal of American History* 56, no. 4 (March 1970): 840–58.

"U.S. Radio At War." *Time* 38, no. 24 (December 15, 1941): 48–49.

"Veterans' Swing." *Newsweek* 18, no. 10 (September 8, 1941): 19.

"Voices of Defeat." *Life* 12, no. 15 (April 13, 1942): 86–100.

Waldon, Webb. "William Allen White." *American Mercury* 52, no. 207 (March 1941): 322–29.

"Was Mr. Knox Speaking For the Administration?" *Christian Century* 58, no. 42 (October 22, 1941): 1293.

"White Heat." *Newsweek* 17, no. 1 (January 6, 1941): 15–16.

Wilkins, Robert P. "Middle Western Isolationism: A Reexamination." *North Dakota Quarterly* 25 (March 1957): 69–76.

Wood, Robert E. "Our Foreign Policy." *Vital Speeches of the Day* 7, no. 5 (December 15, 1940): 130–33.

"Wreck of a Friendship." *Time* 37, no. 14 (April 7, 1941): 64.

Unpublished Works

Carlson, Ronald E. "Organization and Activities of the Chicago Chapter of the Fight For Freedom Committee." Master's thesis, University of Chicago, 1961.

Rogers, William Cecil. "Isolationist Propaganda, September 1, 1939 to December 7, 1941." Ph.D. dissertation, University of Chicago, 1953.

INDEX